DATE DUE

Harvard Economic Studies / Volume 141

Russian Research Center / Study No. 71

This study is cosponsored by the Department of
Economics and the Russian Research Center.
Neither the Department nor the Center assumes re-
sponsibility for the views expressed.

The Service Sector in Soviet Economic Growth

A Comparative Study

GUR OFER

Harvard University Press   Cambridge, Massachusetts
1973

Preface and Acknowledgments

In this book I try to explain why the service industries occupy such a small place in the Soviet economy. The discussion embraces two fields: the general theory of economic development and industrial structure and the nature of the socialist economic system and its growth strategy. The first helps to ask questions and formulate hypotheses; in the second lies much of the explanation that we seek. As will be seen, a good deal of the discussion focuses on the interactions between the two and I hope that the book will thus be of interest to scholars in both fields.

The book grew from my Ph.D. dissertation which was completed in early 1968. Since then it has been rewritten and reorganized, but no systematic effort was made to incorporate new material or to bring the figures up to date. The one exception is the historical analysis of Chapter 8 on which most of the work was done in 1968-1969. In view of this the reader should be aware that the "present" of the book relates to the situation in the Soviet Union around the time of the then most recent population census (1959) and up to the end of the Krushchev era, and, with a few exceptions, no secondary material that appeared after the end of 1967 was used. The question of how the returns of the 1971 population census fit our analysis is left for further investigation.

I would like to thank my dissertation advisers Abram Bergson and Simon Kuznets who went much beyond their adviser's duty in reading the last draft of the book and adding many helpful comments to those they made before. Yoram Ben-Porath, Richard Caves, and at least two anonymous referees read part or whole of various drafts and made many valuable suggestions. Special thanks are due to Susanne Freund for her patient editorial work on numerous drafts and to Adèle Zarmati who assisted her.

Financially, the study was supported mainly by the Russian Research Center at Harvard, where I spent two years as a graduate student fellow and one year as a research fellow. Further research and much of the production cost of the final draft were financed by various research funds of the Hebrew University of Jerusalem. Editorial help and technical facilities were provided by the Maurice Falk Institute for Economic Research in Israel.

Jerusalem   Gur Ofer
July 1972

Contents

Tables

FIGURES

The Service Sector in Soviet Economic Growth

A COMPARATIVE STUDY

Abbreviations and Symbols

DIP	disposable income proportion
FIK	farm income in kind
FT	final trade
FTEQ	full time equivalent
GNP	gross national product
ISIC	International Standard Industrial Classification
LED	level of economic development
LF	labor force
MTGS	tradable goods share at current market prices
PR	labor force participation rate
RU	proportion of rural in total population
TGS	tradable goods share
n.e.s.	not elsewhere specified
—	zero
0	negligible (less than half last digit shown)
..	not available

1. Introduction

An outstanding feature of the Soviet economy is the relatively small volume of services produced. The place of most types of services in the economy is notably small when the USSR is compared with other countries at the same or even lower levels of development. To the student of modern economic growth such a limited service share is rather paradoxical. The commonly accepted relationship between the sectoral structure of a modern economy and the level of its economic progress also obtains as regards the place of services relative to other sectors. On the one hand, high income elasticities of final consumer demand for services and, no less important, the need for services to support the increasingly specialized and sophisticated production system seem to call for a substantial increase in the service share as income rises. The high elasticities have been considered a normal manifestation of the structure of human tastes, and the supporting function of services in production, almost a technological necessity. On the other hand, the service sector is believed to lag behind other sectors in technological progress, thus increasing even further the relative amount of inputs it absorbs.

The long-trend changes of the industrial structure in Russia and the Soviet Union, presented in Table 1, indicate that at least on the face of it the Soviet Union's record is not completely detached from the development factors mentioned above. Over a period of seven decades, four of them under socialism, during which per capita income rose from roughly $100 to $1300, one can identify all the by now well-established trends found in the industrial structure of market economies: a decline in the labor share of agriculture and increases in the shares of manufacturing and related industries and the service industries. The fact that the share of the service sector has been small throughout the Soviet period must indicate that some of the structure-development relationships do not appear to obtain in the Soviet Union, at least not in the same degree as elsewhere.

1

Table 1. Industrial Distribution of the Labor Force, Russia and the Soviet Union, Selected Years, 1897-1964[a] (Percent)

Year	Total civilian labor force	A sector	M sector	S sector
1897	100	77	12	11
1926	100	71	18	11
1940	100	54	28	18
1959	100	41	38	21
1964	100	33	43	24

[a]A = agriculture; M = mining, manufacturing, construction, and transport and communications; S = services.
Source: Appendix Table E-1.

The main purpose of this study is to inquire into this paradoxical feature of Soviet development—to explain how the Soviet economy has managed to achieve the high level of development it has reached and still keep the service sector so small. One explanation might be that the Russians follow Marx in his conviction that the service industries are unproductive and create no material value. Thus, having full control of the economy, the government saw to it that services did not absorb too large a part of the scarce factor resources available. This, however, represents a highly oversimplified view of Marx's ideas on the matter. It will be argued in this study that it also represents a highly oversimplified view of the ideological framework of the Soviet regime, and, still more, of the degree to which the Soviet authorities allow doctrine to interfere with practical economic needs. In any event a central thesis of this book is that the novel economic and social system of the Soviet Union is to a large extent responsible for the small size of the service sector; but that purely ideological considerations of how "productive" service activities are can be only a small part of the explanation. The most important single cause of the limited service sector is, rather, the strategy of economic growth implemented by the Soviet authorities during more than four decades. By strategy we mean the rate of growth aimed at, the sectoral priorities involved, and the principal means of achieving growth. The effect of the strategy of growth has been to curtail mainly the production of services connected with final consumption and urbanization (retail trade, personal and public services). Other factors at work in limiting the scope of services turn out to be the organization and mechanics of central planning, and the abolition of private ownership of productive assets. They are responsible mainly for substitution of the government-run planning apparatus for wholesale trade and financial and other business services. To some extent, however, the conviction that some service activities, especially administration and distribution, are unproductive has also been influential.

This study seeks to explain the place of services in the Soviet economy mainly through the comparative approach; that is, the size of the service industries in the Soviet Union is compared with that in other countries at the same level of economic development. This approach seems to be justified in view of the data presented in Table 1 above which show that despite the different economic systems some major patterns may be common to both market and planned economies. Another purpose of this study, which logically precedes the explanation of the service gap, is to further investigate the functional relationship between the size of the service sector and the process of modern economic growth. In addition to the frequently used income-per-capita criterion, I use several alternative definitions of the level of economic development (LED); the study investigates how the relative quality of the labor force of the different sectors changes with the level of economic development and how it affects the industrial structure; and finally it illustrates theoretically the factors behind changes in the size of a key service sector—commerce—with economic growth. These themes are first explored generally, with reference to market economies, primarily in order to lay the groundwork for the comparative delineation of the place of services in the Soviet economy; at the same time, the initial exploration may help to clarify further the system of relations between the place of services and economic development. On the other hand, the study will, it is hoped, illuminate—with special reference to the service sector—the extent to which development patterns observed in market economies also apply to a country such as the Soviet Union with a radically different economic system. This important issue seems as yet to have been little explored.

As understood in this study, the service (S) sector includes the following industries:[1] trade and finance, which make up the commerce (C) subsector; and public administration, public services, and private services, lumped together as other services (OS) mainly because of lack of data. (Transport services are included with manufacturing and construction in the M sector.)

I deal primarily with one aspect of the size of the service sector, labor input. Specifically, the key variable is the proportion of the labor force employed by the service sector as a whole or by its component industries. From the theoretical point of view, the share of the service sector in GNP is no doubt a more meaningful variable, but the conceptual as well as the statistical problems involved in its use make the labor share a more dependable and solid starting point. When necessary and feasible, I supplement the discussion of labor shares by referring to the share of services in inputs.

1. See Chap. 2, note 6, for details of what is included in each category.

The principal focus of the study is on the place of services in the Soviet economy in 1959. A brief survey of the historical development of the industrial structure is, however, included, mainly in order to shed some light on the dynamics of the 1959 situation and also to test whether the factors that explain it can also explain the historical development.

Likewise, the main comparative approach used in this study is a cross-country analysis at a given point of time—circa 1960; the development features are investigated as if the range of countries whose data are used represent one continuous development process from underdevelopment to full development. Clearly, the cross-country pattern does not need to be identical with the historical pattern. Again, I do not devote much space to possible time series/cross-section differences and their influence on our findings.

Chapters 2 and 3 lay the groundwork of the study by estimating the service gaps in the Soviet Union. First, a theoretical relation is established between industrial structure and the level of economic development and the customary definition of LED is broadened by adding to the income-per-capita criterion indexes of the level of urbanization and the labor force participation rate. This is followed by an estimate of the quantitative relations between the industrial structure and LED (defined in alternative ways) and the size of the services sector and its component industries. The estimates are based on cross-section data for between thirty and sixty market economies and define "normal"[2] services labor shares which are then compared with the Soviet data in order to estimate the Soviet service gaps; most of them turn out to be positive (that is, the normal exceeds the Soviet share). A different set of gaps is estimated for each definition of LED.

Chapters 4 and 5 are devoted to an attempt to correct the gap estimates in two main directions. First, I inquire whether in the Soviet Union some service workers are located outside the service industries or even outside the labor force. Second, the gaps, originally estimated from the number of workers, are corrected for their quality characteristics. This correction entails a general analysis of how interindustry differences in the quality of labor change with economic growth and it is followed by a comparison of the findings with the specific quality characteristics of the Soviet labor force.

Chapters 6 and 7 focus on the gap in commerce, the stress being on final trade services (retail, catering, and their wholesale base). It is this sub-branch that has the largest gap and the one that is least affected by the corrections just mentioned. We formulate two models in which we examine four variables that

2. The word "normal" (without the quotes) will be used in this specific sense of "estimated for a given LED."

may explain the demand for trade and the trade industry's productivity: (a) the amount of goods distributed through trade channels; (b) the amount of services per unit of goods distributed; (c) the efficiency of the distribution network; and (d) the amount of services per unit of goods supplied by customers in their own time. The normal level of each factor and of the model as a whole (in relation to LED) is determined and then compared with the corresponding Soviet level.

The foregoing exercises explain, or at least suggest explanations for, virtually all of the service gaps by what may seem to be a somewhat heterogeneous collection of specific factors. In Chapters 8 and 9 I consider whether a single major factor—the socialist economic system—may not underlie most of the specific factors. First, an empirical test is applied to the relation between the Soviet industrial structure and "socialist economic system." This test relies on (a) data for seven other socialist countries in Eastern Europe; and (b) data for four years (other than 1959) during the socialist period in Russia. I then establish analytically the connection between socialist economic system and the size of the Soviet service industries. In doing so, I incorporate most of the explanatory factors previously analyzed. I conclude with an assessment of future developments in the Soviet service industries.

By far the most surprising finding is that the Soviet Union has a positive gap—a deficiency, to make it plain—in public administration services. This finding contradicts all that is known from Soviet and Western sources alike, and also what one would logically expect in a centrally planned system. Although I am convinced by the evidence, such as it is, more research into this point is undoubtedly needed.

The study by no means gives full answers to all the questions posed nor does it attempt to discuss all of them to the same depth. In the spirit of the empirical tradition, I offer some topics for further research. First, the incorporation into the analysis of the industrial structure of product and capital would improve our ability to identify the factors that affect the industrial structure as countries develop and the differences in the industrial structure between the Soviet Union (or socialist economies) and market economies. Specifically, a better distinction could be made between demand and efficiency factors and the effects on factor proportions could be better identified. Second, the measure of labor input used in this study needs to be greatly improved. Data on hours of work must be introduced as well as much more detailed labor quality criteria and weights. Third, a much deeper analysis of some of the deficiencies and surpluses in the service shares of the Soviet Union is needed; most important here is the deficiency found in public administration services. Further study is also needed on the relationship of this sector with economic development in both market and centrally planned economies. Finally, much more research effort should be directed to the historical and dynamic aspects of the problems—aspects whose treatment is here condensed into half a chapter and which touches only lightly on questions of the historical responsibility for the Soviet Union's deficiency in services and the factors affecting changes in the industrial structure as a socialist country develops.

2. The Service Sector and the Level of Development

The industrial structure of any economy—the industrial distribution of product, labor force, and any other input—is determined by factors on both the demand and production sides. The main demand factors are the level and distribution of income, tastes, the size of the government sector and its policy, and the relative prices of goods and services. These prices are of course determined simultaneously by demand and supply. On the supply side, the shares are affected by the availability of inputs and relative levels of technology and productivity. The two sets of factors differ in their effect on the industrial distribution of product on the one side and labor force—which we are specially interested in in this study—or of any other major input on the other. Although the industrial distribution of product is predominantly determined by the demand factors, the proportion of labor (or capital) directed to any sector is determined by the relative shares of all other inputs and by the sector's production efficiency relative to the rest of the economy, as well as by the sector's output share. To be specific, the labor share of any industry will be larger, the larger its output share and the lower its relative labor productivity. Labor productivity in turn will be lower, the lower the amount of other inputs per unit of labor and the lower the level of total productivity (output per unit of combined inputs)—compared with the rest of the economy.[1] Finally, the relative input proportions, like the capital-labor ratio, are at least partly determined by the nature of technical changes: the more labor using these are in a given sector relative to other sectors, the higher is the sector's labor share.

All of this is of course true for the service sector and its component industries. Particularly important for the service sector, in addition to the factors just mentioned, is, first, the intermediate demand for services by other

1. A formal presentation of the relation between product and labor shares may be found in Victor R. Fuchs's 1968 study (see note 2 below).

branches of the economy. This is important mainly for the C subsector because a high proportion of its services is rendered to firms. While the demand for most intermediate products is ultimately determined by final demand, the demand for commercial and business services is determined to a large extent by the general set-up of the economy—the degree of division of labor and specialization of enterprises. The more sophisticated the structure, the greater the number of links between units, and the greater the demand for services to mediate these links. Second, governments usually have more effect on the size of the public segment of the service sector (public administration, education, public health, and so on) than on the size of any other industry, for the simple reason that they directly generate most of these services.

Many students of economic growth have asserted that the level of development of a country implies the level of many of these factors and that when the level of development changes many of the factors change with it in a certain predictable pattern.[2] Thus, declining relative demand for agricultural products with economic development explains the decline in both the product and labor share of agriculture; the fact that the labor share falls more steeply than the product share is in turn explained by relative advances in agricultural labor productivity. Demand factors are dominant in raising the shares of manufacturing and related industries. The increase in the service shares is explained by a mixture of demand and productivity factors working in the same direction—demand, both final and intermediate, goes up, while it is argued that relative labor productivity declines with economic development. The outcome is usually that in the service sector and most of its component industries the labor share increases much more than the product share.[3]

The main conclusion is that a thorough investigation of how the industrial structure or the service shares change with the level of economic development must include a study of the changes in the shares of product, labor, and other inputs. It also follows that a careful investigation of the labor shares alone may

2. Among the leading studies in the field the following have been concerned with the service sector: Colin Clark, *The Conditions of Economic Progress*, 3rd ed. (London, 1957); the following parts of Simon Kuznets, "Quantitative Aspects of the Economic Growth of Nations," in *Economic Development and Cultural Change*: "II. Industrial Distribution of National Product and Labor Force," *EDCC*, 5 (supplement to no. 4, July 1957); "III. Industrial Distribution of Income and Labor Force by States, United States, 1919-1921 to 1955," *EDCC*, 6 (no. 4, part II, July 1958); Simon Kuznets, *Modern Economic Growth Rate Structure and Spread* (New Haven, 1966); G. J. Stigler, *Trends in Employment in the Service Industries* (Princeton, 1956); Victor R. Fuchs, *The Service Economy* (New York and London, 1968); Victor R. Fuchs, ed., *Production and Productivity in the Service Industries* (New York and London, 1969).

3. Fuchs 1968, pp. 3-5, concludes that the dominant factor affecting labor shares is labor productivity.

be able to account for both demand and productivity factors since all those that have been mentioned affect the labor share. This point is emphasized, since the study concentrates on labor shares and only occasionally turns to the industrial distribution of product and other inputs. The admitted deficiencies of this choice are to my mind outweighed by the well-known conceptual and measurement problems encountered in defining, measuring, and comparing service product shares. A major problem that concerns us directly—to mention only one—is the practice of defining service product shares by their labor inputs, thus assuming constant labor productivity over time. The service product statistics are considered by many students of comparative development to be so poor as to warrant basing international comparisons on material national product rather than GNP in order to avoid using them. To all this one must add the special situation in the Soviet Union where a major part of the service sector is defined as nonproductive and thus not included in the national accounts statistics.

The close relation between the level of economic development and the factors affecting industrial structure make the former a summary variable which can be used to predict the industrial structure of a country. Alternatively, it can be shown how far industrial structure is explainable by this summary variable. The main problem here is that such a summary variable has not been quantitatively defined and there is no agreement on its conceptual definition.

There are two possible ways of approaching the problem, both leading to virtually the same practical conclusion. The first is to insist on a unique index for LED, made up as a weighted average—with agreed-upon weights—of several indicators associated or identified with economic development, such as per capita income, the level of urbanization, or the level of literacy. When this hypothetical index is related to the industrial structure in many countries, it produces estimated, or normal, structures for each country. Clearly the divergencies between the actual and the normal structure depend upon the weights assigned to the development indicators, and each set of weights will produce different-sized gaps that require explanation by non-development variables. For example, if too low a weight is assigned to the level of urbanization, the service gap in highly urbanized countries might be larger than when the factor is given a higher weight. If it is maintained that the low weight is the "true" one, then indeed some of the extra service share must be explained by a higher than normal level of urbanization that is not connected with economic development.

The second approach is to relate the industrial structure of the economy to two dimensions of LED: the level of an aggregate index, with any set of weights, and the relative importance of the different weighted indicators in the composition of this given level. Different patterns of economic growth (more urbanization, less income, for example) may thus have their own effect on the industrial structure. Neither approach, of course, precludes the possibility that in a particular country one or other of the so-called development variables has nothing to do with LED.

I do not propose to commit myself exclusively to either approach. Rather, I shall try to relate the industrial structure of many countries to a cumulative list of variables generally identified with LED and to offer alternative sets of "normal patterns "of change in the structure.

Four development variables were chosen, all of them generally believed to be closely associated with economic development. They were chosen because of their specific connection with the shares of the various services and because in the Soviet Union their levels are in general radically different from those in other developed countries. By this choice we hope to measure as much as possible of the impact of development variables on service shares and to get as full an explanation as possible for the Soviet Union's specific service shares, while using a reasonably small number of variables.

The first and basic indicator is GNP per capita. In using it I follow those who think that this variable is the ultimate goal of modern economic growth and that it represents, in measurable units, the impact of many other factors at work in the process of economic growth. It is expected, and has been found on many occasions, that a higher level of per capita income (y) will be accompanied by higher service shares.

In letting y represent LED we look on it as a measure both of the income that generates demand and of the general level of productivity and efficiency of the economy. A better measure representing the production side would be GNP per *worker.* The difference between the two arises from variations, at given per capita incomes, in the rate of labor force participation of the population. To illustrate, a country with the same y as another but with lower labor force participation rates is operating with a higher labor efficiency and should thus have a higher share of services in the labor force.[4] In order to take these effects into account we choose the rate of participation in the labor force (PR) as our second variable. When it is put in a regression together with income per capita, the estimation process will produce coefficients for the two variables that *together* take into account both the income per capita and the product per worker of the LED at the correct weights.

4. I here ignore the possible effect in the opposite direction (of increased demand for market services) that occurs when a higher percentage of women goes to work. I return to this in Chap. 7.

The other two development variables considered in the study are the proportion of rural in total population (RU) and the ratio between the labor shares of the A and M sectors (A/M).[5] The latter variable is quite close to RU and is used as a substitute for it only for countries for which there are no available data on RU. The main reason for considering RU lies in the assumption that this LED indicator has a special impact on the services (S) share. At a given per capita or per worker income we would expect to find higher S shares in countries with lower RU. The factors that can a priori be expected to work in this direction are, first, that more services are needed simply to make city life feasible; second, that the higher level of specialization of production in cities makes people buy more services from firms instead of providing them for themselves; and third, that the structure of urban tastes favors more services. A fourth factor that may work both ways is that the production of services for urban populations is much more efficient. Assuming that prices of services fall in proportion to labor input, this factor increases the quantity of services demanded in cities but at the same time reduces the labor input needed per unit of service, and vice versa in rural areas. The net effect depends upon whether the price elasticity is lower or higher than unity.

The regression analysis that follows is designed to test the relation between the service shares and the development variables and to establish a normal pattern for the shares as the development variables change. It is based on data for between 43 and 62 countries in the early 1960s (mostly 1960; the countries are listed in Appendix Table A-1).

Because of data limitations the least-squares method could be applied only to the S sector as a whole and to its two major subdivisions,[6] the C and OS subsectors (all other services). As indicated above, several alternative combinations of the development variables are used. This is done not in order to choose the "best" equation but in order to get a broader view of the possible effects of different LED definitions. Naturally, we run into the problem of multicollinearity in the regression analysis, as a direct result of the fact that all the independent variables stand for and are highly correlated with LED and thus

5. Sector notation is: A, agriculture; M, mining, manufacturing, construction and transport and communications; S, services, subdivided into C, commerce, and OS, other services (see also next note).

6. The C sector comprises trade (retail and wholesale trade and catering establishments) and finance (banking, insurance, and real estate). The OS sector comprises public administration, including government, police, and social institutions (including nonprofit institutions); public services, comprising education, science, health, and welfare; private services, including culture and entertainment, hotels, personal services (such as laundries, barbers), and domestic services; and business services.

with each other.[7] Statistically this may result in lower significance levels (higher standard errors) for the individual coefficients, but not for the entire equations. In other words, when the independent variables are highly correlated with each other, the distribution of the combined explanation of the variance in the dependent variable among the individual regression coefficients is not necessarily the correct one. This means that in analyzing the results one should concentrate on the total effects of the combinations and give less weight to the separate coefficients. Accordingly, we shall consider an equation with an extra independent variable worth presenting only if the added variable has a coefficient of the expected sign and the equation as a whole has a higher $\bar{R}^2$, that is, if it can explain more of the variance in the dependent variable.[8]

Some additional remarks on the technical characteristics of the variables used are in order.

In the regressions we use two standard labor force concepts: LF(a), which includes all family workers in the labor force, and LF(b), which excludes them. Neither of them is an accurate measure of labor input; the most important difference is that LF(a) overstates the A share (and understates the M and S shares) and LF(b) understates the A share (and overstates the other two). In the present context, there is however one theoretical point in favor of LF(a): One can consider the proportion of unpaid family workers in agriculture as a measure of the relative importance of subsistence agriculture inside the A sector. This subsector of A has itself been used in some studies[9] as a variable measuring the level of development. Its existence probably depresses the service share more than does the rural proportion as a whole, because its demand for market services is probably lower than that of the "industrialized" A sector, based on paid labor. Assuming that this is so, the overestimation of the A share, and the corresponding underestimation of the S shares, could be interpreted as an allowance for the higher weight of "backwardness" in an A sector with a high proportion of family workers. In addition, the LF(a) data of other countries correspond better to their Soviet counterpart than LF(b) data,

---

7. The simple correlation coefficients among the independent variables are:

	log y	PR	RU	A/M
log y	1.00	0.43	−0.75	−0.69
PR		1.00	−0.19	−0.07
RU			1.00	0.64
A/M				1.00

These figures are based on 43 countries and use labor force definition (a).

8. Let me emphasize that we are not here choosing the best equation on the basis of a higher $\bar{R}^2$. Rather, I assume that all the equations are theoretically "correct" and exclude those equations whose additional variable adds nothing to what we know.

9. I. Adelman and C. Taft-Morris, "A Factor Analysis of the Interrelationship Between Social and Political Variables and Per Capita Gross National Product," *Quarterly Journal of Economics,* 79:555-578 (November 1965).

since there is a different definition of unpaid family worker in the Soviet Union. These arguments can also be adduced in favor of using an LF(a) type of measure for the *PR* variable.[10]

Initially the regressions were calculated on three alternative series for *y:* the two UN series, one based on official exchange rates, and the other on calculated purchasing power parities, and a third one which essentially gives private consumption per capita estimated in a rather unusual way by W. Beckerman and R. Bacon.[11] The correlations among the three series approach unity and the regression results based on them are quite close; I therefore present only the UN purchasing power series, since it represents the theoretically correct approach; I make no attempt to evaluate individual observations of the series. Finally, log *y* is used in all regressions, since it gives a better fit than *y*.

A selection of the regression results based on the LF(a) concept and on observations for 43 countries is presented in Table 2. As was to be expected, there is a strong and significant positive relation between the S, C, and OS shares in the labor force and *y* (lines 1, 6, and 11, respectively). The variable *y* alone explains about two-thirds of the variance in *S* and *C* and slightly less than half of it in *OS*.[12]

Adding *PR* as a second independent variable raises the explained proportion of the variance in the *S* and *OS* shares. In both sectors we get highly significant and negative coefficients (lines 3 and 13). Yet the addition of *PR* does not contribute at all to the *C* equation, for reasons that are not immediately clear. The negative sign that we get for *PR* in the *S* and *OS* equations confirms the expected relation to the product per worker variable, though the coefficient itself is, of course, not the product per worker coefficient.[13] We see that, at the same *y*, the share of services declines as *PR* rises, at least for S and OS.

The combination of *y* and *RU* also gives a better explanation of the service shares than *y* alone (lines 4, 9, and 14). All the *RU* coefficients are negative, a finding that supports the hypothesis that urban areas use more services than rural ones. Again, the improvement in the explanation of the services shares is considerable for *S,* and even more so for *OS,* but very small for *C*. This difference between the two major subsectors deserves further consideration.

10. Both LF concepts used in the regressions are for total labor force, with the armed forces included in the OS sector.

11. W. Beckerman and R. Bacon, "International Comparison of Income Levels: A Suggested New Measure," *Economic Journal,* 66:519-536 (September 1966). The UN series are from *Yearbook of National Accounts Statistics 1964,* Tables 6a and 6b.

12. The regressions using LF(b) yield a somewhat lower $\bar{R}^2$ for 42 countries, but a higher $\bar{R}^2$ for 61 countries.

13. The coefficients are for the equation $S = a + by + cPR$, and differ from those we would have obtained had the equation been $S = a' + b'y + c'Y/L$ where *y* and *Y* are respectively per capita and total GNP, and *L* is labor force.

Table 2. *Service Shares as Functions of LED Variables*[a]

Dependent variable	Independent variable	$\bar{R}^2$[b]	Regression coefficients			Regression elasticities[c]		
			log y	PR	RU	log y	PR	RU
S 1.	log y	0.65	8.12 (0.91)			1.7		
2.	RU	0.64			-0.40 (0.05)			-0.8
3.	log y, PR	0.74	9.63 (0.86)	-0.50 (0.12)		2.0	-0.6	
4.	log y RU	0.71	4.66 (1.33)		-0.22 (0.07)	1.0		-0.4
5.	log y, PR, RU	0.77	6.82 (1.34)	-0.41 (0.12)	-0.16 (0.06)	1.4	-0.5	-0.3
C 6.	log y	0.67	3.79 (0.40)			2.0		
7.	RU	0.50			-0.16 (0.02)			-0.8
8.	log y, PR	0.68	4.04 (0.44)	-0.08 (0.06)		2.2	-0.3	
9.	log y, RU	0.68	3.11 (0.64)		-0.42 (0.03)	1.7		-0.2
10.	log y, PR, RU	0.68	3.47 (0.73)	-0.07 (0.06)	-0.03 (0.03)	2.1	-0.3	-0.0
OS 11.	log y	0.43	4.34 (0.75)			1.5		

No.	Variables	R̄²[b]						
12.	RU	0.53			−0.24 (0.03)			−0.7
13.	log y, PR	0.59	5.59 (0.70)	−0.41 (0.10)		1.9	−0.9	
14.	log y, RU	0.54	1.54 (1.09)		−0.17 (0.05)	0.5		−0.5
15.	log y, PR, RU	0.64	3.35 (1.10)	−0.34 (0.10)	−0.13 (0.05)	1.2	−0.7	−0.4

[a] The regressions are for 43 countries and are based on LF(a) data (see Appendix A). Figures in parentheses are the standard errors of the coefficients.

[b] All R̄² are significant at 1 percent or less.

[c] Percentage change in the dependent variable in response to a 1 percent change in the independent variable at the point of average values for the variables.

Source: Industrial distribution of labor force—UN, *Demographic Yearbook 1964*, Table 12 (Tables 9 and 11 for a few countries); and ILO, *Year Book of Labour Statistics*, Table 4a of 1964 issue and Table 2a of 1965 issue.

GNP per capita (y)—UN, *Yearbook of National Accounts Statistics 1964*, pp. 383ff., Table 6b and corresponding table in other issues of the *Yearbook*. For several Latin American countries unpublished UN data were used (Economic Commission for Latin America).

Where necessary, the figures were converted to 1960 US $ over the implicit United States GNP price index from U.S., Department of Commerce, *Survey of Current Business* (July 1966), p. 37, Table 7.6.

The OS finding can be explained by the direct connection between some of the OS services and the urban way of life, such as local government, personal services, entertainment, and to some extent even education and health services. Looking at line 12 in the table, it can be seen that the *RU* variable may be even more important than per capita income in accounting for the OS result. It is, however, much more difficult to explain the finding for C. One possible explanation of this rather surprising result is the large labor input per unit of commercial services supplied to rural areas. This factor may offset part of the effect of the smaller rural use of these services.[14]

When *A/M* replaces *RU,* roughly the same results are obtained for the group of 43 countries. The results are also unchanged if the calculation is extended to 62 countries (for some of which no *RU* data are available).

Finally, combining all three development variables produces only a slightly better total explanation of the variance than the two-variable regressions. All in all, by using all three variables we can account for close to 80 percent of the variance in the *S* share and less than this for each of the two subsectors.[15]

To complete the picture, the pattern of change of the *A* and the *M* shares was also estimated. All the estimated relations produced the expected result of declining *A* shares and rising *M* shares as economic development takes place. In the equations for the *A* share, all the development variables have the "right" sign and all are statistically significant; but though all the development variables have the "right" sign in the estimations of the *M* shares only GNP per capita appears to be statistically significant. The final equations, based on LF(a) and a sample of 43 countries, are:

$$A = 121.022 \underset{(4.614)}{} - 18.330 \underset{(2.007)}{} (\log y) + 0.483 \underset{(0.180)}{} (PR) + 0.238 \underset{(0.092)}{} (RU); \qquad \bar{R}^2 = 0.90$$

$$M = -31.886 \underset{(11.929)}{} + 11.517 \underset{(1.639)}{} (\log y) - 0.083 \underset{(1.46)}{} (PR) - 0.077 \underset{(0.074)}{} (RU); \qquad \bar{R}^2 = 0.82.$$

The use of *RU* as an independent variable to explain the *A* share is admittedly circular. However, the results are very similar when this variable is eliminated.

Analysis of countries whose service shares show large deviations from the regressions line may improve the theory and will also serve as a benchmark for evaluating the Soviet and other socialist experience. We concentrate on deviations of the *S* shares.

Table 3 shows all the country observations whose deviation from the esti-

14. This point is discussed further in Chap. 6.
15. As with the log *y* regressions, the estimations based on LF(b) were somewhat weaker, but when 61 countries are included the correlation coefficients are higher.

Table 3. Deviation of S,A, and M Shares from Estimated Regression Lines, Selected Countries[a] (Percentage Points)

Country	log y			log y, PR, RU		
	S	A	M	S	A	M
Standard error of regression	5.8	8.3	5.6	4.6	6.9	5.7
Positive S deviation						
United States (I)	7.7	3.1	-10.6	(3.8)	8.6[b]	-12.2
Israel (II)	10.3	-14.4	4.0	5.3	-7.4	2.0
Puerto Rico (II)	9.2	-6.7	-2.4	5.7	-3.1	-2.6
Uruguay (II)	12.1	-13.8	1.6	8.1	-7.6	-0.6
Japan (III)	(3.5)	-7.5	3.9	8.4	-13.4	5.1
Chile (III)	6.4	-11.4	5.1	(1.1)	-4.1	3.1
Jamaica (III)	(3.9)	-1.8	-2.1	8.2	-7.7	-0.4
Panama (III)	6.6	5.3	-11.9	6.2	5.6	-11.8
Ceylon (IV)	(4.6)	-3.0	-1.7	8.7	-8.7	-0.0
Negative S deviation						
Switzerland (I)	-7.3	-0.7	8.0	(-2.2)	-7.6	9.9
Sweden (I)	-6.7	1.6	5.0	-6.3	1.3	4.9
Norway (I)	-7.1	4.5	2.5	-4.7	0.7	3.9
Italy (II)	-7.0	0.8	6.2	-5.3	-1.8	7.1
Finland (II)	-6.3	4.7	1.5	(-3.4)	1.3	2.1
Greece (III)	-7.6	12.0	-4.4	-6.3	11.0	-4.7
Mexico (III)	(-4.0)	9.7	-5.6	-6.6	13.0	-6.4
Turkey (III)	-16.4	28.9	-12.5	-9.5	20.1	-10.5
Thailand (IV)	-6.4	13.0	-6.8	(+2.9)	1.7	-4.6

[a]Countries are ranked in descending order of per capita income (the roman figure indicates the country group)--see Chap. 5. Figures in parentheses are below one standard error of regression. The regressions cover 62 countries, listed in Appendix Table A-1.

[b]This deviation predicts a negative A share (-1.7 percent). This is explained by the extreme position of the United States on the regression line (and hence the high standard error of prediction).

Source: See source to Table 2.

mated S share exceeds one standard error of estimate. The corresponding A and M deviations are also reported. The figures are based on the regression analysis for the group of 43 countries, using the LF(a) concept, and are measured from regression lines with (log y) and (log y, PR, RU) as independent variables. Table 4 presents similar information for the C and OS sectors.

In all, eighteen countries have residuals large enough to qualify under our criterion, half of them positive and half negative. Only in two cases (Turkey and Uruguay) do deviations exceed two standard errors of estimate.[16] Most of the residuals are within 20 percent of the actual S share.

16. When other variables are added to log y this is true only of Turkey.

Table 4. Deviation of C and OS Shares from Estimated Regression Lines, Selected Countries[a] (Percentage Points)

Country	C sector		Country	OS sector	
	log y	log y, PR, RU		log y	log y, PR, RU
Standard error of regression	2.5	2.5	Standard error of regression	4.7	3.8
Positive deviation			*Positive deviation*		
United States (I)	4.6	3.8	Israel (II)	11.5	7.5
Australia (I)	3.8	3.3	Puerto Rico (II)	6.3	(3.3)
Puerto Rico (II)	2.9	(2.4)	Uruguay (II)	10.7	7.4
Japan (III)	6.2	7.1	Chile (III)	6.8	(2.5)
Ghana (IV)	6.1	6.9	Jamaica (III)	4.9	8.4
			Panama (III)	7.6	7.2
			Ceylon (IV)	(3.6)	6.9
Negative deviation			*Negative deviation*		
Switzerland (I)	-2.7	(-1.8)	New Zealand (I)	(-3.7)	-4.1
Sweden (I)	-3.0	-2.9	Australia (I)	(-3.3)	-5.4
Norway (I)	-2.7	(-2.1)	Italy (II)	-6.5	-5.1
France (I)	-2.6	(-2.3)	Finland (II)	-4.8	(-2.4)
Austria (II)	-2.9	(-2.0)	Mexico (III)	(-3.1)	+5.2
Greece (III)	-3.1	-3.0	Turkey (III)	-10.1	-4.5
Turkey (III)	-6.2	-5.0	Ghana (IV)	-8.2	-4.6
Honduras (IV)	-3.4	-3.2	Morocco (IV)	(-2.9)	-4.5
			Thaliand (IV)	-6.4	+1.0

[a]See note a to Table 3.
Source: See source to Table 2.

In most cases the addition of *PR* and *RU* as independent variables reduced the size of the deviation, and the *S* residual is raised for only four countries.

Casual examination of the sign and size of the residuals reveals no pattern: there are both negative and positive residuals of varying size at all levels of development. Such independence of *S* residuals and level of development is supported by Durbin-Watson values for the relevant regressions. Nor do we find a systematic pattern even when the complete structure of residuals is examined, that is, the relationship between the *S, A,* and *M* residuals and LED. Two major types of residual structure in relation to LED are theoretically conceivable. In one, the residual pattern shows that the country is either more or less developed in its structure than is indicated by the battery of independent variables; in this case the *S* residual should be accompanied by an *M* residual of the same sign and an *A* residual of the opposite sign. In the other type of residual structure, no such pattern is visible: an example is Italy whose negative

S residual is fully offset by a positive *M* residual, with the *A* share almost normal.

The structure of residuals belongs to the first category in only seven of the eighteen countries listed in the table. In all the others, the residuals cannot be eliminated by a change in the LED ranking, since every change in ranking that closes some gaps will widen others. In the group with negative *S* deviations it is the less developed countries whose residual structure belongs to the first category, while countries with an "inconsistent" structure are the more developed. There is no such pattern in the group with positive *S* deviations.

Several types of explanation for the existence of large *S* residuals may be suggested. First, there is the possibility of errors of measurement or reporting of both dependent and independent variables. The most important deficiency of this type is the lack of comparability in the data for different countries: the figures for all the countries used in this study were taken as they appear in the sources without any critical examination of their comparability.[17]

Other explanations for the residuals may lie in specific circumstances and factors affecting single countries or groups of countries. Of these, the following have most often been mentioned: first, a large import surplus can cause a positive *S* residual, all other factors being equal; this results mainly from the fact that a heavy import surplus tends to be goods intensive so that local production becomes more services intensive.[18] Second, small countries tend to have higher service shares mainly as a result of their inability to benefit from the economies of scale which arise mainly in manufacturing.[19] Third, "bulging" in service industries results from a failure to bridge the gap between the growth of total (or urban) population and the development of "productive" industries to absorb the flow.[20]

Although these factors are usually discussed as explaining larger than normal *S* shares, their influence creates both negative and positive residuals in a general regression (run on other variables)—some countries are affected by them and some are not (or are affected in the opposite direction). A cursory glance at our list of *S* residuals does not reveal any size effect. Both very large and very

17. The sources themselves (mostly the UN national accounts yearbooks) warn against using the figures in close comparison studies.

18. See Gur Ofer, *The Service Industries in a Developing Economy: Israel as a Case Study* (Jerusalem and New York, 1967), the sources cited there, and the discussion pp. 40, 43-53. See also Fanny Ginor, "The Impat of Capital Imports on the Structure of Developing Countries," *Kyklos,* 22:104-123 (Fasc. 1, 1969).

19. See among others Hollis B. Chenery and Lance Taylor, "Development Patterns: Among Countries and Over Time," *Review of Economics and Statistics,* 50.4:391-416 (November 1968).

20. See Ofer, pp. 130-142.

small countries have positive S residuals. All the countries with negative residuals are small to medium in size.

Some of the countries with positive S residuals have substantial and persistent import surpluses, among them Israel, Puerto Rico, Panama, and Jamaica. To these countries one may add Jordan, South Korea, and Taiwan, which are included in the larger group of 62 countries.[21] On the other hand, there are two countries (Greece and Algeria) where a high proportion of capital imports is associated with negative service residuals; in other countries such as the United States, Japan, Chile, and Ceylon the positive residual is not associated with heavy capital import.

As regards bulging, each potential case must be investigated rather carefully. Some probable examples are mentioned elsewhere, including Puerto Rico and Japan.[22] It would probably be worthwhile to check the situation in Uruguay, Chile, Jamaica, Ceylon, Trinidad, Egypt, Syria, South Korea, and Taiwan.[23]

The list of countries with large C and OS deviations (Table 4) is not quite the same as the S list. Thus, of the 18 countries with large S residuals, 8 also have large C residuals, and 12 have large OS residuals. In addition there are 5 countries with large C deviations and 4 with large OS deviations not matched by particularly large S deviations.

Of the 13 large C residuals (8 of them negative) only 2 positive (Japan and Ghana) and 1 negative (Turkey) residuals exceed two standard errors; few of the others exceed 3 percentage points. In most cases there is some small decline in the size of residuals when all the LED variables are included in the regression. This is also true for the 16 large OS residuals, 7 of them positive. In 3 positive and 1 negative case the OS residuals exceed two standard errors: the typical size of the residual is between 5 and 6 percent. These residuals, particularly the negative ones, will later be compared with the corresponding Soviet residuals.

The empirical results confirm once again that there is a clear positive relation between level of development and the labor share of the service industries. This is true for each of several alternative definitions of LED. Moreover, the explanatory power of the theory increases as more complex LED definitions are used. The regression analysis is used also to estimate what is here called a normal pattern of change of the services labor shares with LED; this is the pattern of change against which the Soviet Union labor service shares will be evaluated later so as to determine how the Soviet industrial structure diverges from the normal.

21. See App. A for the complete list of countries.
22. Ofer, pp. 134-135.
23. The last five show positive S residuals in the 62-country regressions.

3. The Industrial Structure of the Soviet Union

By the late 1950s the Soviet Union could be described as a developed country. In terms of GNP per capita it ranked among the ten or fifteen richest countries in the world; its industrial sector was large and modern; it had captured a leading position in science and technology and the educational level of the population was high. On the other hand, the Soviet population is still behind most of the developed countries in its very high proportion of rural population—it was not until 1960 that urban population reached 50 percent of the total.

The Soviet development has been achieved in a notably short period, shorter than in many other countries, and it was achieved by a different economic and social system—one centrally planned and strictly directed.

The late 1950s may prove to be a major turning point in the history of Soviet growth. This period saw the end of almost a decade of prosperous, undisturbed, and rapid economic growth that followed a period of reconstruction after the second World War and it marked the beginning of a slowing down in the rate of growth that extends to the present. This slowdown has brought the Soviet authorities to a radical rethinking of some fundamental aspects of their system and to some reorganization in practice.

The choice of 1959 as our main date of investigation—which was, of course, dictated by the date of the latest Soviet population census at the time this study was written—may mark a turning point also in the patterns of change of the Soviet industrial structure.

The Soviet Service Sector: 1959

The two principal methods used in the Soviet Union to measure and record the industrial distribution of the labor force are the annual-average method and the population census. The Soviet industrial distribution of the civilian labor force for 1958-1959 is presented according to both methods in Tables 5 (thousands) and 6 (percent). The annual-average method is based mainly on reports from enterprises, and its standard unit of measurement is "full-time employed equivalent." In the censuses, of which four have been taken during the Soviet period, information is supplied by individuals, and everyone who is engaged in work, whether part-time or seasonal, as well as everyone out of work at the time of the census who has worked during the past year, is counted as a member of the working population. It is not surprising that the 1959 census shows about 4 million more employees[1] (about 7 percent of the total) and nearly 8 million more kolkhozniks (about 25 percent of the total) than the annual average figures. The largest absolute difference, of course, occurs in agriculture, where almost everyone is confronted with a triple choice as to where to work—household, private smallholding, or kolkhoz—and a second triple choice, in reporting his work status.

Though in principle the annual averages should give more accurate figures of the labor input of different branches, census figures are more familiar and provide more comparable data for more countries. Moreover, the census data are used as a benchmark for correcting some of the results of the annual-average method. Fortunately, as one can see in Table 6, the two alternatives yield similar percentage distributions of the Soviet labor force. This is so, to be sure, only when the more inclusive concept of labor force [LF(a)] is used, that is, when we include in the labor force farmers working on their private lots.[2]

The only serious divergence between the two series in the service sector is in public administration and social institutions (line 12 of Table 5) where the census figure exceeds the annual-average figure by about 800,000 persons, or by about 50 percent. As a result the census labor share of this service is more than half of one percentage point above the annual-average share. The literature provides various clues to the sources of this difference.[3] Apparently an unspecified number of part-time pensioners and various groups of volunteers are included in the census but excluded from the annual-averages figures. For the most part and for reasons that will become clear shortly I shall use the high figure, but it is as well to keep the lower one in mind. The differences in the

1. This term is used here to comprise the *rabochie* and *sluzhashchie* categories in the Soviet classification. The distinction is roughly that between blue and white-collar workers or between wage and salary earners.

2. As in Chap. 2, I use two labor force concepts: (a) includes and (b) excludes family workers in private enterprises. For the Soviet Union, (a) includes and (b) excludes all workers on private lots in agriculture.

3. TsSU, *Itogi Vsesoiuznoi Perepisi Naselenia 1959 g. SSSR* (Census of Population 1959) (Moscow, 1962), p. 96 (henceforth *Census 1959*), and U.S., Congress, Joint Economic Committee, *New Directions in the Soviet Economy,* 89th Cong., 2nd Sess., 1966 (henceforth *New Directions*), pp. 722-723 (on "Volunteers"). See also the discussion in Chap. 4 below.

Table 5. *The Soviet Civilian Labor Force, by Industry (Thousands)*

Industry	Annual average		Census, January 1959	Adjusted estimate
	1958 (1)	1959 (2)	(3)	(4)
1. Agriculture (a)[a]	44,291	42,459	49,386	48,771
2. Private subsidiary lots	*12,704*	*11,677*	*9,865*	*9,865*
3. Agriculture (b) [line 1 less line 2]	*31,587*	*30,782*	*39,521*	*38,906*
4. Manufacturing[b]	20,992	21,654	23,832	23,348
5. Construction	5,312	5,860	6,558	6,906
6. Transport	5,668	5,972	5,030	4,939
7. Communications	664	691	708	818
8. Electric power	..[c]	..[c]	..[c]	1,091
9. Other material production	..	..	151	..
10. Trade	4,190	4,389	5,160	5,192
11. Finance, credit and insurance	..	..	..	..
12. Government and local administration, social institutions, social security, and credit	1,554	1,533	2,329	2,761
13. Education, science, and art	5,933	6,287	6,403	5,867
14. Health and welfare	3,059	3,245	3,305	3,302
15. Housing, personal and domestic services	1,832[d]	1,913[d]	1,637	2,466
16. Unclassified services	..	..	682	..[e]
17. Not known	295	349	191	191
A(a) [line 1]	44,291	42,459	49,386	48,771
A(b) [line 3]	31,587	30,782	39,521	38,906
M [lines 4 through 9]	32,636	34,177	36,279	37,102
S [lines 10 through 16]	16,568	17,367	19,516	19,848
C [lines 10 plus 11]	*4,190*	*4,389*	*5,160*	*5,452*
OS [lines 12 through 16]	*12,378*	*12,978*	*14,356*	*14,396*
Total[f] LF(a)	**93,790**	**94,352**	**105,372**	**105,912**[g]
LF(b)	**81,086**	**82,675**	**95,507**	**96,047**

[a]All figures include collective farmers working in nonagricultural activities. *Indicators* estimates them at 2,700,000, about one million of them in services; the Census records only 547,000 collective farmers engaged in nonagricultural activities, only 108,000 of them in services. See the discussion in Chap. 4 below.

[b]Includes workers in producer cooperatives and private artisans.

[c]Included in other branches.

[d]Includes 200,000 artisans.

[e]Belongs to lines 12 and 15 but cannot be broken down and is here included in line 15.

[f]The totals include line 17 (not known). LF(a) includes workers on private subsidiary lots, and LF(b) excludes them. In the international data difference between the two concepts is "unpaid family workers."

[g]This is the Census total *plus* 540,000 militarized police.

Source: Annual averages–based on U.S., Congress, Joint Economic Committee, *Current Economic Indicators for the USSR* (89th Cong., 1st Sess., 1965; henceforth *Indicators*), pp. 67-69, Table VI-2, and pp. 71-73, Table VI-4. *Census 1959* and adjusted estimate, see Appendix Table B-1.

Table 6. The Soviet Civilian Labor Force, by Industry (Percent)

Industry	Annual averages		Census, January 1959
	1958	*1959*	*1959*
1. Agriculture (a)	47.4	45.2	47.0
2. Private subsidiary lots	*13.6*	*12.4*	*9.4*
3. Agriculture (b) [line 1 less line 2]	*33.8*	*32.8*	*37.6*
4. Manufacturing	22.4	23.0	22.6
5. Construction	5.7	6.2	6.2
6. Transport	6.1	6.4	4.8
7. Communications	0.7	0.7	0.7
8. Electric power	..	..	..
9. Other material production	—	—	0.2
10. Trade	4.5	4.7	4.9
11. Finance, credit, and insurance	..	..	..
12. Government and local administration, social institutions, social security, and credit	1.7	1.6	2.2
13. Education, science, and art	6.3	6.7	6.1
14. Health and welfare	3.3	3.5	3.1
15. Housing, personal, and domestic services	1.9	2.0	1.6
16. Unclassified services	—	—	0.6
A(a) [line 1]	47.4	45.2	47.0
A(b) [line 3]	33.8	32.8	37.6
M [lines 4 through 9]	34.9	36.3	34.5
S [lines 10 through 16]	17.7	18.5	18.5
C [lines 10 plus 11]	*4.5*	*4.7*	*4.9*
OS [lines 12 through 16]	*13.2*	*13.8*	*13.6*
M+S	52.6	54.8	53.0
Total LF(b)	86.4	87.6	90.6
LF(a)	**100.0**	**100.0**	**100.0**

Source: Table 5 and notes there.

other service branches are small enough to allow the use of either estimate quite freely.[4]

The last columns of Tables 5 and 6 present our adjustments of the industrial distribution of the Soviet civilian labor force. The adjusted figures are based on the census total, except for the addition of 540,000 militarized police. The adjustments were made in order to allocate unclassified residuals and to transform the Soviet classification to one as close as possible to the International

4. Outside the service sector, there is also a substantial difference in the share of transport. The two sources may differ in their definition of the branch as regards the inclusion or exclusion of segments serving other industries.

Industry	Adjusted estimate		
	(i)	*(ii)*	*(iii)*
1. Agriculture (a)	46.1		
2. Private subsidiary lots	*9.3*		
3. Agriculture (b) [line 1 less line 2]	*36.8*	40.6	
4. Manufacturing	22.1	24.4	41.0
5. Construction	6.5	7.2	12.1
6. Transport	4.7	5.1	8.7
7. Communications	0.8	0.9	1.4
8. Electric power	1.0	1.1	1.9
9. Other material production	—	—	—
10. Trade	4.9	5.4	9.1
11. Finance, credit, and insurance	0.3	0.3	0.5
12. Government and local administration, social institutions, social security, and credit	2.6	2.9	4.9
13. Education, science, and art	5.6	6.1	10.3
14. Health and welfare	3.1	3.4	5.8
15. Housing, personal, and domestic services	2.3	2.6	4.3
16. Unclassified services	—	—	—
A(a) [line 1]	46.1		
A(b) [line 3]	36.8	40.6	
M [lines 4 through 9]	35.1	38.7	65.1
S [lines 10 through 16]	18.8	20.7	34.9
C [lines 10 plus 11]	*5.2*	*5.7*	*9.6*
OS [lines 12 through 16]	*13.6*	*15.0*	*25.3*
M+S	53.9	59.4	**100.0**
Total LF(b)	90.7	**100.0**	
LF(a)	**100.0**		

Standard Industrial Classification (ISIC). With only a few exceptions (mentioned below), the adjusted figures do conform to ISIC, and this is especially so with regard to the distinction between services and other industries.[5] A full

5. The only service/nonservice discrepancies between the Soviet and the ISIC distribution are (a) only part of "electricity, gas, water, and sanitary services" (ISIC order 5) is included in the Soviet S sector; the rest, including electricity, is classified in the M sector; (b) the Soviet item "project survey organizations" (which are basically offices for evaluating and planning construction projects) is under the Soviet definition included in construction; some of the activities covered by this item may in other countries belong to business services, a category that hardly exists in the Soviet Union. [These remarks are based on TsSU, *Slovar po Otrasliam* (industrial classification) (Moscow, 1959).]

account of the adjustments made can be found in Appendix Table B-1. Table 7 presents a detailed breakdown of the service labor force, based on the adjusted figures.

As seen in Tables 5 and 6 the service sector in the Soviet Union accounts for no more than one-fifth of the total and only one-third of the nonagricultural labor force. This is undoubtedly low for a developed country such as the Soviet Union. The commercial sector employs about 5 percent of the labor force and one-quarter of the service workers. Our definition of this sector (in Table 7 and throughout the study) deviates from ISIC in two ways. The first is intentional: we include the catering industry in this sector, instead of in personal services. The second is that we exclude real estate from the sector; this item is left in "housing, personal, and domestic services," partly because of identification problems. Catering comes to about one-fifth of the C labor force while housing may be estimated at less than half a million workers or close to 10 percent of the C labor force.

Public administration (which also includes social organizations such as the Communist Party, the trade unions, the Komsomol) employs 2½ percent of total labor force. This is more than shown by the census (Tables 5 and 6) since we have shifted some municipal-type workers (such as firemen, policemen, and parks workers) from the housing industry, as well as 540,000 militarized police from the army. It is possible that the defense administration is classified as part of the armed forces in the Soviet Union.[6] Since this is done in varying degrees in other countries as well, and since no indication is available as to how far it is done in the Soviet Union, nothing was added to the public administration figure on this account. It is unlikely that more than half a million employees are affected.

Public services (education and health) employ about 9 percent of total labor force and form the largest segment of the S sector. The scope is quite similar to that of the ISIC item.

Finally, about 2 percent of the labor force and just over one-tenth of those engaged in services are employed in "housing, personal, and domestic services." The main elements of this cluster of services can be found in Table 7. They include some municipal workers and dwelling services. The figure for domestic and other services is a residual and should be considered the upper limit as reported in the census; this point is discussed further in the notes to Table 7.

6. The fact that the census records only 632 women in the Soviet army of 3.6 million suggests that this is not so (*Census 1959,* p. 96, Table 30).

Table 7. The Soviet Services Labor Force, by Industry, 1959[a]

Industry	Thousands	Percent
1. Trade	*5,192*	*26.2*
2. Catering	1,167	5.9
3. Retail	2,357	11.9
4. Wholesale[b]	1,668	8.4
5. Finance, credit, and insurance	*260*	*1.3*
6. Government and social institutions	*2,761*	*13.9*
7. Government administration	1,707	8.6
8. Security services (police)	839	4.2
Regular police	299	1.5
Militarized police	540	2.7
9. Social institutions[c]	215	1.1
10. Education, science, and art	*5,867*	*29.6*
11. Education	4,081	20.6
12. Science	1,471	7.4
Scientific institutes	971	4.9
Scientific services	500	2.5
13. Art	315	1.6
14. Health and welfare	*3,302*	*16.6*
15. Housing, personal, and domestic services	*2,466*	*12.4*
16. Culture and recreation	530	2.7
17. Hotels and housing	961	4.8
18. Personal services	293	1.5
Baths and laundries	92	0.5
Barbers and beauty shops	131	0.7
Photographers	27	0.1
Other, clerical and accounting	43	0.2
19. Unallocable services[d]	682	3.4
Total	**19,848**	**100.0**

[a]The subtotals (lines 1, 5, 6, 10, 14, and 15) were broken down by one of two methods: (i) according to the percentage subindustry distribution in the annual-average source (averaging the 1958 and 1959 data); and (ii) according to the occupational distribution in the Census, whenever the annual-average source was sufficiently detailed.

[b]Supply of intermediate materials and equipment, and other wholesale.

[c]Party, unions, Komsomol, consumer cooperatives, etc.

[d]The figure of 682,000 is the residual left in Table 33 of the Census as "other non-material production," and it is not entirely clear what this residual covers. There is, however, some indirect evidence that the item consists mainly of domestic services: in the official classification key for occupations prepared for the Census, the group "Housing and communal economy" includes an item (#650) "Domestic worker, midwife, and nanny"; similarly, in the official census instructions persons privately employed as "Domestic workers, nannies, and private drivers" are required to give the name of the employing family as their place of work. If domestic workers are included in the labor force there cannot be more than 682,000.

According to the branch classification key, "religious institutions" are not included among the "branches of the national economy" but are classified together with "workers in the process of changing their place of work." They may therefore be included among the 682,000.

Source: Subtotals (and total services) from Table 5, adjusted estimate.

The Service Gaps in the Soviet Union: 1959

In this section the data on the industrial structure of the Soviet Union are combined with the normal pattern of change with LED estimated in the last chapter, and the Soviet deviations from the norm are determined.

I begin by deriving the figures for the Soviet variables: (a) GNP per capita in 1959 is estimated at about $1000 (in 1960 prices), using the Western concept.[7] (b) According to the census, the Soviet values of *RU* and *PR* are respectively 52.2 and 52.0 percent.[8] (c) The industrial distribution of the civilian labor force (as presented in the last section) is adjusted to include the armed forces in the OS (and S) sectors in order to make the Soviet figures comparable with the international data. With this adjustment the Soviet S shares [LF(a)] become: $S = 21.1$ percent, $C = 5.0$ percent, and $OS = 16.1$ percent.[9]

The gaps between normal and actual Soviet service shares are shown in Table 8. We refer to the gaps emerging from the regressions with y as "basic gaps" and examine [column (5)] the extent to which the inclusion of other development variables helps to close them.

On the basis of GNP per capita alone the Soviet Union has a relatively large gap for the S sector. The actual Soviet figure is 15 percentage points below the normal level, or less than 60 percent of the norm. There is an even larger gap in the C sector—the Soviet C share is no more than 40 percent of what we would expect in a country with a per capita income of $1000. The gap is actually somewhat wider than this because the C sector is defined more broadly in the Soviet Union than in most other countries. The OS gap is smaller, with the Soviet share only 5.3 percentage points below (or 75 percent of) the norm. It should be remembered, however, that these OS shares include the armed forces and that the proportion of labor force in the armed forces is higher in the

---

7. The figure is based on *New Directions*, p. 109, Table 8. This source gives figures for 1958 and 1960 expressed in 1964 US $ but computed from fixed-prices growth indexes of value added for individual sectors in the Soviet Union and weighted by 1959 weights. For further details see *New Directions*, pp. 128-130, Appendixes A and B, and sources given there. The figure obtained for 1959 is $226 billion (in 1964 prices). It is converted into $211 billion at 1960 prices by the implicit price index of the United States gross product from U.S., Department of Commerce, *The National Income and Product Accounts of the United States, 1929-1965*, Table 8.1, pp. 158-159; the 1959 average population (put at 110.55 millions) is from U.S., Congress, Joint Economic Committee, *Current Economic Indicators for the U.S.S.R.*, 89th Cong., 1st Sess., 1965 (henceforth *Indicators*), p. 27, Table II-1. The final figure is $1001. The procedure employed is not theoretically foolproof but there are good reasons to believe that there is no serious bias.

8. *RU* from *Census 1959*, p. 13, Table 1; *PR* is based on *ibid.*, p. 96, Table 30.

9. The census (p. 96, Table 30) gives a figure of 3,623,000 for the armed forces, from which we have already deducted 540,000 police. The adjusted shares are thus obtained by adding 3,083,000 to total civilian labor force and to the relevant subdivisions.

Table 8. The Service Gaps in the Soviet Union[a] (Percent)

Dependent variable	Independent variable	Service share Actual (1)	Service share Estimated (2)	Standard error of estimate[b] (3)	Gap (2)–(1) (4)	Percent of basic gap[c] closed by adding variables (5)
S	1. log y		36.0	5.8	14.9	0
	2. RU		29.0	5.9	7.9	47
	3. log y, PR	21.1	29.6	5.0	8.5	43
	4. log y, RU		33.1	5.2	12.0	19
	5. log y, PR, RU		28.6	4.6	7.5	50
C	6. log y		14.6	2.5	9.6	0
	7. RU		11.3	3.1	6.3	34
	8. log y, PR	5.0	13.5	2.5	8.5	11
	9. log y, RU		14.0	2.5	9.0	6
	10. log y, PR, RU		13.3	2.5	8.3	14
OS	11. log y		21.4	4.7	5.3	0
	12. RU		17.7	4.3	1.6	70
	13. log y, PR	16.1	16.1	4.0	0.0	100
	14. log y, RU		19.1	4.3	3.0	43
	15. log y, PR, RU		15.3	3.8	−0.8	115

[a]LF(a) data.
[b]At the point of average values for all the regression variables.
[c]Basic gap is that in lines 1, 6, and 11 (i.e., with log y only).
Source: Actual USSR, see text, p. 28.
       Other countries, see sources to Table 2.

Soviet Union than in most other countries. The gap is therefore somewhat greater for civilian OS.[10]

The service gaps in the Soviet Union are narrower when computed on the basis of any combination of development variables. In other words, adding to the analysis some or all of the other variables helps to explain, or close, part of the basic gaps. This is so because the Soviet Union is less urbanized and employs a higher percentage of population than other countries at the same level of income per capita. Thus the Soviet Union is in a sense less developed than is indicated by income per capita alone and should have lower normal S shares. When all the development variables are used together, the gap in the S sector declines from 15 to 7.7 percentage points, or to about half its basic level. A major part of this decline is due to the inclusion of *PR*.

10. The armed forces are about 3 percent of total labor force in the Soviet Union. If we assume that the normal figure is between 1 and 2 percent, then the gap for civilian OS will be 1.2 percentage points higher.

The C and OS gaps are not equally affected by *RU* and *PR*. As with the international regression estimates, the large basic gap in the C share is not much affected by the additional variables. The basic gap is reduced by only 0.6 points when *RU* is added to the regression and by 1.3 points when both *PR* and *RU* are included. In trying to explain why the addition of *RU* makes so little difference, it may be observed that compared with other countries, especially those with similar per capita income, the Soviet relative A share is much higher than the relative *RU;* this may be due either to different rural/urban definitions or to the existence of a larger nonagricultural rural population in other countries: the larger the agricultural sector within the rural population, the smaller one would expect the C (and for that matter the S) share in total labor force to be. Moreover, the nonagricultural population demands more commercial services than do farmers, although it is just as scattered, and may therefore impose a larger than average burden on the trade industry. For these reasons we have also estimated the Soviet C gap with *RU* replaced by the A labor share in the regression: for the (log *y*, *A*) equation the gap comes to only 6.7 points, that is, the contribution of the large agricultural sector to closing the basic gap is 2.9 percentage points or close to one-third of the basic gap.[11] Considering the deficiencies of the estimate for A, the figure of 2.9 points probably overstates the gap-closing effect of this variable.

When *y, PR,* and *RU* are combined to define LED, the OS share in the Soviet Union becomes close to normal (that is, the gap almost vanishes), and apparently this is also true for the civilian share.

How do the gaps in the Soviet service industries compare with the residuals found in other countries? Comparing Tables 3, 4, and 8, we see that the Soviet S and C gaps are rather large, while the OS gap is not exceptionally so, even according to the regression with log *y* alone.

The Soviet S gap is larger than all but one (Turkey) of the negative residuals reported in Table 3 (log *y*) and double the next largest negative residual according to the log *y* regression; when all the LED variables are included, the difference between the Soviet Union and the others is much smaller. This last result indicates that the addition of the other two development variables does more

11. The equation (43 countries) is
$$C = 9.740 + 1.122 \log y - 0.129A \qquad \bar{R}^2 = 0.72$$
$$(0.981) \qquad (0.044)$$
The standard error of estimate is 2.3. This type of equation was not introduced in the general analysis of Chap. 2, mainly because it is undesirable to use *A* as an independent variable since by definition $A + M + S = 1$, and there is a strong likelihood that this rather than the functional relationship will show up in the results. This shortcoming is, we hope, less disturbing for the C sector which accounts for only a small percentage of total labor force.

to reduce the Soviet S gap than that of other countries with large negative residuals. It is tempting to draw the conclusion that in its development structure—that is, the mix of development indicators—the Soviet Union differs significantly from the other countries represented in the regressions.

The Soviet C gap is, relative to those in other countries, even larger than the S gap. The Soviet C gap (Table 4, log y) is at least three times the largest C gap for other countries (again Turkey is the exception). For this sector the differences between the Soviet Union and the other countries with large negative residuals do not narrow when other LED variables are added. This is in line with the generally low response of the C shares to the other LED variables. Thus, the negative gap in the C share in the Soviet Union still remains exceptionally large when all the development variables are considered.

The Soviet gap in the OS share is not exceptionally large (Table 4); furthermore it vanishes when all the LED variables are included—something that does not happen for other countries with large negative OS residuals. Again, the most serious service gap is located in the C sector and the use of a more elaborate LED definition helps to reduce the gap in the sector with a relatively small gap in the first place. How far this is true for each industry in the C and OS sectors is discussed in the next section.

Gaps in the Shares Within the C and OS Sectors

The association between the industrial structure of the labor force and LED can be found at various levels of labor force aggregation. It seems reasonable, however, to assume that the predictive power of the highly aggregative LED variables diminishes over successive stages of disaggregation: as we disaggregate the word normal becomes less justified and two countries with the same LED are more likely to differ in the labor force shares of individual industries. Aggregation may be based on close substitution of products and services in their final or intermediate uses or on similarity of production technique. In either case, small differences in tastes, production techniques, and relative prices—differences that have nothing directly to do with LED—can result in shares that diverge more from the normal at lower levels of aggregation. Much of the additional variance disappears when similar products and services are aggregated in the above sense.

Disaggregation also weakens the relationship with the LED variables because statistical difficulties are aggravated. For one thing, international divergences in the industrial classification of the labor force increase and the data becomes less comparable. For another, the more detail is required, the fewer countries it is available for.

We compare the detailed Soviet C and OS shares with those of only a small number of countries, chosen primarily because potentially comparable data exist for them. These countries are the United States, France, Austria, and Japan, and their GNP per capita is, compared with the Soviet Union, much higher, higher, similar, and lower, respectively. The Soviet per capita GNP figure of $1000 compares with $2500 estimated for the United States; $1414 for France; $860 for Austria; and $430 for Japan (all around 1960 and in 1961 US dollars; see Appendix Table A-1 below). The ranking of the different countries is the same when other LED combinations serve as the criterion. With the important exception of the Japanese C sector, the actual shares of the C and OS sectors in these countries are reasonably close to their corresponding normal shares as estimated by the regression.[12]

Table 9 presents the by-industry breakdown of the C sector labor force in the Soviet Union and the four countries mentioned (in percent of total and C sector labor force). Unfortunately, the large C sector excess found for Japan in the regressions prevents us from examining a typical C sector for a country less developed than the Soviet Union. Even so, it seems clear that the Soviet C gap is spread over all the subsectors, although there is some concentration in retail trade and banking and insurance.[13] This emerges from the within-commerce distributions which show that these two industries employ a smaller proportion of the C labor force in the Soviet Union than in the other countries. The gaps in wholesale trade and catering are somewhat smaller.

12. The actual and estimated (normal) shares of the C and OS sectors in the countries included in Table 9 and 10 are as follows (circa 1960):

Country	C sector		OS sector	
	Actual	Normal	Actual	Normal
United States	28.5	25.4-28.6	22.6	22.1-22.3
France	23.1	22.9-22.7	13.3	15.7-15.5
Austria	18.5	20.7-16.6	11.1	12.4-12.0
Japan	14.9	17.7-13.5	17.6	9.9- 9.4

The left-hand normal figure is from the log *y* regression and the right-hand figure for the most extreme estimate among the other combinations. The "actual" C and OS figures given here differ from those in Tables 9 and 10 mainly because the regressions are based on total labor force while Tables 9 and 10 are based on civilian labor force. There are also some, mostly very small, differences between the sources, and small adjustments were made in Tables 9 and 10 to make the figures comparable. (No such adjustments were made in the regression data.) One major adjustment is that in Tables 9 and 10 catering establishments have been shifted from OS to C for the United States.

13. The Soviet banking and insurance figure does not include real estate. This item could add up to half a percentage point to the figure.

Table 9. C Sector Labor Shares in Five Countries,
by Industry, circa 1960 (Percent)

Industry	USSR 1959	USA 1960	France 1962	Austria 1960	Japan 1961
A. *Percent of total civilian labor force*					
Total commerce	5.2	22.9	14.7	12.4	17.4
Retail trade	2.2	12.7	7.5⎫	9.4	8.8
Wholesale trade	1.6	3.9	3.6⎭		4.8
Catering	1.1	3.0	1.9	1.8	2.2
Banking and insurance	0.3	3.3	1.7	1.2	1.6
Total civilian LF (a) (thousands)	105,721	65,143	18,558	3,279	43,681
B. *Percent of commerce labor force*					
Total commerce	*100*	*100*	*100*	*100*	*100*
Retail trade	43	56	51⎫	76	51
Wholesale trade	31	17	24⎭		27
Catering	21	13	13	14	13
Banking and Insurance	5	14	12	10	9

Source: USSR–Table 7.

USA–Department of Commerce, Bureau of the Census, *U.S. Census of Population 1960: United States Summary, Detailed Characteristics* (Washington, 1963), pp. 1-565, Table 210.

France–Institut National de la Statistique et des Economiques, *Recensement Général de la Population de 1961, Résultats du Sondage au 1/20 pour la France Entière; Population Active* (Paris, 1964), pp. 72-73, Tables 2 and 3.

Austria–Oesterreichisches Staatisches Zentralamt, *Volkszählungs Ergebnisse 1961: Heft 15 Die Berufstätigen nach Ihrer Wirtschaftlichen Zugehörigkeit* (Vienna, 1964), Table 1 and 2.

Japan–Bureau of Statistics, Office of the Prime Minister, *1960 Population Census of Japan; Part 3: Labor Force Status, Industry, Employment Status, Hours Worked and Unemployment* (Tokyo, 1963), Tables 3 and 5.

Table 10, panel A, gives similar information for the OS labor force.[14] It is particularly important to disaggregate this sector because it contains many heterogeneous services that may respond quite differently to changes in the level of development, and the variance of subsector gaps may turn out to be large.

Panel C gives an impression of the effect of RU on the various gaps, since this variable was found to be important with respect to OS. This is done by com-

14. Lines 14 to 16 (panel A) show the labor force shares of industries not included in the Soviet OS sector. Line 17 gives available figures for the share of the armed forces (included in the regressions but not in the OS total of Table 10).

Industry	USSR 1959	USA 1960	France 1962	Austria 1961	Japan 1960
A. Percent of total civilian labor force					
1. Total OS	**13.2**	**22.0**	**17.4**	**16.8**	**12.1**
2. Public administration	2.6	5.1	4.8	6.1	3.9
3. Government	1.6	4.3	3.4	5.2	2.3
4. Police	0.8	0.4	0.7	0.9	0.9
5. Social institutions	0.2	0.4	0.7	..	0.7
6. Public services	8.7	9.8	7.3	5.5[a]	4.3
7. Education and science	5.6	5.3	3.5	2.8[a]	2.5
8. Health and welfare	3.1	4.5	3.8	7	1.8
9. Private services	1.9	7.1	5.3	5.2	3.9
10. Culture and recreation	0.5	1.0	0.4	..[a]	0.7
11. Hotels	0.5	1.0	0.8	1.7	0.7
12. Personal services	0.3	2.0	1.1	2.1	1.8
13. Domestic services	0.6	3.1	3.0	1.4	0.7
Noncomparable items[b]					
14. Other business services	..	1.0	1.0	..	1.0
15. Religious services	..	0.5	0.5	..	..
16. Other communal services	0.4[c]	..	..	..	..
17. Armed forces[d]	2.9	2.6	2.1	..	..
Total civilian labor force (thousands)	105,721	65,143	18,558	3,279	43,681
B. Percent of OS sector labor force					
1. Total OS	**100**	**100**	**100**	**100**	**100**
2. Public administration	20	23	27	36	32
3. Government	12	19	19	31	19
4. Police	6	2	4	5	7
5. Social institutions	2	2	4	—	6

Industry	USSR 1959	USA 1960	France 1962	Austria 1961	Japan 1960
6. Public services	65	44	42	33[a]	36
7. Education and science	42	24	20	17[a]	21
8. Health and welfare	23	20	22	16	15
9. Private services	15	33	31	31	32
10. Culture and recreation	4	5	2	..[a]	6
11. Hotels	4	5	5	10	6
12. Personal services	2	9	7	13	14
13. Domestic services	5	14	17	8	6
C. *Percent of M + S labor force*					
1. Total OS	**24.6**	**23.5**	**22.1**	**21.8**	**18.3**
2. Public administration	4.9	5.4	6.0	8.0	5.9
3. Government	3.0	4.6	4.3	6.8	3.5
4. Police	1.5	0.4	0.9	1.2	1.3
5. Social institutions	0.4	0.4	0.8	—	1.1
6. Public services	16.1	10.5	9.2	7.1[a]	6.4
7. Education and science	10.3	5.7	4.4	3.6[a]	3.7
8. Health and welfare	5.8	4.8	4.8	3.5	2.7
9. Private services	3.6	7.6	6.9	6.7	6.0
10. Culture and recreation	0.9	1.1	0.5	..[a]	1.1
11. Hotels	1.0	1.1	1.1	2.2	1.1
12. Personal services	0.5	2.1	1.5	2.7	2.7
13. Domestic services	1.2	3.3	3.8	1.8	1.1
Total M + S labor force (thousands)	56,950	60,624	14,660	2,519	29,335

[a]Culture and recreation included in education.
[b]Not included in line 1.
[c]Housing services not elsewhere included in OS (arbitrary assumption).
[d]Percent of total labor force.
Source: See Table 9.

paring the nonagricultural labor force shares of the various services, thus making the extreme assumption that the agricultural population does not consume any OS services at all. Since this is definitely not so, the method overestimates the effect of *RU* on the gaps; and since the rural population uses the various services in different proportions, the relative gaps of the industries are also biased.

In the three major OS subdivisions the largest gap is in private services (see line 9 in panels A and B of Table 10). Our sample of four countries suggests that the labor force share of this subsector increases with income per capita. The Soviet share is about half the Japanese share and a much lower proportion of the shares of the other three countries. Private services constitute only about 15 percent of the Soviet OS labor force, although in the other four countries the subsector employs almost a third of OS labor. Within private services the gap seems to be concentrated more in personal services (laundries, barber shops, and so on) and domestic services than in culture and entertainment. When the effect of the urbanization variable is estimated, the gap narrows a little but does not vanish.

The most remarkable finding of this analysis is the gap in public administration. Though our small sample shows no consistent trend of association with income per capita, the Soviet share is clearly lower than that of the other four countries. The gap is even wider when we examine only government administration and social institutions. In these two branches the Soviet Union employs less than half the proportion of labor force employed in the United States, France, and Austria, and about two-thirds of the Japanese proportion. This is surprising, since the natural expectation is to find a large government administrative apparatus in a country with a centrally planned and directed economy.[15]

Here, too, the gap is reduced when the shares are computed for the nonagricultural labor force. But the remaining gap is still substantial despite the fact that the procedure used overstates the urbanization effect.

The gaps in private services and public administration are partly offset for OS as a whole by an excess in public services, most of it in education and science. The Soviet labor share of this industry is (along with the United States share) the highest in our table and probably one of the highest in the world. The figure for health and welfare services is higher in the Soviet Union than in Austria and Japan. There is quite a lot of evidence that the labor share of public services increases with per capita income.[16] The Soviet Union thus

15. It should be remembered that the higher of the two Soviet estimates is used here.
16. See for example Kuznets 1958, p. 64, Table 6.

employs a higher proportion of its labor in these public services than countries at the same income level. Part B of the table shows, of course, an even greater excess.

The business and religious services included in the OS sector in most countries are not all reflected in the Soviet figure. Some (particularly business services) are classified elsewhere, while others either do not exist or are not recorded in the labor force at all. The omission of these branches and institutions widens the Soviet gap for the OS sector as a whole.

To complete the picture, let us also look at the gaps in the Soviet A and M sectors (Table 36 in Chapter 8 below). There is a very large negative basic gap of 22.2 points in agriculture, a gap equal in size to the normal estimated A share (22.6). When the other LED variables are added to the regressions the surplus diminishes to 12.8 points, which is still 25 percent above the norm. As with the S gap, this decline is peculiar to the Soviet Union among the group of countries with large positive S gaps. In the M sector there is a small positive gap of 7.3 points, compared with an estimated share of 41.4 percent, which is only slightly diminished by the inclusion of other development variables.

There are large deficiencies in the service industries and they are concentrated mainly in the C sector and in public administration and personal services. The findings suggest some of the directions in which explanations for the gaps might be found. For one thing—unlike in other countries—LED variables other than income per capita influence the size of most Soviet gaps rather strongly. This implies that Soviet development structure, that is, the relation among the LED variables, differs from that of other countries (see Chapter 2). We have still to inquire into the causes of this special development structure.

Second, the structure of the major gaps (in the S, A, and M sectors) is consistent with a lower level of development for the Soviet Union than indicated by the LED variables; that is both the S and M shares are below the norm while the A share is exceptionally high. It looks as if some other features that go with development are missing and that their inclusion may further explain the gaps. This is to some extent done in later chapters.

A possible explanation of both the Soviet sensitivity to the LED variables and the fact that the gap structure is consistent with a lower LED is that the per capita GNP estimate used for the Soviet Union is too high and thus creates artificially large basic gaps, overstating the Soviet level of development, and distorting the development structure by making y too high for the given PR and RU values. This explanation must be ruled out. To be sure, there do exist lower valuations of the Soviet per capita GNP. Although the value used here is based on a calculated purchasing power parity ratio of 0.91 new rubles per 1961 US dollar, the value based on the official exchange rate (1.11 rubles/$1) is only about $800. Also, a recent estimate of Abram Bergson's, as well as some of his earlier ones, come out somewhat below $1000, even when calculated on a similar purchasing power parity basis.[17] The $1000 figure has been used because at the time of compilation it was the most recent available and because it is based on the purchasing power parity principle used for most of the other countries in the regressions. But although the real figure may be somewhat lower, the point is that relatively small variations in *y*, well within the range of possible values, do not substantially change any of the findings of this chapter. To give a few examples, if the *y* value for the Soviet Union were as low as $600 the basic S gap would still be at the high level of 10.8 percentage points (compared with our figure of 14.9) and the final gap with all the LED variables included would be 5.9 points (compared with 7.5). For the S share to be normal, *y* would have to assume a value below $200—which is altogether implausible. Similar numerical results obtain for all the other gaps. As regards the development structure (that is, the relation between *y, PR,* and *RU*), *y* must again assume a very low level if it is to correspond to the rather high levels of the other two variables. I conclude that if indeed the Soviet Union is in some ways less developed than indicated by its LED variables, it is because it may mean that these variables do not represent the entire development phenomenon, and not that *y* is exaggerated.

Lastly, not all the findings can be explained by deviations in the level of development or its structure. Most notably, the gap in the C sector was only slightly affected by additional development variables. Moreover, although the gap structure of the major sectors does correspond to a lower level of development for the Soviet Union, the gap structure within the S sector does not; the C gap is much larger than the OS gap, and there is wide variation within each of these two subsectors, especially in OS. Other factors, not connected directly with the development variables, must be responsible for at least part of the gap picture. That, too, is a matter looked into below.

17. Bergson's most recent calculations for 1955 give a figure of about $900 (calculated as the geometric average of the figures comparing the per capita GNP, based on dollar and ruble prices, of the United States and the Soviet Union). Bergson's figures are in his "The Comparative National Income of the USSR and USA" (preliminary draft; October 1969; henceforth Bergson 1969), pp. 5-6, Table 2. Other calculations are based on various sources for GNP and population growth in the United States and Soviet Russia. These calculations were not available at the time of writing.

4. Services Performed but Not Recorded in the Service Industries.

As already mentioned, the country data on the industrial distribution of the labor force are not entirely comparable. Despite the efforts of the United Nations to standardize accounting practices, international differences in the conceptual and definitional framework and in statistical methods persist. Some of these are due to differences in industrial organization and as such cannot be ironed out by a uniform set of definitions; it is this type of divergence which is particularly important as regards the Soviet Union with its radically different economic system. While the preceding chapter contained an attempt to adjust for the more technical kind of differences, the present chapter compares differences in the industrial location of certain services which are, I believe, due to basic organizational differences between the socialist or Soviet economic system and the market economies.

Occupational Structure within the M Sector

In most countries, including the Soviet Union, the industrial distribution of the labor force is defined according to the principle that all the workers of a given enterprise should belong to the same industry, that is, the industry to which the major activity of the enterprise belongs. Accordingly, a cafeteria will be classified in the catering industry only if it is an independent enterprise; if it is run by, say, a steel mill it will be classified in manufacturing. It is clear from this that a different organization of production units may produce different industrial distributions of the labor force, despite the fact that the same types of activity are carried on.

In this section (and the next) we look at such organizational differences between the Soviet Union and other countries and examine whether they could have produced some of the service gaps found in the preceding chapter. The question is whether more service activities are incorporated within the production industries in the Soviet Union than in other countries.

Three considerations come to mind. First, for various reasons the Soviet system favors enterprises that engage in many side activities, including the supply of workers' services such as cafeterias, medical units, cultural centers, and nurseries—services that in most other countries are performed by independent enterprises.[1] Second, since it is run by the state, the production enterprise is simply the bottom level of what is essentially a complete hierarchy of administrative bodies on top of it. The cutoff between "production" and "administration" may thus be fairly high on the ladder in the Soviet system so that a higher proportion of the people in the linking institutions are included in the production industries. One would like to know whether this explains the gap in public administration found in the preceding chapter.[2]

Finally, one must consider the possible effect of the Soviet ideological bias against nonproductive work—which includes the white-collar and service-type occupations, even when they are performed within the "productive" industry, as well as all the service industries. This bias, which can be traced to Marx, has two contradictory effects on the location of service activities in the Soviet industrial system. First, overriding the main principle of classification, various service activities (such as factory cafeterias, health units, and so on) are taken out of production enterprises and classified in the appropriate service industries. This practice offsets at least part of the opposite effect of multiactivity enterprises. Second, the bias exerts pressure on enterprises to keep their "nonproductive" manpower to a minimum. Aside from the effects of this pressure on the actual employment of service-type workers, it may also encourage a tendency to disguise service units inside productive departments.

In order to check on "excess" services in the Soviet Union's productive industries (excluding agriculture for the moment), we compare the *occupational* structure of the labor force in different countries. We concentrate on white-collar workers who are performing administrative and commercial functions and on small-services workers who perform cleaning and other janitorial services. The international comparison is hampered by the fact that the scope and coverage of the same occupation vary widely among countries. To overcome this problem, at least to some degree, groups of closely related occupations as well as single occupations, are compared. In this way, possible substitution among closely related services, in definition as well as on the job, is taken into account. There may, however, also be substitution beyond the white-collar

1. See, e.g., M. S. Weitzman, *Comparison of U.S. and U.S.S.R. Employment in Industry, 1939-1958* (Washington, 1963), p. 20.
2. The possibility that there is substitution between commercial and administrative services is dealt with below, Chap. 8.

category (between technician and skilled worker or foreman) or the small-services category (between janitor and unskilled worker).

Another problem concerns the choice of countries with which to compare the Soviet Union. There is no clear theory of how the internal occupational structure of industries changes with the level of development, partly because of the classification problem. The general assumption is that the proportion of white-collar workers rises with economic growth. Taking this possibility into account, we arrange the countries for which there are occupational data in per capita GNP groups and give more attention to the group of countries with incomes similar to that of the Soviet Union. Another reason for doing this is that the Soviet service gaps were defined vis-à-vis countries of the same LED, and any explanation of the gaps should be based on the same comparison.

The 18 countries for which there are reasonably comparable data have been arranged in two groups: those with higher income (group I) and those with lower income (groups II-III) than the Soviet Union.[3] In the Soviet figures I have included all the occupations that might be included under service occupations in any other country even when the probability seemed to be small, so that the Soviet proportions are probably biased upwards. Considering the findings, the bias is in the "right" direction.

The calculations are presented in Table 11. Judging by the country group averages, the proportion of white-collar workers appears to rise with income per capita. This is true for all occupational groups in manufacturing and for most of those in construction and transport. It is also true for all white-collar workers in each of the three industries [columns (1) and (2)]. In manufacturing and transport the proportion of small-services workers increases from group II-III to group I. However, the variances of the proportions of both white-collar and small-services workers in each income group are too large to enable us to reach any firm conclusion from the figures.

The proportion of clerical and accounting, administrative and management, and sales workers in the manufacturing labor force is much lower in the Soviet Union than in the two country groups—less than half the group I figures and no more than two-thirds of the group II-III figures. Out of 19 countries, the Soviet Union ranks lowest in the first two occupations and third from bottom in the third.[4] It is fairly clear that there is a gap here, in addition to the one found in the service industries. Despite the gap in the service industries, which reduces

3. The grouping follows that used in Chap. 5 (p. 59). In the present comparison, however, the lower limit for group II-III is $400 at 1960 prices.

4. D. Granick arrived at the same conclusion, comparing white-collar workers in manufacturing (and mining) in the Soviet Union and the United States for 1954-1956. He showed in addition that in the 1930s the picture was reversed when Soviet manufacturing employed more white-collar workers than United States manufacturing. See D. Granick, *The Red Executive* (Garden City, N.Y., 1961), pp. 141-144.

Table 11. White-Collar and Small-Services Workers in the M Sector, Soviet Union and Other Countries[a] (Percent[b])

Industry and country group	Total (3) through (6) (1)	Total excluding engineers, etc. (3) through (5) (2)	White-collar				Small services
			Clerical and accounting (3)	Administration and management (4)	Sales and supply (5)	Engineers and technicians (6)	(7)
Manufacturing							
Group I	20.4	16.7	9.0	4.8	2.9	3.7	2.3
Group II-III	14.6	13.1	7.4	3.8	1.9	1.5	1.8
Soviet Union[c]	15.7	8.6	4.7[d]	2.8	1.1	7.1	4.2
Soviet Union rank[e]	15	19	19	17	16-17	1	2
Construction							
Group I	10.5	7.8	3.4	4.2	0.2	2.7	0.8
Group II-III[f]	9.8	7.1	3.8	3.2	0.1	2.7	1.1
Soviet Union	14.1	7.6	3.3[d]	3.6	0.7	6.5	3.2
Soviet Union rank[e]	5	8-9	8	8	1	1	2

Transport

Group I	27.9	18.2	13.5	3.7	1.0	9.7	4.8
Group I-III	20.0	16.6	13.4	2.6	0.6	3.4	4.0
Soviet Union	19.1	12.7	8.6[d]	3.4	0.7	6.4	5.1
Soviet Union rank[e]	16	17	16	8-9-10	7-8	7	6

[a]Group I (11 countries): Belgium, Canada, Denmark, France, Netherlands, New Zealand, Norway, Sweden, United Kingdom, United States, West Germany. Group II-III (7 countries): Argentina, Chile, Finland, Ireland, Israel, Japan, Puerto Rico.

[b]Percent of labor force in each industry.

[c]Includes mining (not included for other countries). The potential discrepancy is negligible.

[d]Including workers in stores described as blue-collar workers (*rabochie*, see note 1 in Chap. 3) in the Soviet sources. There are 352,000 of them in manufacturing, 38,000 in construction, and 124,000 in transport. If we exclude them, the percentages for the clerical and accounting category become 3.2, 2.7, and 6.1 for the respective industries.

[e]Rank out of 19 countries (18 countries for construction, see note f).

[f]Excludes Puerto Rico owing to lack of data.

Source: Soviet Union—based on *Census 1959*, pp. 146-158, Table 44. Other countries—M. H. Horovitz, M. Zymelman, and I. L. Herrnstadt, *Manpower Requirements for Planning: An International Comparison Approach*, vol. II: *Statistical Tables* (Boston, 1966), country tables.

the amount of services that the enterprise can receive from outside, the Soviet enterprise "manages" to operate with less administrative and sales staff than a similar enterprise in many other countries, among them many less developed ones.

This conclusion must be qualified by the much higher Soviet proportion of engineers and technicians (probably mainly the latter) in manufacturing. In many countries engineers, and to a smaller extent technicians, perform managerial, administrative, and even clerical tasks. It appears that this is more so, on the average, in the Soviet Union. One reason may be that the campaign against excess administrative apparatuses concentrates more on clerical and managerial workers than on technical occupations. There are many references in the Soviet press to the effect that engineers as well as managers have to engage in clerical work simply because there are not enough clerks.[5]

When engineers and technicians are pooled with other white-collar workers (thus assuming that more of them carry administrative-clerical jobs in the Soviet Union than in other countries), the Soviet figure for manufacturing is no higher than the group II-III average and is still below the group I average [column (1)]. Of the 19 countries, the Soviet Union ranks fourth from the bottom (only Finland, Argentina, and Chile have lower proportions). Even on this basis, and given that the Soviet figures are somewhat overstated, the size of the administrative apparatus, including the part of it engaged in sales and supply, is lower than in other countries at a comparable level of development.

The picture in transport is similar to that in manufacturing, except that here the distribution of workers between the managerial and technical groups is more in line with other countries. In construction, on the other hand, we find higher relative proportions of white-collar workers in all categories, which brings the Soviet Union to fifth position in the ranking. One possible explanation is that in the Soviet Union the "project survey organizations" are included in this industry (see Chapter 3, note 5); in other countries, at least part of the work of such agencies is done in engineering offices classified as business services.

The Soviet proportion of workers in small services in all three industries is

5. See Joint Committee on Slavic Studies, *Current Digest of the Soviet Press* (henceforth *CDSP*), 14.4:30 (February 21, 1962); V. Komarov, "O Ratsionalnom Ispolzovani Kadrov Spetsialistov," *Voprosi Ekonomiki,* no. 9 (September 1966), pp. 15-25; and U.S., Department of Commerce, Joint Publications Research Service, *Translations on USSR Labor* (henceforth JPRS-*Labor*), no. 127 (August 30, 1966), pp. 7-14. Komarov specifically makes the point that the Soviet Union/United States difference in the occupational structure of white-collar workers does not reflect a different structure of the jobs performed; many engineers and technicians carry out clerical jobs because enterprises are under pressure to reduce the number of clerks. See also H. N. Shishkina, *Trudovie Resursi SSSR* (Moscow, 1961), pp. 51-52.

one of the highest among the countries considered. In most countries the great majority of persons in this category are in janitorial-cleaning-maintenance jobs, so that the only plausible definitional substitution is between them and other unskilled workers. More substantial reasons for the difference may be that, in line with the general tendency not to use outside services, Soviet enterprises provide cleaners and watchmen services for themselves rather than hire them from specialized service firms.

A rough estimate of the "surplus" small-services workers in the M sector is made by assuming that it consists of all workers in excess of the group II-III proportion. According to this, it amounts to about 2 to 2½ percent of total M sector employment or to between 700,000 and 800,000 persons, most of whom would be considered part of business services in other countries.

Table 12 compares the occupational structure of manufacturing industries in the Soviet Union and the United States. Here the occupational categories are more comparable than in Table 10. However, we are now comparing countries which differ greatly in productivity and this probably accounts for much of the difference in occupational structure. The general picture is very similar to the one observed in the preceding table, only the gaps are wider. The higher proportion of planners and inspectors in the Soviet Union as well as the similar proportion of bookkeeping personnel is at least partly explained by the fact that the Soviet Union has a centrally planned and controlled economic system. But the proportion of engineers, managers and executives of all kinds, and supply and sales personnel is smaller in the Soviet Union, and the proportion of clerical workers is much smaller. The Soviet excess use of small-services workers found in Table 11 is confirmed here.

The puzzle of Chapter 3 is still a puzzle at this point in the discussion. The personnel missing from the C sector have not been found within the production enterprises nor has the supposedly large administrative apparatus, which was not classified under public administration, been found there.

Services in Agriculture

Socialized agriculture: As with other industries, there may be administrative sales and supply agencies classified as agriculture which should be classified as public administration or trade. The identification of such workers is much more complex for agriculture, since in the Soviet Union this industry is organized in a way that differs radically from what is usual in most of the countries of comparison.

Table 12. Manufacturing Labor Force, by Occupation,
Soviet Union and United States

Occupation	Thousands		Percent	
	Soviet Union	United States	Soviet Union	United States
1. Craftsmen, operatives, and laborers	*19,061*	*12,462*	*80.1*	*71.4*
2. Total white-collar workers (lines 4 through 11)	*3,735*	*4,704*	*15.7*	*26.9*
3. White-collar workers excluding engineers, etc. (lines 6 through 11)	*2,034*	*3,755*	*8.6*	*21.5*
4. Industrial technicians	1,242	343	5.2	1.9
5. Engineers, architects, scientists	459	606	1.9	3.5
6. Other qualified persons (art, sport, law)	31	32	0.1	0.2
7. Managers and executives (industrial)	473	898	2.0	5.1
8. Managers and executives (commercial and financial)	250	560	1.1	3.2
9. Planners, economists, statisticians, and inspectors	164	16	0.7	0.1
10. Accountants and book-keepers[a]	538	410	2.3	2.4
11. Clerical workers[a] [b]	578	1,839	2.4	10.5
12. Small services	*995*	*290*	*4.2*	*1.7*
13. Subtotal (lines 1 + 2 + 12)	**23,791**	**17,456**	**100.0**	**100.0**
14. Service and white-collar workers n.e.s.[c]	–	409		2.3
15. Not known	–	319		
16. Total manufacturing labor force (lines 13 through 15)		*18,184*		

[a]The distinction between the line 10 and line 11 categories may not be the same in both countries.

[b]See note d in Table 11.

[c]Comprises 175,000 newsboys, 35,000 cafeteria workers, and 199,000 qualified persons. In the Soviet classification these come under services even when employed by manufacturing.

Source: Soviet Union—See source to Table 11.

United States—*United States Census of Population 1960 Occupational Characteristics* (Washington, 1963), Table 2.

Soviet agriculture is essentially an industrialized[6] sector with large production units employing what amounts to hired workers and with an industrial-type managerial and administrative organization. This is literally so for State farms (*sovkhozi*) which employ one-sixth to one-fifth of the agricultural labor force and virtually so for collective farms (kolkhozi) which employ the remainder, especially since the early 1960s, when money remuneration was introduced. This organization contrasts with the individual-proprietor-based agriculture of almost all the other countries.

In contrast to the typical owner farmer who manages his farm with little specialized help, keeps his own records, serves as his own supply and sales manager, and works on the farm—all these functions are performed by special employees in the state or collective farm. In addition, large units of production tend to absorb functions usually performed for the individual farm by outsiders. Finally, many personal, municipal, and social services are performed by the central administrations of collective farms and to a lesser extent by the State farms—these are not only production units but also social, administrative, and geographical entities. It is therefore probable that there is some mixing of production and service functions and there is some evidence that some of the workers involved in these services are in fact classified into the agricultural labor force.

It may therefore be argued on the one hand that some of the apparent excess of white-collar workers in Soviet agriculture relative to other countries is justified because it is due to the difference in organizational patterns. On the other hand, there seems to be a strong tendency in the USSR to include in agriculture service workers who should be reclassified under services.

According to the 1959 Census, there were 2,450,000 persons in agriculture, or 6.2 percent of the socialized agricultural labor force, who may be classified as white-collar workers since they perform managerial and administrative functions. Data on the occupations and functions of such persons are presented in Table 13. To the regular white-collar occupations (defined in the Census as nonagriculturists by occupation), we have added 760,000 workers defined by the Census as agriculturists by occupation as well as industry: farm managers, brigade leaders, and some of their staff. Most other Soviet sources treat these people as belonging to the administrative and service staff of the kolkhoz or sovkhoz.

The Census does not list any small-services workers in agriculture, but other

---

6. The term "industrialized" is used here to refer to the internal organization of the production unit rather than to its external links. Most agricultural sectors in more or less developed countries are industrialized in the latter sense, i.e., they sell most of their produce and purchase a substantial part of their inputs.

Table 13. Services in Soviet Agriculture

Occupation	Thousands	Percent
All service workers	**3,425**	**8.8**
White-collar workers	*2,455*	*6.3*
Accounting and clerical	713[a]	1.8
Storekeepers	209	0.6
Trade workers	69	0.2
Managers and executives	944[b]	2.4
Engineers and technicians	121	0.3
Agricultural specialists	399	1.0
Small services	*970[c]*	*2.5[c]*
Labor force in socialized agriculture[d]	**38,837**	**100.0**

[a]Including 29,000 listed as "agriculturists by occupation," while the others are listed as accounting and clerical personnel.

[b]731,000 (142,000 managers of specialized farms and 589,000 brigade leaders) are listed as agriculturalists by occupation.

[c]Assumed to be 2.5 percent of the agricultural force (this is the average of the two Nimitz figures, see note 7 in Chap. 4).

[d]Including forestry (411,000).

Source: Total agricultural labor force—*Census 1959,* Table 44. White-collar workers—*Census 1959,* p. 146, Table 44, and p. 161, Table 47; also *Census 1959,* p. 159, Table 45, for a more detailed occupational breakdown of "agriculturists." Small services, see note 7 in Chap. 4.

sources indicate that such workers do exist. Assuming that the Census listed them as farmers, I have "borrowed" a figure from N. Nimitz's calculations on the occupational structure of the labor force in agriculture. Thus their number can be estimated at between 2 and 3 percent of the socialized agricultural labor force (800,000 to 1,200,000).[7]

The figures of Table 13 on the whole agree with most other sources on agricultural employment, though the total number of workers classified in agriculture with service type occupations may reach 4 million.[8] The problem is

7. N. Nimitz, *Farm Employment in the Soviet Union, 1928-1963* (Santa Monica, 1965), pp. 128-129. This source gives two figures for "administrative services in collective farms":3.5 percent and 6.8 percent. The second includes and the first excludes "postal services, expediting, transport services to administration, and maintenance of administrative building" (p. 129). My assumption is that at least half of these workers belong to the small-services category.

8. *Collective farms:* Nimitz's figure for the proportion of white-collar and small-services workers is 6.8 percent (see preceding footnote). If it is assumed that brigade leaders are not included and 1.9 percent is added on this account (as in the Census), we get a figure of between 8 and 9 percent. Figures for individual collective farms range from 6 percent in a highly praised farm to 13, 16, and even 18 percent in some that are criticized sharply for this [*CDSP,* 13.21:23-24 (June 21, 1961), and 14.42:21-22 (November 14, 1962)]. These sources also give detailed lists of the positions included in the white-collar and small-services category, among them store managers, most specialists (such as milking-machine operators), and managers (such as assistant brigade leaders or pump-house managers in the poultry section).

now to determine how many of them can properly be reclassified into our service industries.

Comparisons of the Soviet occupational structure of agriculture with that in other countries are of little help. When proprietors are listed as farmers, the proportion of white-collar workers is much higher in Soviet agriculture than in any of the other countries, and when proprietors are classified as managers the white-collar proportion is higher in the other countries.[9]

Viewing the agricultural industry in the Soviet Union as an industrialized branch one might compare its white-collar proportions with urban industrialized industries inside the Soviet Union. As can be seen from Tables 11 and 13, the white-collar proportion is much lower in agriculture (6 to 7 percent) than in manufacturing (15 percent).

According to the Census only 108,000 kolkhozniks are employed in service activities, 85,000 of them in education and health, with 11,000 in trade and the remaining 8,000 in other services.[10] This seems to me too small a figure, considering that at the beginning of 1959 there were about 70,000 collective farms in the Soviet Union with a population of about 65 million. It is thus likely that some kolkhozniks serving the population were classified as farmers.

From fragmentary evidence on tasks performed by the administrative and service staff of collective farms one gets the impression that although most of them are engaged in servicing production, some of them, such as the food-store manager and the wood-store manager, serve the community. Some of the administrative staff are also expected to deal with the population's problems rather than directly with production.

Agricultural administration above the kolkhoz level is apparently not classified as agriculture. Exceptions to this may be: (a) the administrative staff in

---

State farms: Nimitz gives the occupational distribution of "basic production personnel." We assume that all workers in other activities were reported in the Census according to the procedure applied to M sector enterprises (that is, cafeteria workers were included in catering, and so forth). The figure for white-collar and small-services workers are (percent of state farms labor force):

Marketing	1.5
Materials purchasing	5.2
Branch administration	6.0
Farm administration	2.2
Total	*14.9*

[Nimitz's main source is TsSU, *Selskoe Khoziaistvo SSSR* (Moscow, 1960), pp. 452-453.] *Collective and state farms combined:* The average (including small-services) is about 10 percent, which is slightly above the corresponding Census figure. In absolute figures we get about 4 million white-collar and small-services workers (that is, 10 percent of the 39 million in agriculture).

9. Data for other countries are from M. H. Horovitz, M. Zymelman, and I. L. Herrnstadt, *Manpower Requirements for Planning and International Comparison Approach,* vol. II: *Statistical Tables* (Boston, 1966).

10. *Census 1959,* pp. 104-105, Table 33.

the MTS/RTS[11] which might have some administrative-control functions on the collective farms; (b) similar staff in agricultural services institutions. Nimitz estimated the administrative and service staff in the MTS/RTS at 242,000 and 123,000 in 1958 and 1959, respectively, and the total staff of the agricultural service institutions at 140,000 and 160,000, most of whom are employed directly in agriculture (in veterinary, seed, pest control, irrigation, and drainage services).[12]

There are many complaints in the Soviet press about excess administrative and service staff in collective farms. The same complaints, however, are constantly voiced about other industries as well.

Taking all this into account, we can make the following estimate of the number of service workers to be reclassified out of agriculture into the service industries: (a) We assume that as many as five people per collective farm are actually service workers, about half of them in distribution and half in administration, yielding a total of about 350,000. (b) There may be a few hundred thousand administrative workers (mainly in MTS/RTS) who belong to public administration. (c) Some of the 6.7 percent of workers on the state farms (see note 8 in this chapter) engaged in marketing and material purchasing should probably be reclassified under the trade industry. Their total number is about 300,000. In all, about a million workers are thus shifted out of agriculture and added, in about equal numbers, to public administration and trade. This leaves some 2.5 million people performing managerial, executive, and small-services jobs in agriculture.

The collective-farm market: A considerable part of Soviet agricultural production is sold to the urban population through the collective-farm markets, in which many of the traders are the farmers themselves. These people are classified in the Census together with other agricultural workers on their own subsidiary plots, that is, they are considered to be outside the socialized labor force.[13] The number of such retail traders is not known. Several estimates made by casual Soviet observers put it anywhere between 500,000 and 900,000 in the late 1950s and early 1960s.[14] Taken at face value, this means that as many as 20-30 percent of the total number of retail workers do not appear as such in the Census figures.

11. Machine-tractor stations and technical repair stations. The former were abolished in 1957.
12. Nimitz, pp. 141-146.
13. This can be inferred from the Census instructions [TsSU, *Vsesoiuznaia Perepis Naselenia 1959 g.* (Moscow, 1958), p. 46].
14. The two extreme figures are given by A. A. Vasileev, *Kolkhoznaia Torgovlia i Zagotovki* (Moscow, 1960), p. 12. The lower figure is the number of traders on ordinary days. At times, the author says, the number goes up to 800,000. There are 900,000 trading pitches in all urban markets together. In another source (quoted in *New Directions,* p. 724), the estimate is 700,000 persons (some time in the early 1960s).

A second approach to the estimation of the number of collective-farm market traders is to estimate the number of persons needed to sell the amount of merchandise sold in these markets, assuming the average level of sales per person in the socialized Soviet retail industry (the state and cooperative networks). This method would yield an underestimate because sales per person must be much lower in collective-farm markets than in the retail industry— collective farmers spend much time in going to and from the market and they usually sell their own rather small amount and assortment of goods. On the other hand, we should get a good estimate of the number of workers adjusted for quality or productivity, and this is more meaningful for our purposes.[15] Working along these lines yields an estimate of between 90,000 and 120,000 "retail-trade equivalent" workers, depending on the prices applied to collective-farm market sales.[16]

A combination of two conclusions emerges when this result is compared with the direct estimates: the rate of sales per worker in the collective-farm markets is much lower than in the average retail enterprise, or the direct estimate is too high in the sources quoted above, or both. If the whole difference is explained by the lower sales per worker the rate on the kolkhoz market is no more than 20-25 percent of the rate for a retail worker elsewhere in the Soviet Union.

Public Administration in Public Services

We first compare the occupational structure of the public service industries in the Soviet Union and other countries in order to determine whether some workers classified in health and education do not properly belong to public administration. Assuming that the occupational distribution is meaningful, Table 14 demonstrates that the proportion of both clerical and executive and small-services workers in both education and health is lower, or no higher, in the Soviet Union than in the other country groups or single countries. On the face of it then, there is again no evidence of the existence of misclassified public administration workers in the public services, and the conclusion reached for the M sector again holds. In services, however, the distinction

15. We adjust the labor force distribution for differences in quality in the next chapter. By adding collective-farm traders at average quality, the necessity of making further adjustments for this category of workers is avoided.

16. Sales per retail worker in the socialized industry came to 31,940 rubles in 1959 (here and elsewhere reference is to new rubles), total sales of, 65.5 billion rubles and 2.1 million workers. In the same year sales in the urban collective-farm markets came to 3.83 billion rubles at market prices [TsSU, *Narodnoe Khoziaistvo SSSR v 1960 g.* (Moscow, 1961), p. 735 (henceforth *Narkhoz*)]. We then get 3.83 × 31.940 = 119.9 thousand. A calculation that takes into account also the fact that prices are higher in the collective-farm markets than in socialized trade gives an estimate of only 91.4 thousand (the deflator is 1.31, according to Bergson 1969). These estimates take no account of intercommodity differences in the sales per worker rates.

Table 14. Administrative and Small-Services Workers in Public Services, Soviet Union and Other Countries[a] (Percent[b])

| Service and country group | Administrative | | | Small services |
	Total	Clerical and accounting	Managers and executives	
Education				
Group I	8.7	6.9	1.8	13.8
Group II-III	7.6	6.8	0.8	14.9
Soviet Union	8.3	4.4	3.9	14.5
Soviet Union rank[c]	8	13	2	7
Health				
Group I[d]	10.9	9.0	1.9	20.2
Group II-III[e]	11.9	9.8	2.1	19.7
Soviet Union	6.2	4.5	1.7	6.4
Soviet Union rank[c]	12	14	8	14

[a]The occupational data for public services are not as comparable as those for the M sector in Table 11. Group I (10 countries): Belgium, Canada, Denmark, Netherlands, New Zealand, Norway, Sweden, United Kingdom, United States, West Germany. Group II-III (6 countries): Chile, Finland, Ireland, Israel, Japan, Puerto Rico.
[b]Percent of labor force in each industry.
[c]Rank out of 17 countries (education) and 15 countries (health, see notes d and e).
[d]Excluding New Zealand.
[e]Excluding Chile.
Source: See source to Table 11.

between administrative and professional jobs is rather vague in the occupational classification. It is probable that when a teacher, for example, moves to an administrative job in the Ministry of Education he will continue to be classified in censuses and the like as a teacher. As there is no direct evidence on the Soviet practice of industrial classification of the ministries responsible for the various public services, there is still a possibility that public administrative workers in these ministries were classified under "public services" rather than "public administration."

Three sources of supply of services in the Soviet Union are *not* recorded in the labor force. These are services provided to the community by organized groups of volunteers, services offered commercially by private people, which are illegal in varying degrees, and finally services supplied by households to themselves in their free time. The third source is discussed in a later chapter.

Volunteers:[17] Volunteers perform various services for their communities in almost all countries. It seems, however, that they are much more important in

17. The discussion in this section is based largely on *New Directions,* pp. 722-723, and U.S., Congress, Joint Economic Committee, *Dimensions of Soviet Economic Power,* 87th Cong., 2nd Sess., 1962 (henceforth *Dimensions*), pp. 641-642.

the Soviet Union, both in numbers and in the wide range of their activities. The recruitment of volunteers to perform urgent tasks and to participate in the various campaigns for harvesting, road building, propaganda, and so forth, has been an important element in Soviet life all along. A new drive to organize groups of volunteers to perform a wide range of administrative and other services on a regular basis was initiated by Khrushchev at the 21st Congress of the Communist Party in 1957.[18] Since then and up to the present the number of such volunteers has grown substantially and by 1959 had reached several millions.

A major purpose of the volunteer drive is clearly to limit or even reduce the number of paid employees at all levels of government.[19] If the statistics are consistent, the labor force in public administration declined by about 400,000 between 1953 and 1955, and by another 100,000 between 1955 and 1959. Since 1959 it has stayed at almost the same level.[20] Some of this stagnation in the size of the sector at a time of rapid economic growth and urbanization can be attributed to services provided by the volunteers. Another purpose of the volunteer drive was to induce workers whose skills were needed to carry on working after retirement age.[21]

The activities performed by the volunteers can be listed under three main headings: civilian-municipal services, economic services, and political-cultural activities.[22]

The first category includes the Volunteer People's Guards (the largest group) who carry out some police functions, the Comrade Courts, which deal with small disputes, the Volunteer Fire Brigade, many street, parks, houses, and sanitation committees, and general administration on the local and municipal level. By 1962, over two million volunteers were said to be participating in such activities.

18. *CDSP*, 11.21:21 (June 24, 1959).
19. See, e.g., Shishkina, p. 51.
20. *Indicators*, pp. 71-72, Table VI-4. The decline from 1953 to 1955 may be connected either with a real reorganization or with a reclassification of workers after the death of Stalin. See also Appendix Table E-1 below.
21. The pension laws in force from 1956 to 1964 allowed only token pay for people who chose to go on working after formal retirement. Since 1964 the amount of pay allowed has been increased substantially. See *CDSP*, 16.14:29 (April 29, 1964).
22. In addition to sources already cited in this section, the following provide information on the various activities and the number of persons involved: on activities in the party organizations, see P. Pigalev, "Obshchestvennie Nachala v Rabote Partiinykh Organov," *Kommunist*, no. 7 (May 1962), pp. 60-69, and *CDSP*, 14.2:30 (February 7, 1962); on economic activities, see S. Kunin, "Shire Privlekat Obshchesvenost k Uluchsheniu Ucheta i Otchetnosti," *Vestnik Statistiki*, no. 2 (1962), pp. 16-22; on economic control and inspection in trade enterprises, see *CDSP*, 11.18:32 (June 3, 1959), and G. Dikhtiar, "Soviet Trade in the Period of the Full-Scale Building of Communism," *Problems of Economics*, 5:45-52 (August 1962); on volunteer police force, see *CDSP*, 11.10:3 (April 8, 1959) and 15.7:7 (March 13, 1963); on comrade courts, see *CDSP*, 13.33:8 (September 13, 1961) and 13.43:13-15 (November 22, 1961).

Economic functions include a variety of statistical and auditing committees, stores committees, retail trade inspectors, economic analysis bureaus, and technical economic councils. Their functions vary from general consultation to plant and organization management, specific financial auditing, and inspection of performance of enterprises. This group of volunteers usually consists of engineers, accountants, economists, and other specialists.

The last group of activities corresponds to similar ones carried on by groups of volunteers in many other countries. It includes parents' school committees, political committees, and cultural boards.

In most cases the volunteer groups work apart from the parallel staff departments, but in some cases nonstaff workers are incorporated in regular administrative departments and work alongside the paid officials. There are even several examples of volunteers running stores.[23]

In 1959 there may have been at least two million and maybe up to three million volunteers, about half of them in the People's Guards and most of the rest in other municipal and cultural activities; several hundred thousand people were probably involved in various economic activities.[24]

Much more difficult than estimating the number of volunteers is to estimate their contribution to output in units of full-time paid public administration employees. Little can be suggested in this direction except for the obvious point that *on the average* a volunteer contributes less than a staff employee. If the full number of volunteers were added to public administration, the sector would be spuriously inflated owing to the difference between the gross number and its full-time-paid equivalent. Nevertheless, the relative contribution of the Soviet volunteer to public administration services is probably higher than in many other countries. Several hundred thousand persons can probably be added to the services labor force on this account.

Illegal Services

Shortages, supply gaps, and bottlenecks, whenever and wherever they appear, call for somebody to remedy them—in return for high profits, of course. In the Soviet Union, where such bottlenecks are plentiful, there must be, and there

23. See *CDSP*, 11.21:21 (June 24, 1959) and *Biuleten Ispolnitelnogo Komiteta Moskovskogo Gododskogo Soveta Depitagov Trudiashchikhia*, no. 5 (March 1962), p. 15.
24. We can illustrate the number of people involved from information about volunteer activities in two small towns. In one town of 75,000 inhabitants there were (in 1959) 250 volunteer committees with about 4,000 *aktivi* (volunteers in public affairs) of the women's organizations alone [A. I. Lukianov and B. M. Lazarev, *Sovetskoe Gosudarstvo i Obshchestvennie Organizatsi* (Moscow, 1960), pp. 150-153]. In another town, with about 50,000 inhabitants, there were said to be more than 5,000 *aktivi* [*CDSP*, 13.38:8-9 (October 18, 1961)].

are, many people involved in supply and trade activities, as well as in the supply of various small personal services. The labor inputs in these operations are not recorded in the labor force statistics, since these activities are performed on a private basis and are illegal in varying degree. Despite this, not only private citizens but also collective farms and even local economic councils at times feel constrained to use the services of these operators. I make no attempt to guess their number; their mere existence, however, proves the point that the legal socialized supply and trade agencies are inadequate either in size or in efficiency.[25]

Let me summarize the findings of this chapter industry by industry. Up to half a million administrative workers classified according to the Soviet setup under various industries may belong to public administrative services as conventionally defined; some of them are in agriculture, and some come from the volunteer movement outside the labor force. After adjustment the public administration sector is still smaller than normal and certainly not as large as it is alleged to be in a centrally planned economy. Indeed, far from there being a surplus, there is an actual shortage of administrative and clerical workers in the economic and control agencies within the M sector. This finding is most surprising, and it increases the public administration gap to be explained.

Persons engaged in trade and supply outside the trade industry are found in agriculture, as suppliers of both the rural population and agricultural production and as salesmen of agricultural products in the collective-farm markets. They are also found as private operators outside the established Soviet system and to a lesser degree among the volunteers. Together there are probably no more than half a million such workers (in "full-time equivalent"), and they thus cover barely 10 percent of the C sector gap.

Most of those classified in business services in other countries seem to be employed directly by the industries using their services in the Soviet Union. This is true of small services as well as design and engineering services. This may explain some of the gap in private services. Other private services are also supplied by persons outside the socialized economy, in many cases illegally.

25. See, e.g., *CDSP*, 11.34:18 (September 23, 1959); 12.42:32 (November 16, 1960); 14.28:31 (August 10, 1960); 13.51:32 (January 18, 1961); 18.33:24 (September 7, 1966); and 19.11:27 (April 5, 1967). It is possible that some cases on the borderline between legal and illegal operations were recorded as trade workers by the Census. This may explain why the Census figure for trade exceeds the annual-averages figure by more than the typical amount (see Table 5).

5. The Quality of the Service Labor Force

The various labor shares so far presented on which our findings rest are all based on the rather generally defined unit of labor: an "employed person." Even if uniformly defined across countries, an employed person may represent widely different amounts of labor input for different industries both within and across countries. If so, our findings, for both the general relation between labor shares and LED, and the service (or other) gaps found between the Soviet Union and the normal pattern, clearly require correction. An attempt to correct for relative quality of labor differences across industries and countries is the subject of the present chapter.

When the basic input unit is an employed person (presumably on a yearly basis) the most obvious quality criterion is actually a quantitative one: the number of hours of work per worker. Unfortunately there are not enough data to incorporate this factor in a systematic and precise manner, and we must be satisfied with a qualitative discussion.

Apart from hours worked, the three principal criteria of labor quality generally used are the proportion of males, the proportion of workers in the prime-age groups (defined here as 25-64), and the average level of education. I shall not justify the choice of these quality criteria here but refer the reader to the elaborate analysis of Denison and others.[1] One comment may be in order: when we talk about labor quality the interest centers on the actual productivity of given groups of workers and not on their potential productivity. Social

---

1. See, e.g., E. F. Denison, *The Sources of Economic Growth in the United States* (New York, 1962; henceforth Denison 1962), chaps. 6 and 8; E. F. Denison, *Why Growth Rates Differ: Postwar Experience in Nine Western Countries* (Washington, 1967; henceforth Denison 1967), chaps. 7, 8, 9, and 16; and D. Schwartzman, *The Decline of Service in Retail Trade: An Analysis of the Growth of Sales Per Manhour, 1929-1963* (Pullman, Wash., 1971), chap. 4.

discrimination to prevent entrance of women to certain professions provides an example of the disparity between the two.

The three quality criteria must first be assigned productivity weights; they are defined as the relative productivity of women (compared with men) and of non-prime-age (compared with prime-age) workers, and the relative loss (or gain) in labor productivity as a result of one less (or more) year of schooling.[2] In reality these productivity weights vary between countries and industries and are therefore very difficult to estimate. To reduce the problem to manageable dimensions I make a few simplifying assumptions (unquestionably at the cost of precision):

1. The productivity effects of the quality factors are assumed to be additive. This would be realistic if the factors were independent (for example, if the productivity differential between men and women at the same level of education and in the same group were the same no matter what the educational level or age group).
2. In principle there should be specific productivity weights for every country. With a few exceptions, we assume the same productivity weights for all countries for a given factor.
3. The productivity weights are assumed to be the same for all industries. Again this is clearly not so in reality. Compared with men, women are relatively more productive as nurses than as farmers, and differences in education are more important in one industry than in another.

We estimate productivity weights from three sets of data. A general group of weights is estimated from a cross-section table of hourly wage by age and educational level, based on the US 1960 Census of Population,[3] and from the extensive body of data and discussion contained in Denison's two works (note 1 in this chapter) on the United States and Western Europe. A second set of weights is estimated from Soviet wage data but is of limited value because of the small number of observations. In every case, the productivity weights are estimated on the assumption that the wages used represent marginal productivities. Needless to say, these productivity weights are at best crude approximations. The results based on them should be evaluated accordingly.

For the age criterion, the assumption is that workers outside the 25-64 age group are 70 percent as productive as those within it, all other factors being held constant.[4]

2. A formal development of the quality adjustment is presented in Appendix C.
3. The table is given by Schwartzman, p. 46, Table 4-1, and is based on the 1/1000 sample of the US 1960 census.
4. See Appendix C, part IV.

For the sex criterion, it is assumed that women are 60 percent as productive as men, with age, education, and hours kept constant.[5] This single weight undoubtedly covers quite a wide variation. The relative productivity of women probably rises with LED. This can be explained in terms of women staying longer in the labor force and augmenting their stock of experience, as well as in terms of returns to education, the steady penetration of women into jobs earlier barred to them, and the increase in demand for labor in jobs where the relative productivity of women is higher. According to C. D. Long,[6] the relative productivity of women increased by 15 percentage points in the United States in the first half of the twentieth century. In addition, women are relatively more productive in services than in the A and M sectors, and within the S sector they are relatively more productive in health services than, for example, in trade. These differences in the sex productivity weights will be accounted for only qualitatively.

Lastly, there is the education criterion. For the highly developed countries, a productivity differential of 5 percent is assumed for each year of additional formal education.[7] As the level of development rises and education becomes more plentiful, productivity per additional year of schooling should go down. Following Denison, we assume that for countries in the middle income range the weight will be 67 percent above the group I figure, or 8.3 percent per additional year of schooling.[8] Since there are no data on the level of education for the group of least developed countries, there is no point in assigning any productivity weight and arbitrary assumptions must be made about the effects of education in this income range.

The ideal procedure for incorporating the quality factors into the analysis of services labor shares would be to adjust each share by the quality coefficients in each of the countries involved, and then to rerun the regressions of Chapter 2 with the adjusted data. This, however, cannot be done, mainly because of the small number of countries for which we have educational data; in any case our crude productivity weights do not justify such refinements. Instead, we employ a method which seems good enough for the data. In order to learn about the patterns of change with LED of the by-industry differences in the relative quality of labor we first examine the quality characteristics for four country groups (for which data are available) arranged in descending order of per capita income. The observed patterns are then used to correct the unadjusted service

5. See Appendix C, part IV.
6. Quoted by Denison 1962, pp. 81-82.
7. See Appendix C, part IV.
8. Denison 1967, p. 85, Table 8-3.

shares and to compare the adjusted Soviet shares with the adjusted normal shares computed in the preceding step.

The four country groups have the following GNP per capita ranges (at purchasing power parity in 1960 US dollars): group I: $1000-$2500, which includes the United States, the rich Commonwealth countries, and most of the countries of Northwestern Europe, all of which are more developed than the Soviet Union; group II: $500-$999, which includes the less wealthy countries in Western Europe, South Africa, Israel, and the most advanced countries of Latin America; group III: $250-$499, which includes Turkey and Japan, the less developed countries in Southern Europe, and the less wealthy countries of Latin America; and group IV: $70-$249, including the least developed countries, mainly in Asia and Africa, as well as the poor Latin American countries. Though the grouping is according to GNP per capita, it conforms, with few exceptions, to that according to all our other definitions of LED.[9]

The International Findings

The tables of this section cover 28 countries in all four groups for the age criterion, 50 countries, also in all four groups, for sex distribution, and 6 countries (only one each in groups II and III, none in group IV), for educational level.

Table 15 presents a general view of the changes that take place in the quality variables as LED rises. The proportion of workers in the prime-age group rises with LED, both in total labor force and in most of its subdivisions; the exception is the C sector, and as a result the prime-ages proportion rises more moderately in the S sector than in the rest of the economy. In addition, as LED rises, the proportion of males in the labor force declines, in all sectors and in almost all income ranges. The decline is greatest in the S sector and negligible in the A sector. Although in the OS sector most of the change takes place in the early stages of growth, in M and C it comes only at higher levels of income. The age and sex trends are contradictory in their effect on quality changes. The only unambiguous change, observed without weighting, is the decline in the quality of the C sector labor force.

The decline in absolute quality due to changes in age and sex composition is likely to disappear when differences in educational level are taken into account. Unfortunately, such differences cannot be allowed for here because of

---

9. For other LED definitions, countries are ranked by their S share as estimated by the regression.

Table 15. Males and Prime-Age Workers, by Industry and Country Group[a] (Percent[b])

Country group	Total labor force	A	M+S	M	S	C	OS
A. Percent aged 25-64							
Group I (8)	75.0	75.0	75.0	78.0	71.3	69.8	72.0
Group II (4)	71.1	70.4	71.1	71.8	69.0	67.5	71.1
Group III (6)	70.3	68.9	72.4	72.4	73.1	75.2	72.4
Group IV (10)	67.7	67.0	68.4	69.1	68.4	73.8	65.7
B. Percent males							
Group I (11)	69.6	80.7	67.5	80.7	50.1	57.8	45.2
Group II (11)	75.0	84.0	71.3	84.8	59.3	74.3	49.5
Group III (9)	72.5	78.3	73.2	84.1	60.9	75.4	53.7
Group IV (19)	80.4	82.8	76.4	84.4	69.9	74.8	69.9

[a]According to per capita income (see p. 59 for income ranges). Figures in parentheses give the number of countries included.

[b]Percent of labor force in each cell of the table. The figures are the X_{kij}'s (k = age, sex). See Appendix C for the formal presentation of the computations.

Source: UN, Demographic Yearbook 1964, Table 9.

lack of data, but the UN series on the educational level of total labor force in many countries clearly indicates that the rise in educational level with per capita income is large enough to become dominant and to raise the absolute quality of the labor force in every major sector of the economy.[10] Other factors that may affect the absolute quality of the labor force are the increase in the relative productivity of women and the decline in the number of hours worked. The first tends to raise quality and the second to reduce it. According to Denison, however, part of the loss in productivity due to the reduction in hours is made up by self-generated increases in productivity. In the range of 48 to 52 hours a week (on a yearly average) or more, the compensation is very close to 100 percent, and it reaches about 30 percent at 40 hours a week.[11] Thus the overall loss from reduction of hours is not very large and is concentrated in the high income ranges.

Tables 16 and 17 present the final stages in the computation of the effect of the quality factors on the unadjusted labor force shares of the four country groups.[12] In Table 16 the relative quality advantage or disadvantage of each industry compared with total and non-A labor force is shown for each country

10. UN, Demographic Yearbook 1963, Table 14.
11. Denison 1962, p. 40, and Denison 1967, pp. 59-63.
12. The other stages of computation are explained in Appendix C.

group. The comparison within the non-A labor force is made in order to isolate the important effects of the relative quality changes in the A sector. The computations for the group IV quality differentials were based on an arbitrary assumption regarding differences in educational level, namely, that the group IV interindustry quality differentials stemming from differences in educational level contribute twice as much to the industry quality differentials between groups IV and I as to those between groups II and I.[13]

This means basically that educational differentials narrow as income rises. Over the entire income range as well as in the upper (groups II to I) range there is a decline in the relative labor quality of the S sector and its two subdivisions. In effect, there is a change from relatively superior quality for these industries in group IV countries to relatively inferior quality in group I. The decline is more marked in OS and smaller for C. Though all the quality factors estimated contribute to this decline in relative quality, the relative decline in the educational levels is the most important. The increase in the relative proportion of women is important in the OS sector in the lower income range and in the C sector in the higher range. This pattern indicates the way women penetrate into the non-A labor force, first to the OS industries (domestic service and education and health services) and only later to trade (and the M sector). According

Table 16. *Quality Adjustment Coefficients, by Industry and Country Group*[a] *(Percent)*

Country group	A	M+S	M	S	C	OS
A. Sectors compared with total labor force						
Group I	+1	−0	+4	−8	−6	−9
Group II	−8	+2	+5	+0	+1	−0
Group I+II	−5	+1	+4	−4	−3	−4
Group III	−10	+5	+7	+4	+6	+4
Group IV	−19	+6	+6	+10	+4	+15
B. Sectors compared with M+S labor force						
Group I			+4	−8	−6	−8
Group II			+3	−2	−1	−2
Group I+II			+3	−5	−4	−5
Group III			+1	−1	+0	−1
Group IV			−1	+4	−2	+9

[a]$R_{ij} = \prod_k (q_{kij} + 1) - 1$ (see Appendix C).

Source: Age and sex, see Table 15; education, unpubl. data of M. Zymelman. See also text and Appendix C.

13. See Appendix Table C-1 and notes in Appendix C.

Table 17. *Estimated Service Labor Shares,*[a] *Unadjusted and Adjusted for Quality, by Country Group (Percent)*

Sector	Country group				Change over income range	
	I	II	III	IV	IV −I	II −I
S sector						
Unadjusted[b]	39.8	33.3	27.3	20.4	−19.4	−6.5
Adjusted[c]	36.5	33.3	28.3	22.4	−14.1	−3.2
C sector						
Unadjusted[b]	17.0	11.6	9.4	8.2	−8.8	−5.4
Adjusted[c]	15.9	11.7	9.9	8.5	−7.4	−4.2
OS sector						
Unadjusted[b]	23.4	20.0	16.7	13.1	−10.3	−3.4
Adjusted[c]	21.3	19.9	17.3	15.1	−6.2	−1.4

[a]The C and OS shares do not add to S since the unadjusted shares are estimated from separate regressions.

[b]W_{ij}.

[c]$W_{ij}^* = (R_{ij} + 1)(W_{ij})$ (see Appendix C).

Source: Unadjusted share—estimated from the regression of log y on service shares (see Table 2).

Adjustment coefficients—Table 16 (the computation was done with less rounded figures than those shown there).

to our calculations, age is the least important factor. Its major contribution is in reducing the relative quality of C sector labor in the lower income range.[14]

The relative decline in the quality of S labor must be reflected in a relative increase somewhere else in the economy. This occurs in the A sector, although the relative quality of M labor also declines slightly. The contribution of the A sector to the relative decline in the quality of the non-A labor is double-edged; on the one hand, the relative quality of its labor increases by 20 percent over the whole income range (9 percent over II to I). On the other, the labor share of the sector declines sharply over the whole range, so that it contributes to the average smaller and smaller weights of labor of lower-than-average quality. Nevertheless, not all the relative quality changes are connected with the A sector (see panel B in the table). The relative quality of the S sector and its two subdivisions still decline markedly within the non-A labor force.

The service shares must now be adjusted for quality differences. This is done in Table 17. We compute the *estimated* service shares for the four groups of countries (unadjusted in the table) and then adjust them with the quality coefficients of Table 16. It is found that the quality adjustments modify the unadjusted increase in the S, C, and OS shares substantially over all income

14. The findings for the separate factors are based on Appendix Table C-1 and underlying worksheets.

ranges, but especially over the upper range where it skims off half the increase in the S share and more than half the increase in the OS share. In all cases, though, even the adjusted shares still grow with income. The adjustments and the rate of decline in the relative quality of services labor are biased upwards if the productivity weights of women in these industries are higher than the 0.6 weight used here, or if the productivity of women increases with LED. I tend to accept both these possibilities.

The probable effects on quality of several other factors should be added to those estimated in this section. These other factors are interindustry differentials, the decline in the number of hours worked, and changes in the amount of part-time work (to the extent that they are not measured in the source data). Although we cannot measure their intensity, we can at least indicate the direction in which they work.

If we accept Denison's conclusion that all reductions in hours above the limit of a 48-hour week are fully compensated by increased productivity in the remaining hours, then we need not worry about this effect in the lower income range, where the working week is mostly above this limit. For the upper income range, over groups II to I, hours in general decline more sharply in industries with more employees than in those with many self-employed. This is supported by 1929 to 1963 data for the United States on the by-industry pattern of decline in hours (in percent compounded per year):[15]

Total labor force	−0.6
A sector	−0.4
M sector	−0.6
S sector	−0.7
C sector	−0.5
OS sector	−0.8

If this pattern also holds for the II to I income range, then the decline in hours may further reduce the relative quality of the S and OS sectors but may tend to increase the relative quality of the C sector. These effects are partly offset by the compensating increase in productivity, which may be as high as half the original effect (assuming that the reduction is in the 40- to 50-hour-week range) and which is likely to be especially large in services where the least productive hours (when the fewest customers come) are cut first.[16]

15. During the period 1929-1963 the United States moved from about $1700 per capita GNP (in 1958 dollars) to about $2900 [U.S., Department of Commerce, *Survey of Current Business,* 46:37 (July 1966)]. The data on hours are from Schwartzman, p. 40, Table 3-1, with additional details kindly supplied by the author.

16. Denison 1967, p. 13.

Another factor reducing the relative quality of services labor may be a *relative* increase in the proportion of people working part-time. Only part of the adjustment needed for part-time workers finds its way into census figures, because some seasonal workers do not register as workers if the census takes place when they are not employed. Also, as with shorter hours, there seems to be productivity compensation, because part-time employment helps enterprises to adjust their services to variations in the volume of customers, on a daily or weekly basis.

If all these factors were taken into account, the quality adjustment coefficients for services would perhaps be somewhat larger than those shown in Table 17. Even so the adjusted service shares would still rise over the whole income range, though the OS and perhaps the S shares may not rise over the groups II to I range.

The Relative Quality of the Soviet
Labor Force by Industry

Table 18 presents the labor quality characteristics in various industries in the Soviet Union. The data are presented for both labor force concepts LF(a) and LF(b).[17] The main reason for this is that there are no good data on quality for workers occupied on private plots in agriculture, so that in order to compute figures for LF(a) I have had to make several crude assumptions about them. The LF(b) figures are much more reliable, although even they involve several arbitrary assumptions, mainly with regard to age distribution.[18]

Two sets of results emerge from the table: first, the direction of the inter-industry differences in the level of the quality factors is very similar to that found in other countries; specifically, the S labor force is more concentrated in prime ages, employs a higher proportion of women, and is better educated than the labor force of the other sectors. Also, the A labor force is less educated and has a low proportion of male workers; both these characteristics are more pronounced when workers on private plots are included [compare the A figures for LF(a) and LF(b); see also Table 15].

17. See definition in Chap. 3, note 2.
18. It is assumed that the 20-24 age group constitutes 50 percent of the 20-29 age group, for all industries. This assumption may overestimate the proportion in the prime-age group in A and M and underestimate it in the S sector. It is also assumed that two-thirds of workers aged 60 and over belong to the 60-64 group. Third, in compiling level of education, census data, presented in terms of type of school completed, are translated into average number of years. The conversion was done with help of Dewitt's scheme of the structure of the Soviet educational system [N. Dewitt, *Educational and Professional Employment in the USSR* (Washington, 1961), facing p. 22; and *Dimensions,* p. 244]. See also notes to Table 18.

Table 18. Some Quality Aspects of the Soviet Labor Force, by Industry[a]

Quality criterion	Total labor force	A	M+S	M	S	C	OS
LF(a)							
Percent aged 25-64	72.4	71.6	72.7	69.5	79.4	78.5	79.7
Percent males	46.3	37.9	53.0	61.3	36.9	38.5	36.5
Education							
(years of schooling)	5.6	4.3	6.8	6.2	7.8	6.6	8.3
LF(b)							
Percent aged 25-64	72.6	71.9					
Percent males	50.2	46.0		as above			
Education							
(years of schooling)	5.8	4.7					

[a]$X_{ki(su)}$; see Appendix C.
Source: See Appendix Table C-2.

Second, Table 18 (together with Table 15 above) shows that the main difference between the Soviet labor force and that of other countries is the much higher proportion of women employed in total labor force and in most of the sectors; compare figures of 46 to 50 percent males in the Soviet Union with figures of between 70 and 80 percent for the four groups of countries in Table 15. Such a major difference in the composition of the labor force may affect not only the relative labor force quality of various industries but also, as is shown below, the relevant sex productivity weights. For this reason an attempt must be made to estimate a set of Soviet productivity weights and compare it with the general set of weights based on the cross-country data.

The system of Soviet weights was estimated by a regression of quality characteristics of the Soviet labor force in 1959 on monthly wages (for 1958), the units of observation being the eleven industries that make up the labor force. The small number of observations is the greatest weakness of this estimate. A second problem is the extent to which wages in the Soviet Union represent productivity. Although the labor market is considered one of the freest in the Soviet Union, one may ask how free it really is. For one thing, just a few years later, in 1964, a wage reform raised relative wages in most services by more than 20 percent.[19] Wages could correspond to productivity either before or after such a change, if at all, but hardly at both periods. In the regression itself

19. See the various decrees in *Trud* (July 16, 1964), p. 1, and *Sotsialisticheski Trud* (August 1964), p. 3.

it was not possible to isolate a significant coefficient for any prime-age group of workers despite several variants tried by shifting the age boundaries.[20]

The estimates of productivity weights for women and for level of education produced by the regression are 0.21 for women relative to men and 13.8 percent for every year of additional education. The coefficients from which these weights were calculated are highly significant, as is also the entire equation.[21]

These weights are quite different from the general set since the Soviet age and education weights are higher and the sex weight much lower. Some of the differences between the two sets of weights may be due to statistical factors,[22] and some, mainly those for the sex productivity weight, may be explained by lower-than-equilibrium pay in the Soviet Union to workers in services and agriculture where the concentration of women is greatest.[23] Some of the differences, however, may reflect real factors. The higher weight for additional education (13.8 percent per year in the Soviet Union compared with 8.3 percent in the general set of weights for middle-range countries) may indicate that the stock of human capital is still relatively small compared with other countries or compared with Soviet growth targets.

The explanation of the differences in the sex weight is much more complex. The much higher proportion of women employed in the Soviet labor force may in theory have two contradictory effects on the productivity weight, effects based on the reasons for assuming that women are less productive in the first place. Women are said to be less productive than men while performing the same job because of their family responsibilities; as a result of them women do

---

20. The reason may be statistical: either the small number of observations does not allow for enough variation in the levels of the factor, or the fairly high correlation between prime age and level of education ($R = 0.55$) makes the coefficient of the latter absorb the effect of the former as well.

21. The equation is

$$W = -530.8 + 11.5 \text{ (percent males)} + 119.5 \text{ (years of education)} \qquad \bar{R}^2 = 0.72$$
$$(260.2) \quad (2.3) \qquad\qquad\qquad (26.1)$$

where W is the annual wage. The estimate is based on the quality factor level as in Table 18 (based on the Census) and monthly wages as reported in *Narkhoz 1964*, p. 555 (for 1958). The productivity weights are derived from the estimated equation by computing the change in the wage produced by a small change in the quality characteristics.

22. The eleven observations that we have create a relatively high and almost entirely spurious negative correlation between the proportion of males and the level of education ($R_{\text{males, education}} = -0.51$); this is a result of a high proportion of women and a high level of education in the service industries. This may have resulted in a simultaneous increase of the coefficients for both the sex (percent of males) and education variables; we have already mentioned the possible absorption of the age factor in the education coefficient.

23. The wage reform in the service industries is some evidence as regards services—its official justification was very much along these lines. See references cited in note 19 in this chapter.

not stay in the labor force as long as men and have (at a given age and educational level) less on-the-job training and experience; family responsibilities are also the cause of many interruptions in a woman's work routine. Women are said to be less qualified than men for specific jobs, mainly those requiring physical strength, while they are believed to be better qualified for other jobs (such as nursing and teaching), because of their special characteristics. If women are employed according to their relative advantage, that is, if they enter first those jobs in which they have most advantage or least disadvantage, then more women in the labor force means a lower productivity weight because additional jobs will be less and less suitable for them. Women are also said to be less productive than men because of job discrimination: they may be employed in jobs in which they are not able to realize their full potential because they are conventionally barred from other jobs. If these restrictions are lifted then the unused potential can find its way into higher productivity of women.[24]

In the Soviet Union one again finds factors working in opposing directions: there is no question that the Soviet Union has lifted many of the social restrictions on jobs for women—indeed women are encouraged to take almost any job—and, despite many complaints by women about existing restrictions, they work at jobs which far fewer of their counterparts do in the West, as physicians, store and office managers, or scientists, for example.[25] This factor may increase women's productivity relative to men's. Other factors, however, seem to work in the opposite direction; first, as we have seen, more women are employed relative to men in the Soviet Union. Other things being equal, they are bound to take some jobs in which they have a smaller relative advantage. Secondly, though fewer restrictions are put on jobs for women, fewer of the traditional women's jobs are available in the Soviet Union because of its peculiar industrial structure—the number of secretarial jobs in particular and services jobs in general is small. Taking these two factors into account it is not surprising that many women still perform hard physical labor in agriculture and in the M sector. (The other side of equality of job opportunity is that women may or even must also take up hard labor.) In view of all this I am inclined to think that the productivity weight for women in the Soviet Union should not be higher and may even be lower than the general weight—as is indicated by the estimated Soviet weight.

Table 19 shows the interindustry quality differentials and the resultant over-

24. H. Sanborn, "Pay Differences Between Men and Women," *Industrial and Labor Relations Review,* 17:534-550 (July 1964).
25. See N. T. Dodge, *Women in the Soviet Union* (Baltimore, 1966), chap. 10, esp. pp. 198-199; and *Indicators,* pp. 94-97.

Table 19. Interindustry Quality Differentials, by Quality Criteria, in the Soviet Union, General and Soviet Weights (Percent)

Quality criterion	A	M+S	M	S	C	OS
A. Weighted relative interindustry quality differences[a]						
1. General weights						
LF(a)						
Age	−0.3	0.1	−1.0	2.3	2.0	2.4
Sex	−4.3	3.4	7.6	−4.8	−4.0	−5.0
Education	−10.8	10.0	5.0	18.3	8.3	22.4
M+S						
Age			−1.0	2.2	1.9	2.3
Sex			4.1	−7.9	−7.2	−8.1
Education			−5.0	8.3	−1.7	12.4
2. Soviet weights						
LF(a)						
Age	0.0	0.0	0.0	0.0	0.0	0.0
Sex	−11.8	9.4	21.0	−13.2	−11.0	−13.8
Education	−17.9	16.6	8.3	30.4	13.8	37.3
M+S						
Age			0.0	0.0	0.0	0.0
Sex			10.6	−20.6	−18.6	−21.1
Education			−8.3	13.8	−2.8	20.7
B. Adjustment coefficients[b]						
1. General weights						
LF(a)	−15	14	12	15	6	19
LF(b)	−11	10	8	11	2	15
M+S			−2	2	−7	6
2. Soviet weights						
LF(a)	−28	27	31	13	1	18
LF(b)	−20	18	21	5	−6	10
M+S			1	−10	−21	−5

[a] $q_{ki(su)}$ (see Appendix C).
[b] $R_{i(su)}$ (see Appendix C).
Source: Panel A computed from Table 18 and weights shown in Appendix C.

all quality adjustment coefficients, computed on the basis of both the general and the Soviet set of weights. As can be seen, the differences are quite marked. In order to avoid repetition the findings of this table are discussed along with the comparisons of the Soviet Union with other countries.

We compare the relative labor force quality measures of the Soviet Union with the corresponding estimates of three different groups: the average of groups I and II, group II, and group III. Each comparison corresponds to one of the LED definitions in the regression analysis of Chapter 2. Each comparison also indicates the quality adjustments that should be made to the Soviet service shares to make them conform with the shares in the comparison group.

The per capita income criterion ranks the Soviet Union between groups I and II; the quality adjustments in the Soviet service shares should therefore be made in accordance with the relative quality of the labor force in the corresponding service industries of countries of similar income per capita, represented here by the average of groups I and II. When LED is defined by income, level of urbanization, and labor participation rate together, the Soviet Union falls into group III.[26] Thus, the adjustment of the gaps established by this development definition must be done with respect to country group III. Likewise, when the level of development was defined by y and *PR,* or y and *RU,* the Soviet Union was ranked by the regression on the border between groups II and III and inside group III, respectively. Since the numerical results of these two last cases are very close, the comparison with the average of groups II and III is omitted.

Table 20 summarizes the results of these comparisons. All the comparisons in panel A of the table show that the relative quality of the S labor force in the Soviet Union (and of OS and, with some exceptions, C) is higher than the relative quality of the corresponding sectors in the other groups of countries with the same LED. The Soviet relative quality advantage in the S sector moves from as low as 3 percent to as high as 20 percent, depending on the comparison made. The relative quality advantage rises as we move from group III to the higher income groups and is higher for Soviet LF(a) than LF(b). The Soviet-weight figures are not very different from the general-weight figures; when Soviet weights are used, the relative quality of services is enhanced by the greater weight of education and depressed by the lower weight for the productivity of women. The explanation for the differences in the quality advantage between the various comparisons is fairly straightforward.

The relative quality of workers on their own plots is the lowest in the Soviet economy; this is because this group of workers includes a very high proportion of women and of young and especially old workers, and because the educational level is much lower than average. In all these respects they are even less qualified than the rest of the A labor force; by adding them to the labor force one raises the relative quality of labor in all other sectors, including services, and thus also the relative advantage of Soviet service labor over that of other countries.

26. The countries are ranked according to the size of the regression *estimate* of the relevant service share. The estimated S and OS shares put the Soviet Union into the same group, but the estimated C share never puts it below group II. There is therefore no point in comparing the relative quality of Soviet C labor with that of group III countries.

Table 20. Relative Labor Quality Differentials, by Industry, Soviet Union and Selected Country Groups[a] (Percent)

	A	M+S	M	S	C	OS
A. Total labor force						
1. General weights						
Soviet LF(a) with						
Group I+II	−10	13	7	20	9	24
Group II	−7	11	6	16	5	20
Group III	−6	8	5	12	1	16
Soviet LF(b) with						
Group I+II	−7	9	4	16	5	20
Group II	−4	7	2	12	1	16
Group III	−2	5	1	8	−3	12
2. Soviet and general weights						
Soviet LF(a) with						
Group I+II	−24	26	26	19	5	26
Group II	−21	25	25	15	1	22
Group III	−19	22	24	11	−4	17
Soviet LF(b) with						
Group I+II	−15	17	17	11	−3	17
Group II	−13	16	15	7	−7	14
Group III	−11	13	14	3	−11	9
B. M+S						
1. General weights						
Soviet Union with						
Group I+II			−5	7	−3	11
Group II			−5	4	−6	8
Group III			−3	4	−7	7
2. Soviet and general weights						
Soviet Union with						
Group I+II			−1	−4	−17	2
Group II			−1	−6	−20	−0
Group III			1	−7	−21	−2

[a] $r_i = \prod_k (q^*_{ki} + 1) - 1$ (see Appendix C).

The contribution of each quality factor to the total quality differential can be seen in Appendix Table C-3, where a detailed description of one of the comparisons is presented. The decreasing quality advantage of the Soviet S sector as we move to comparisons with groups of lower LED countries is explained by the general trend of decline in the relative quality of services labor as LED increases. The quality advantage is always larger for the OS than for the C labor force. Though the former ranges from 9 percent to 26 percent, the quality advantage of C labor does not exceed 9 percent and in several comparisons it disappears completely or turns into a disadvantage.

The quality advantage of the Soviet S sector reflects in large part the fact that the gap between the quality of the agricultural and the nonagricultural labor force is wider in the Soviet Union than in other countries. This can be seen in Table 20. In all cases the relative quality of A labor is lower and of M+S labor higher in the Soviet Union than in the other countries. This is so even when the size of the rural population and the labor force participation rate are taken into account as development variables (in the comparison with group III). Only in one case, when workers on private plots are excluded from the Soviet data [LF(b)], is the relative quality of A labor almost equal to that of group III. Admittedly, the lower relative quality of Soviet A labor might be partly spurious owing to a more inclusive definition of Soviet agricultural labor compared with other countries, with the difference made up of lower quality labor. Even if this is so, the quality adjustment takes care of this difference.

Not all relative quality differences in service labor can be explained by the rural-urban difference. With general weights, the relative quality of Soviet services is higher than in other countries, even when only the non-A labor force is taken into account (panel B of Table 20). In this case, however, more than the total relative advantage is located in OS, while the C labor force is relatively inferior to its counterpart in other countries. Thus, it is only the still lower quality of agricultural labor that gives C labor any advantage. When only urban labor is included, the relative quality of the commerce worker is lower than in other countries.

The main contributor to the higher relative quality of the Soviet S sector is level of education, especially that of OS workers. The large proportion of women in *nonservice* industries and the somewhat higher concentration of prime-age workers in the S sector also contribute to this advantage.

While the proportion of women in the labor force of all industries is higher in the Soviet Union than in other countries, their *relative* proportion is higher in the nonservice industries. This affects positively the relative quality of the S labor force but not that of the C sector. The relative proportion of women in the C sector is very high, a fact that contributes much to its lower labor quality.

The quality advantage of the OS sector in the Soviet Union can be explained in part by its peculiar internal industrial structure: the high proportion of education and health services and the low proportion of personal and domestic services which are usually made up of less qualified workers. This internal structure accounts for some of the much higher relative educational level and the somewhat lower proportion of women and very young and old workers. In order to answer the question whether or not these structural differences explain all of the OS quality advantage it is necessary to examine comparative data on the quality characteristics of these industries. Unfortunately, we have no such information for either the OS or the C sectors. The scanty evidence gives the impression that the relative educational level in the Soviet Union is higher in public services and public administration than in other countries.[27] Within the C sector, it may be assumed that women are especially concentrated in retail trade and thus may be pushing its relative labor quality to below that in other countries.

Finally, when general and Soviet weights are used the low productivity weight for women applied to the Soviet data pushes the relative quality of Soviet S labor to below that of M, eliminates the quality advantage of OS labor, and increases even more the quality inferiority of C labor. I think that this result is too extreme.[28]

Table 21 translates the findings of this section into the direct effect of the differences in relative quality of labor on the various service gaps estimated in Chapter 2. It may be seen [column (5)] that the quality adjustments, combined with a small additional contribution of the effect of part-time labor, may close about one-third of the original S sector gap. However, most of the effect is confined to the OS sector, whose small gaps are closed or turned into an excess.[29]

Some remarks on the possible quality effects of differences in the number of hours of work are in order. The problem can be divided into two elements: the length of the work week for full-time workers and the proportion of part-time workers. Part-time work does not as a rule exist in the Soviet Union. Every worker is expected to carry a full-time load, as defined for him. There are, however, seasonal and temporary workers in the Soviet Union who are employed only part of the year. It is assumed here that this category is taken care of and reduced to full-time equivalents by the annual-averages method of labor reporting. In most of the other countries, especially the more developed ones, the opposite occurs: part-time work is an important element in the labor force, especially for women, and especially in services. In so far as the usual census-type reporting inflates part-time labor inputs, this difference between the

27. Such evidence as exists from other countries is from Zymelman (unpublished data).

28. Using mixed weights for the quality criteria, in general and for sex in particular, offsets the relative disadvantage of Soviet M sector because it employs relatively more women than the M sector in other countries.

29. Table 21 uses Soviet LF(a) data and the general set of weights, which are probably more reliable. Using the mixed weights, the quality adjustments would close a greater proportion of the gaps.

Table 21. Quality-Adjusted Soviet Service Gaps[a] (Percent)

| Independent variable | Corresponding country group | Adjusted shares[b] | | Service gap | | Percent of gap covered by adjustment $100 - \frac{(4)}{(3)}$ |
		From the regression (1)	Soviet Union (2)	Unadjusted (3)	Adjusted (1) − (2) (4)	(5)
S sector						
log *y*	I+II	34.7 ⎫		14.9	10.0	32.9
log *y, RU*	II	33.1 ⎬ 24.7		12.0	8.4	3.0
log *y, RU, PR*	III	29.6 ⎭		7.5	4.9	34.7
C sector						
log *y*	I+II	14.2 ⎫		9.6	8.8	8.3
		⎬ 5.4				
log *y, RU*	II	14.1 ⎭		9.0	8.7	3.3
OS sector						
log *y*	I+II	20.6 ⎫		5.3	1.1	79.2
log *y, RU*	II	19.0 ⎬ 19.5		3.0	− 0.5	116.7
log *y, RU, PR*	III	15.9 ⎭		− 0.8	− 3.6	c

[a]Based on Soviet LF(a) and the general productivity weights. Computations were done with less rounded figures than those in the source tables.

[b]$W_{ij} = (R_{ij.} + 1) \ (W_{ij})$ (see Appendix C). For the Soviet Union the R_{ij}'s shown in Table 19 have been raised by 2 percentage points in order to adjust for part-time work.

[c]Denominator too small to give meaningful result.

Source: Unadjusted shares underlying columns (1) and (2), and the unadjusted gap [column (3)] from Table 8.

　　　Adjustment coefficients (R_{ij}'s) for country groups, Table 16; for Soviet Union, Table 19.

Soviet Union and other countries results in an underestimation of the Soviet services labor share.[30] The importance of this factor can be gauged by comparing the industrial distribution of workers[31] in the United States on the basis of full-time equivalent (FTEQ) with a regular distribution based on the number of people engaged.[32] Since the United States is the country with the most part-time work, the differences found between the two distributions can be considered as the upper limit for the effect of part-time work. The results of the comparison show that according to the FTEQ distribution the S share is

30. Assuming, as for the Soviet Union, that seasonal workers are reported in full-time equivalent units in the censuses.

31. Differences in hours worked between employees and self-employed are ignored here. This aspect is dealt with below (Chap. 7) in the discussion of the relative quality of the self-employed. See also the references cited in note 1 in this chapter.

32. Both distributions are compiled by the Bureau of Labor Statistics (U.S., Department of Commerce) on the basis of labor surveys.

lower by 6 percent (not percentage points!) and the A and M shares are correspondingly higher.[33]

It was a little surprising to find that the distribution based on FTEQ (which is based on labor force *Surveys*) was almost exactly similar to the industrial distribution of employed persons as recorded in the 1960 population *Census*. The only exception was that the census share for retail trade was lower by about 10 percent than the FTEQ share; this difference was made up by an opposite difference in wholesale trade. This means that except for these two sectors the inclusion of part-time employment does not affect the distribution in the United States. From these two comparisons, it is clear that population censuses do catch part of the part-time effect, and also that part-time in services may be partly compensated by a more flexible work schedule. We assume that the relative quality advantage of the Soviet Union's service labor force that is due to the lack of part-time work is no more than one-third of the differences indicated by the comparison of the FTEQ and the ordinary labor distributions in the United States. This estimated effect is included in Table 21, column (2).[34]

As for the second element, the length of the working week, there seem to be only very small differences between the Soviet Union and other countries in the length of the working week, and we shall not try to document them here. In many Western countries there seems to be a difference in the number of hours worked between blue- and white-collar workers, with the latter working shorter hours. This is not so in the Soviet Union, and as a result there might be a small additional advantage for the Soviet service labor force; it is not taken into account in Table 21.

Two principal conclusions emerge from this chapter. First, as GNP per capita (and the labor share of services) grows, the relative quality of the services labor force declines. Although the quality decline is not large enough to offset the rise in labor share altogether, it does substantially modify it, in both the C and OS sector and over most of the income range, especially at the upper end. The

33. The C share is lower by 5 percent, its trade component by 7 percent, and the retail industry by 10 percent. The OS share is lower by about 6 percent. This is distributed as a 13 percent decline for private services (33 percent in domestic services), a 7 percent increase in public administration, and no significant change in public services. Labor force data from U.S., Department of Commerce, *Survey of Current Business,* 42.7:28-29 (July 1962), Tables 50-55. The census data mentioned below are from U.S., Department of Commerce, Bureau of the Census, *United States Census of Population 1960; United States Summary* (Washington, 1963), pp. 1-571, Table 214.

34. E.g., the part-time adjustment for Soviet OS labor is assumed to be 2 percent, because in the United States the FTEQ share of this sector was 94 percent of the share computed on the basis of number of persons engaged. See Table 21, note b.

quality adjustments affect the OS more than the C sector. The main reasons for the decline in relative quality are the increase in the proportion of women employed in services and the decline in relative educational level of service workers.

Second, the relative quality of services labor is higher in the Soviet Union than in other countries of the same LED; correcting for quality reduces the Soviet S gap, and the quality adjustment may explain as much as one-third of the unadjusted gap. The allocation of the quality adjustment between the two subsectors of S does not correspond to the size of their gaps; the relative quality advantage of Soviet C labor is only slight, and the quality adjustment only slightly reduces the sector's unadjusted gap. By contrast, the relative quality of Soviet OS labor is considerably above that of OS labor in other countries, so that when the adjusted shares are compared, the OS gap almost disappears or even changes sign. At this level of aggregation the quality adjustments do not, therefore, help much in explaining the largest negative Soviet service gap, the one in the C sector.

6. The Service Gap in Trade: I

This chapter and the next are devoted to the gap in trade, the largest observed in the service sector and one which has been explained to only a limited degree by the factors considered so far. In practice we confine ourselves to final trade (FT): retail and that part of wholesale that mediates between the producer and the retailer; banking and insurance or trade between production units are thus not covered. Our estimates of the gaps in the subdivisions of the C sector, expressed as percent of total labor force, are set out in Table 22.

In the preceding chapters the basic gap was explained as follows. Between 0.6 and 2.9 percentage points are associated with the larger-than-normal rural population or rural labor force (Chapter 3). In addition, after analyzing other special features of Soviet agriculture in Chapter 4, it was estimated that as many as half a million trade workers are classified in agriculture. All in all, no

Table 22.   The C Sector Gap in the Soviet Union, by Sub-Branch (Percent[a])

Industry	Soviet share		Basic gap[b]
	Actual	Estimated	
Total C sector	**5.0**	**14.6**	**9.6**
Retail and catering	3.3	9.4	6.1
Retail	2.2	7.4	5.2
Catering	1.1	2.0	0.9
Wholesale	1.5	3.6	2.1
Finance, credit, and insurance	0.2	1.6	1.4
Final trade[c]	3.5	10.0	6.5

[a]For a rough idea of the numbers involved, 1 percent of the labor force can be taken as approximately 1 million employed persons.
[b]Based on regressions on y alone.
[c]Retail and catering plus 15 percent of wholesale by assumption.
Source: Tables 7 and 8 and underlying worksheets.

more than 3.5 percentage points of the gap can be explained by the large size of Soviet agriculture.

The relative quality of trade workers (including part-time) in the Soviet Union is slightly above that of trade workers in the countries of comparison (Chapter 5, Table 21, and Appendix Table C-3), when total labor force is the basis of comparison. In the Soviet Union part of this small advantage stems from the large size of the agricultural sector, an effect taken into account in the first point listed above[1] so that no additional allowance is warranted. In the retail industry the relative quality of labor may well be somewhat lower in the Soviet Union than in other countries.[2]

The abolition of private ownership of productive property and the legal and conventional limitations on the ownership of private property in general eliminate the bulk of the services of exchange of assets, stocks, and securities that exist under the private ownership system. This explains most of the gap in finance, credit, and insurance in the Soviet Union.

The discussion in Chapter 9 explains an important part of the gap in those branches of wholesale trade concerned with the connections among production units; in the Soviet industrial classification these are "material technical supply" and a large part of the "procurement" divisions;[3] together, they employed 85 percent of total wholesale employees in 1959.[4]

Taken together, all the factors mentioned reduce the 9.6 percent C gap to 3½-5½ percent, depending on the estimate for the agricultural element. The Soviet final trade share is about 3½ percent, while the estimated share is about 10 percent (retail, catering, and 15 percent of wholesale in Table 22); this yields a basic gap of 6.5 percentage points, of which only 1-2½ points are explained by the factors mentioned so far.[5] It is this remaining gap (a deficit of about 5 million workers) that is the topic of this and the next chapters.

The next section of this chapter sets out a simple model enumerating the factors that determine the size of the trade industry. We go on to analyze the

---

1. Compare lines 1 and 2 of panel C in Appendix Table C-3. The small relative quality advantage for total labor force turns into a small disadvantage for the M+S comparison. This is due partly to the relatively low quality of the A labor force and partly to the fact that the Soviet A share is relatively high. When the latter factor is controlled the result falls somewhere between the figures of lines 1 and 2, i.e., close to no relative quality advantage or disadvantage.

2. See the discussion in Chap. 5 above.

3. The agencies responsible for getting agricultural output to the purchaser.

4. Based on the annual-average estimates in *Indicators*, p. 71, Table VI-4; applied to the figures in Table 7 (1.7 million) this comes to 1.4 million.

5. The assumption is that the effects of the first two factors mentioned are evenly distributed over all subdivisions.

pattern of change in trade with LED and set the benchmark for the analysis of the Soviet trade industry presented in the last section.

The Theoretical Framework

The production process within the final trade industry consists of combining ex factory consumer *goods* with trade *services* produced from primary inputs to provide final *commodities* to the consumer.[6] In general, the production function involved can take any form, but as a first simplifying assumption a fixed proportion function between trade services and goods is used. The trade coefficient is defined as the number of service units per unit of goods and is assumed to be constant. This implies the existence of a unit of this kind, which is readily assumed but difficult to define.

The size of the aggregate trade coefficient at any point of time for any country is assumed to be a function of three parameters: (a) the services intensity of the assortment of goods sold by the trade industry; (b) the number of different goods sold; and (c) the "economic distance" between factory gate and consumer.

First, the overall trade coefficient is a weighted average of the trade coefficients of individual goods which are assumed to differ from each other. Different goods do need different amounts of transportation and further processing, different storage facilities, and so on. The overall trade coefficient will thus vary with changes in the assortment of goods sold.

Second, there is a positive relation between the number of goods—including the number of brands, types, styles, and varieties of the same basic good—and the trade coefficient. The increase in services requirement appears in the increased number of firms that each store has to deal with, so that the amount of real inputs in distribution rises; moreover it appears in the need for more display shelves, larger inventories, and finally in higher administrative and accounting inputs, where there is a heavy load of fixed cost per transaction.[7] Increasing the diversification of a product also raises costs to the manufacturer, and it is necessary to determine who suffers more from the process. It may be

6. We thus assume that goods bought for investment or government use do not consume "final" trade services. Note the distinction made here between goods (ex factory) and commodities (including FT services).

7. Diversification is usually associated with increased information to the consumer, which in turn increases productivity in trade. The present discussion distinguishes between diversification and information, and deals only with the former. This point is made partly in response to Goldman's article on this subject [M. I. Goldman, "Product Differentiation and Advertising: Some Lessons from Soviet Experience," *Journal of Political Economy,* 68.4:346-357 (August 1960); henceforth Goldman 1960], on which I rely heavily in the presentation of the diversification variables (see esp. pp. 354-357).

argued on several grounds that the distribution system suffers more. To begin with, the production system can more easily increase division of labor, thus avoiding shortening the production process for each variety of a given good, whereas a store must offer the customer the full range of choice and cannot afford to specialize.[8] Next, much of the specialization that can take place in production increases the demand for distribution services. It is the distribution industry that pays some of the costs of the higher specialization that raises efficiency. Finally, it has been argued that in market economies the higher efficiency inherent in the competition that creates product diversification makes up for the "waste" associated with it, an argument recently extended also to socialist systems. Again, the system as a whole and production in particular might well be more efficient, but any "waste" is mainly in terms of larger inputs in distribution.

Third, the trade coefficient also increases with "economic distance" between producing and consuming units. By economic distance we mean, in addition to geographical distance, distance in time (products are stored over seasons), the number of links involved, and the additional services connected with all these: further processing, storage, packing, refrigeration, and the like.

The absolute amount of labor invested in trade services depends on labor productivity in performing the services as well as on the amount of goods sold and the trade coefficient. Productivity is in turn a function of the quality and effort of labor, of all other inputs per worker invested in the same production, and of technology and organization. The next step is to transform the absolute amount of labor into the share of FT labor in total labor force—the main variable investigated. It follows that this share[9] will be greater, the greater are (a) the proportion of tradable goods (at ex factory prices) in total national product and (b) the trade coefficient; and the lower is (c) the labor productivity in final trade relative to the rest of the economy, which in turn depends on relative labor quality and effort, on the relative level

8. The following would be an extreme example: It takes five firms to supply a given market with one product. If however they each produce a different brand of the product, supplying the same market at the same level of efficiency, the distribution costs will be greater.

9. The FT labor share is here defined as the proportion of FT labor in total labor force *minus* FT labor (see next footnote), and national product is taken *minus* FT services. So defined, the FT share (let us call it the pure share), differs from the regular share in that its denominator is the non-FT instead of the total labor force. The statistical significance of the difference is demonstrated in the following cases: the pure share is about 10 percent greater than the regular share in countries where the FT labor share is 10 percent. In the Soviet Union, where the regular FT share is 4-5 percent, the pure share is only about 5 percent greater. Thus the actual differences between the two shares are, for our purposes, negligible. In what follows, we continue to talk loosely of the FT labor share.

of other inputs per worker, and on the relative level of technology and organization—all in final trade compared with the rest of the economy.

Finally, the most important factors determining the tradable goods share (TGS) in national product are considered: (a) the share of private disposable income in the national income; (b) the propensity of private consumers to spend on tradable commodities, which is the complement of the sum of the propensities to save, to buy other services, and to consume farm income in kind. These propensities are determined by tastes, income, relative prices, and the structural factors that determine the size of farm income in kind. We thus consider income per capita, the proportions of disposable income and of farm income in kind, and the price of consumer commodities (including services) relative to the price of other uses of disposable income as determinants of the tradable goods proportion. [10]

10. The verbal discussion of the theoretical model can be summarized by the following system of equations and relations:
Define Z as consumer commodities consisting of G and X

G	goods at the factory gate
X	final trade services
a	trade-service coefficient
I	services intensity
N	number and variety of goods
D	economic distance

The production function of Z can be written as
(1) $Z = \text{Min}(G; X/a)$
(2) $a = F(I,N,D)$,
with partial derivatives $F_I > 0; F_N > 0; F_D > 0$
The labor input into final trade, L_X, is then calculated as
(3) $L_X = G \cdot a \cdot 1/x(k_X)$ [brackets for "function of"]
where $1/x$ is the labor input per unit of trade service, which is itself a function of k_X (all other inputs per worker and technological level lumped together).
The labor share in final trade, LS_X, is derived from equation (3) as follows:

$$LS_X = \frac{L_X}{L - L_X} = \frac{G \cdot a}{Q - G \cdot a} \cdot \frac{\frac{1}{x}(k_X)}{\frac{1}{q}(k)}$$

where $L - L_X$ is	non-FT labor force
$Q - G \cdot a$	non-FT national product
$1/q$	labor productivity in $Q - G \cdot a$
k	other inputs per worker and technology in $Q - G \cdot a$.

Putting $G/(Q - G \cdot a) = TGS$ (tradable goods share), we get
(4) $LS_X = TGS \cdot a(I,N,D) \cdot \dfrac{q}{x} (k_X;k)$.

(The TGS and FT labor shares are here defined as the proportion of the total *minus* FT labor and product, respectively, in order to keep the shares unaffected by the size of the variable they are assumed to determine.)
Finally, we establish the relation

Several extensions of the model are of course possible, and some of them may be important in empirical applications: (1) Allowing for substitution in production between factory and trade establishments according to their production advantages (for instance, preparing the goods at the manufacturing site to save on expensive services; packaging could be an example). As a result, the trade coefficient becomes variable. (2) Allowing for a second activity by which to produce trade services (such as home self-supply) and giving the consumer the choice between the two. The implications of this extension of the model are very important for an understanding of what happens in the Soviet Union and are dealt with in the next chapter. For the time being, the original more restricted framework is examined.

The Change in the FT Labor Share
with the Level of Development

It was shown in Chapter 2 that the labor share of final commercial services increases with LED; this is still true when the shares are adjusted for quality (Chapter 5). It is generally argued that the trade labor share rises with LED as the combined result of two factors: the relative demand for services of commerce rises, and the trade industry lags behind the rest of the economy in technological change, as well as in the increase of capital per worker. The demand factors are represented by the tradable goods share and by the trade coefficient in our model, while relative labor productivity is the summary variable for the supply side.

The share of tradable goods: As income per capita increases (for a given proportion of disposable income), people tend to spend more of their income on services and less on goods; there is also sometimes a tendency to increase

---

$TGS = h(y; y_d; y_f; P_z/P_s)$

with partial derivatives $h_y < 0$, $h_{y_d} > 0$, $h_{y_f} < 0$, and $h_{P_z/P_s} < 0$,

where y is income per capita

$\quad y_d$ disposable income proportion (DIP) in y

$\quad y_f$ farm-income-in-kind (FIK) proportion in y

$\quad P_z/P_s$ relative price of commodities to that of other uses of disposable income.

The theoretical considerations here are based on, among others, Simon Kuznets, "Quantitative Aspects of the Economic Growth of Nations VII. The Share and Structure of Consumption," *Economic Development and Cultural Change*, 10 (no. 2, part II, January 1962), 6, 12, and 24-30; and Milton Gilbert and Associates, *Comparative National Products and Price Levels* (Paris, 1958), p. 66, Table 21.

the proportion of personal savings. In addition, as income per capita increases, the disposable income proportion (DIP) tends to decline as the share of government and the amount of savings and investment from sources not included in disposable income increase. Though much of what is taken by the government is returned to the population, it is returned in the form of services and not, for the most part, as income. With positive income elasticity for consumer goods, a lower DIP means a lower TGS.

On the other hand, the farm-income-in-kind (FIK) proportion of income clearly declines as LED rises, a decline which helps to raise TGS. This factor seems to be more important at the lower income ranges, since the FIK proportion is already very small in group II countries. The trend of change of the relative price of commodities over the LED range is less clear. Though the price of goods seems to decline relative to the price of services as a result of the rapid technological improvements in goods over the upper income ranges, the trend may be reversed in the lower income range. In the underdeveloped countries there seems to be quite a large element of rent paid to services workers as a result of rural-urban immobility and the control of scarce financial and educational resources by small groups of people. These rents are eliminated in the process of development as the population becomes more mobile, geographically and socially; this offsets the opposite effect of the technological lag on services. Even when the relative-price trends of goods to services are known, there is still no clear picture of the relative price of commodities, since the commodities themselves include services, though in a lower proportion than services themselves.

Existing empirical studies show that although on balance TGS declines over the upper income ranges, it may increase somewhat in early stages of development. The same studies also confirm the hypothesis of the effects of the individual factors on TGS.[11] As most of these studies do not refer directly to TGS, I have tried to make an independent estimate of the relation between it and LED that will fit into our framework. Table 23 is the final result of a series

11. The hypothesis that the relative price of services may go down when income rises over the lower income range is supported empirically by the sharp decline in the relative average product per worker over these ranges. See Kuznets 1957, p. 41, Table 18, and p. 44, Table 20.

Empirical evidence on other points can be found in Kuznets 1962, p. 8, Table 3; p. 24, Table 10; and pp. 30-31, Table 11; and in Gilbert and Associates, chaps. 3 to 6, esp. pp. 86-87, Tables 30-32. In the Gilbert study, the group called "other OEEC countries" includes all the less developed countries, Turkey, Greece, and Portugal (belonging to group III in our classification), Ireland and Austria (in our group II), along with only two advanced countries (Sweden and Switzerland). The figures for this group should be reasonably comparable with our group II data and on this assumption we use some of them below.

Table 23. Tradable Goods Share in GNP at Current Prices (MTGS), by Country Group, circa 1960ᵃ (Percent)

| | Share in GNP of | | | |
| | Tradable goods at current prices (MTGS) | | Final trade (FT) | Farm income in kind (FIK) |
Country group	Assumption (i) (1)	Assumption (ii) (2)	(3)	(4)
Group I (12)	34	32	14	1
Group II (9)	44	40	13	3
Group III (6)	47	44	15	4
Group IV (12)	42	38	14	8

ᵃFor details of the computation and explanation of assumptions (i) and (ii) see Appendix D. Figures in parentheses are the number of countries included in each group.
Source: See Appendix D.

of crude estimates of TGS at current market prices (denoted by MTGS) for the four GNP per capita country groups. The transformation of the MTGS figures into TGS figures, that is, their adjustment for changes in the relative price of goods included in the price of total product, is left for the text, as it was not possible to estimate reliable price indexes. The principal stages of the TGS computation are described in Appendix D.

Bearing in mind the crudity of the estimating procedure, we find that at current prices the share of tradable goods in GNP declines from group III to group I, but that it increases from group IV to group III. Columns (2) and (4) of the table show also that the increase in MTGS over the lower income range is fully explained by the decline in the FIK proportion, while the other factors apparently account for the decline in MTGS over the rest of the income range. The question is how these figures look when converted to constant prices. For this purpose I use the price indexes compiled by Milton Gilbert. He demonstrates that the proportion in GNP of the major groups of commodities declines from "other OEEC" countries (mostly OEEC lower income countries) to the United States by about half as much when calculated in constant prices (of either group) as when calculated in domestic prices. If we are willing to transfer this relation to the transition from group II (and perhaps also group III) to group I, then we may conclude that TGS also declines at constant prices, at least in the upper income ranges.[12]

12. The proportion of consumption of various categories of commodities (including trade markup) in total GNP (including the value added of trade) is there computed at different prices. It can be shown that the differences between Gilbert's figures and ours (which exclude trade markup) are very small for our purposes and that the same is true for Gilbert's implicit price indexes compared with the ones we would use.

The trade coefficient: Both the level of diversification of the mix of tradable goods and the economic distance between the producer and the consumer probably increase with LED and explain the increase in the demand for trade services (at a given level of efficiency). This is intuitively quite clear, but it is not easy to supply a quantitative proof. In any empirical study it is difficult to disentangle increased demand for the service from a lag in its technological progress. The reason for this is, of course, that it is difficult to define and measure the physical output of services. I do not touch on the assortment intensity factor, as it is not known how it is related to LED.

Relative productivity of labor in trade services: Any increase in the FT labor share that is not explained by the increases in the TGS and the trade coefficient must be explained by the technological lag of final trade services with LED and the smaller capital intensity of the innovations and technological changes in trade as compared with the rest of the economy. A slower increase in the amount of capital per worker could be a manifestation of either or both these elements.

The Gap in the Soviet Trade Industry Explained: A First Attempt

In this section the model is applied to the Soviet Union in order to explain the sources of its trade gap. Quantitative measures are offered for only a few of the model variables; for the rest less solid analysis will have to suffice.

The share of tradable goods: The Soviet TGS is considerably below that of most other countries in the world, a fact which explains a large part of the Soviet gap in the trade industry. This low share of tradable goods is a combined result of the high priority given to growth (and defense) and of the high FIK share which is partly due to a policy of economizing on commercial services.

Table 24 presents some of the computations and summarizes the results of the comparisons of the Soviet TGS with those of group II countries and the United States. The comparison with group II is of course the relevant one for the Soviet Union. The comparison with the United States is made for control purposes, as the figures are more reliable. The basic Soviet data differ somewhat in concept and derivation from those of the other countries. First, the Soviet figures in domestic prices are at factor cost, and not at market prices as for the other countries. The reason for this is the familiar fact that most Soviet taxes are turnover taxes on consumer goods; this artificially increases consumer

Table 24. Share of Tradable Goods (TGS) in GNP, Soviet Union and Other Countries[a]

	At domestic prices weights (1)	At US weights (1955 dollars) (2)	At Soviet weights (1955 rubles) (3)
A. TSG, percent			
Soviet Union[b]	32	17	32
Group II:			
Assumption (i)[c]	44	34	..
Assumption (ii)[c]	40	31	..
United States	28	28	40
B. TGS ratios			
Soviet Union/Group II (i)	0.73	0.50	..
Soviet Union/Group II (ii)	0.80	0.55	..
Soviet Union/United States	1.14	0.61	0.80

[a]Soviet Union–1955, 1959 (when rounded, as here, the figures come out the same for both years); Group II–circa 1960; United States–1960.
[b]At factor cost.
[c]The difference between the two assumptions is explained in Appendix D.
Source: See Appendix D.

prices and the Soviet TGS in market prices, much beyond the similar effects of indirect taxation in other countries. Secondly, the Soviet figures were derived directly from retail sales figures and not from consumption figures as for the other countries. To make these figures comparable, retail purchases of investment goods were subtracted from the Soviet figures. Also, the estimate of Soviet FIK is independent of the estimation of TGS, while for the other countries estimated FIK shares were subtracted from private consumption of goods.

The TGS figures at domestic prices and in US 1955 dollars appear in columns (1) and (2) respectively; the latter is the only set of prices for which it was possible to get estimates for both group II countries and the Soviet Union. The United States figures in Soviet prices are shown in column (3).

The numerical conclusion from the different ratios of Soviet TGS to that of other countries is that the tradable goods share in the Soviet Union is about 65 percent of the share in group II countries. This estimate is reached in several steps, most of them based on the hypothesis that on the basis of any relevant set of quantity weights the relative price of consumer goods (even at factor cost) is higher in the Soviet Union than in group II countries.

When US quantity weights are used, the price of goods relative to total GNP (US = 1.00) is 1.62 in the Soviet Union and 1.22 in other OEEC countries.[13] This supports the hypothesis only for the set of quantity weights used. The theory of index numbers does not admit the conclusion that these relations among the relative prices of goods will be invariant with different weights.

There is some independent support for our hypothesis in the fact that in the Soviet Union agriculture and light industry, the major sources of consumer goods, lag in efficiency behind the producer goods industries and also have higher relative prices than services, all relative to countries of the same LED.

An ideal measure of the size of the Soviet TGS relative to that of group II is the geometric average of two estimates of the ratio (TGS_{su}/TGS_{II}) one based on Soviet and the other on group II prices. The figure of 65 percent for Soviet relative TGS is further supported, as it can be plausibly demonstrated that the TGS rates of 0.73 and 0.80 [panel B, column (1)], based on domestic prices, are overestimates, while the ratios of 0.50 and 0.55 based on US prices [panel B, column (2)] are underestimates of this geometric average ratio.[14]

If the TGS in the Soviet Union is only about two-thirds of the normal level, then the relative labor share of its trade industry, all other factors being equal, should be a similar proportion of the normal employment share [see equation (4), note 10 in this chapter].[15] This factor alone can explain up to half of the remaining gap in the final trade industry.[16] It is presently shown, however, that this explanation overlaps other explanations advanced earlier.

---

13. The available information on the relative price of goods to GNP is (US = 1): Soviet Union in Soviet weights, 1.24; in US weights, 1.62; the geometric average is 1.42. "Other OEEC" in OEEC prices, 1.20; in US prices, 1.22. The relative price of goods in the Soviet Union is also higher than in "other OEEC" on the basis of the above mentioned geometric average. (For sources, see Appendix D.)

14. That the Soviet TGS ratio of 0.73 or 0.80 is an overestimate of the ideal measure can be shown as follows: applying Soviet prices to group II increases the group's TGS, and the Soviet TGS is pushed down by applying group II prices so that the ratio between them declines either way.

The ideal index is also below the geometrical average (0.7) of the two TGS ratios between the Soviet Union and the United States [last line of panel B, columns (2) and (3)] since the TGS of the United States is one of the lowest we have recorded. It is clearly lower than that of group II in either US or European prices. The second half of this proposition can be proved by a similar line of reasoning. It should however be remembered that the TGS ratio in 1955 US prices for group II is the most shaky, since we "borrowed" the prices of another country group.

15. a. It is assumed that in the long run it is possible to expand the industry at constant labor productivity as long as all other inputs grow at the same rate.

b. Changing from the comparison of LS_X's to the comparison of trade shares makes a negligible difference to the gap computations. See note 9, this chapter.

16. If the estimated size of final trade employment is 4-5 percent of the labor force (see Table 22), then, with a normal TGS it would be 6-7 percent, compared with a normal share of about 10 percent.

Up to a quarter of the difference between the Soviet Union and group II in the TGS is due to a higher proportion of farm income in kind in the Soviet GNP. According to A. S. Becker's estimates, the proportion was 7.7 percent in 1959,[17] compared with our estimate of about 3 percent for group II. Had the two proportions been the same the relative Soviet TGS would have been in the vicinity of 0.7 to 0.75 of normal.

Three elements can account for this difference in the FIK proportion. First, there could be an error in our arbitrary estimate for group II.[18] Second, as we have seen before, the relative size of the agricultural sector in the Soviet Union is larger than in group II countries. Thus when we apply to the Soviet Union the same assumption used in estimating the group II FIK share (that it is 20 percent of the income originating in agriculture), we get a figure of 5.5 percent for FIK in the Soviet Union.[19] The effect of applying the normal FIK level is presumably taken care of by the introduction of RU or at least A as a variable in the C regressions[20] and it should not be counted again here. Finally, the high Soviet FIK figure may be an indication of the Soviet policy of restricting commercial services in rural areas despite the existing demand for them in the "industrialized" agricultural sector. Even if this is so, much of the extra share of FIK (over the 5.5 percent) may reflect farm products distributed outside the official trade system by farm officials and others. An estimate for these workers was added to the total number of trade workers in Chapter 4 above. The conclusion is thus, that whatever the reason, all the effects of the larger share of FIK in the Soviet Union have already been accounted for somewhere else, or should not be taken into account at all.

About 75 to 85 percent of the effect of the lower Soviet TGS is a result of the lower proportion of disposable income in GNP, itself a direct result of

17. A. S. Becker, *Soviet National Income and Product 1958-1962 Part Two. N.I. at Factor Costs and Constant Prices* (Santa Monica, 1966), p. 33, Table 2.

18. Errors can, of course, occur for many reasons. One is the tendency of most Western students to overestimate the Soviet FIK proportion. This is borne out by new computations carried out by A. Bergson who kindly made them available to the author.

19. The value added of agriculture is estimated at 27-29 percent of GNP, and 20 percent of this comes to 5.4-5.6 percentage points. (A. S. Becker, p. 92.)

20. More probably only when A is included, as may be demonstrated by the following figures (percent):

	Group II	Soviet Union
RU	47	52
Value added share of agriculture	15	27-29
Labor share of agriculture	26	46

The difference in RU is much smaller than the difference in the two agricultural shares. Also, if FIK is a function of the latter, A will represent it much better than RU, at least for the Soviet Union. [Source: Group II, see source of Table 2; Soviet Union, p. 28 above (RU), Table 6 (A labor share), and the preceding footnote (A value added share)].

planning decisions to allocate large shares of the national product to investment, defense, and other public purposes.[21] The Soviet DIP is one of the lowest in the world when calculated at factor prices. An international comparison of the proportion of *private consumption* in GNP has been made by Simon Kuznets.[22] This shows that the Soviet proportion is about 80 percent of that in countries with similar per capita income. The Soviet DIP is even lower (compared with other countries); in the Soviet Union personal savings constitute a smaller share of personal income, and government-supplied services such as education and health (included in private consumption by Kuznets) are relatively larger. In addition, a comparison made on a uniform price basis would yield a smaller Soviet DIP, since even at factor cost private consumption is overpriced in the Soviet Union, compared with investment, defense, and public and government services.[23]

The proportion of goods bought in the Soviet Union out of disposable income above what is indicated by the income elasticity may reflect the fact that some services, which in other countries are purchased from personal income, are supplied by the government and that many other services are scarce. The relatively low price of services (if available) might work in the opposite direction. Compared with the lower income effect, these factors have only a small effect on TGS. To sum up, at least three-quarters of the effect of the lower TGS of the Soviet Union constitutes a new explanation for the trade gap.

The trade coefficient: The Soviet Union apparently produces a much smaller number of types, styles, brands, and varieties of consumer goods than any market economy of the same or even lower LED.[24] There are several reasons for this. A logical conclusion from the assertion that the income elasticity for variety is greater than unity is that the demand for variety on the part of the Soviet consumers must be below that of consumers in other countries of the same GNP per capita, because the Soviet *disposable* income per capita is much lower than in these countries, and consumer demand structure is a function of disposable income. On the supply side, I argue that the price of diversi-

21. See the discussion of growth strategy in Chap. 9 below.

22. Simon Kuznets, "A Comparative Appraisal," in Abram Bergson and Simon Kuznets, eds., *Economic Trends in the Soviet Union* (Cambridge, Mass., 1963; henceforth Kuznets 1963), p. 360, Table VIII-17. The figures are 56 percent for the Soviet Union and 70 percent for the comparable income group.

23. Some indication of the relative prices of these categories in the Soviet Union can be found in U.S., Congress, Joint Economic Committee, *Comparisons of the United States and Soviet Economies,* 86th Cong., 1st Sess., 1959 (henceforth *Comparisons*), p. 385, Table 3, and notes; and Bergson 1969. Both these sources compare Soviet prices with United States prices.

24. See Goldman 1960. Much of the discussion here is based on this article.

fication in a centrally planned economy is higher than in a market economy while the benefits derived from it are smaller, at least in theory. That the price is higher rests on the argument about the higher price per link or transaction under a centrally planned system. The number of administrative and supply operations increases much faster than the number of varieties created. Together with the increase in variety goes an increase in the number of possible bottlenecks and in the need for adjustments. Finally, a central planner is in a better position than an individual competitor to evaluate the total social costs of diversification. The latter observes only his private costs in introducing a new variety, and these may be lower than the social costs.

On the benefit side, a "classical" centrally planned system is not geared to gain from market-type competition and, at least in principle, product differentiation is not needed for efficiency, which is achieved by the managers of the enterprise who operate in accordance with a system of administratively imposed rules. Thus the centrally planned economy does not have to "waste" resources in order to achieve efficiency. The planners may also put a lower value on variety than do the consumers. With less demand and more expensive supply, at least in the planners' eyes, the preference on the supply side for a narrower range of goods becomes clear.[25] It is not possible to estimate quantitatively the effect of this element on the size of the Soviet trade sector, but it could be substantial.[26]

As regards services intensity, we lack a meaningful theoretical model for distinguishing between quantity and productivity in services.[27] One line of retail distribution that clearly has a higher trade coefficient than others is catering ("eating and drinking places"), where other services are offered in addition to the sale of goods. The Soviet Union channels a larger proportion of its tradable goods through restaurants and similar institutions than other coun-

---

25. The Soviet system has also failed to provide a good system of information (by means of packaging, displays, advertisement, etc.) about the narrow variety of goods that are produced. This is an obvious inefficiency in distribution that can be corrected independently and without increasing the number of brands produced. We comment on this apropos of a passage in Goldman's article (1960, pp. 354-355) in which he correctly maintains that marketing and advertisement can raise the efficiency of distribution. We remark here that the process need not necessarily be combined with an increase in the number and variety of goods.

It is interesting to find that there are complaints in the Soviet Union about the difficulties faced by stores in dealing with what they consider as too *many* different products and prices. See *CDSP,* 12.13:39 (April 27, 1960).

26. See V. Tiukov, "Soviet Trade in the Period of Full-Scale Building of Communism," *Problems of Economics,* 5.6:3-10 (October 1962). Tiukov considers that an increase in the assortment of goods is one of two important factors which will in future reduce the productivity of trade.

27. An example of an attempt to tackle the problem for the United States trade industry can be found in Schwartzman, chap. 10.

tries, and this is a reason for employing *more* people in retail than in other countries. However, as the additional services which make the coefficient larger are of the household type and indeed substitute for household services, I shall defer the discussion of this aspect to the next chapter, where the whole question of substitution between market and household production of trade services will be incorporated as an extension of our model.

A second a priori assumption is that the trade coefficients are related to a transaction as a unit and, specifically, that they are smaller per unit of sales in larger transactions.[28] Accordingly, trade lines with naturally larger transaction sizes will in general be less service intensive. One possible distinction between larger and smaller transaction lines could be the division between nonfood and food products. On this basis it can be argued that as a larger part of Soviet tradable goods is made up of food, the trade coefficient of the Soviet assortment is also higher here than in other countries and that this should induce a higher, not a lower, trade employment level. The problem is that the evidence for a high trade coefficient in food is not conclusive, mainly because in different countries the food/nonfood differences in the transaction size vary and also because different sets of prices produce contradictory results. Thus in the Soviet Union food sales per worker are only 60 percent of nonfood sales per worker at market prices, but 93 percent when measured in US dollars. On the other hand, in the United States, sales of food per worker are in general (at least since 1929) higher than those of nonfood.[29] In view of all this, and taking into account that the difference in the proportion of food (other than from restaurants) in Soviet tradable goods is only slightly higher than in group II countries,[30] I decided not to isolate the effect of this factor here, but to estimate it below together with the productivity per worker effects.

The same is done with the distance factor. We shall see below (Chapter 9) that the rigid and inefficient supply system tends to reduce the number of links among enterprises and to make them more self-sufficient. This, of course, applies also to final trade services. In terms of the model, it means shorter

28. *Ibid.,* chap. 8. See also below, where we return to the efficiency aspects of this variable.

29. *Ibid.* p. 207, Table A2-11 for the United States. TsSU, *Sovetskaia Torgovlia Statisticheski Svornik* (Moscow, 1964; henceforth *Sovtorg. 1964*), pp. 218-225, for the Soviet Union. Exchange rates are from Bergson 1969.

30. Based on Gilbert and Associates, pp. 86-87, Tables 30-32 for group II and Bergson 1969 for the Soviet Union. The Soviet proportion of food in total retail sales is about 60 percent at domestic prices and about 70 percent in 1955 US dollars. This may be compared with the respective group II figures of 50 percent and 60 percent. If we take out the sales of food through restaurants the difference will probably drop to 5-7 percentage points. This is not high so long as the differences in the service coefficient of food are within 20 percent or so of the differences in the service coefficient of nonfood.

economic distances between all economic units, on the one hand, and on the other lower relative productivity per worker.

There are, however, two aspects of the Soviet economy that may lead to greater economic distance in final distribution services as well as in intermediate services. The first is the large proportion of rural population in the Soviet Union: low population density increases the economic distance, while the industrial organization of Soviet agriculture should aggravate the problem. We have seen that it is handled by cutting the supply of services to rural areas.[31] The second point is the vast opportunity for specialization and division of labor enjoyed by the Soviet Union because it is the second largest open market in the world in terms of aggregate GNP (after the United States). The costs of additional distribution could be recovered several times over by exploiting scale and regional comparative advantage effects. It seems that the high price of external links (to enterprises as well as to stores) prevents full utilization of this advantage and the distance is kept small, with little regional coordination.[32]

The conclusion is that the service coefficients in the Soviet Union are apparently lower than in comparable countries, mainly because of the lower level of product diversification. It is also possible that the potentialities of distribution are not fully exploited as a result of the relatively high real costs of transactions outside the enterprise created by the planning system.

Relative productivity: If relative labor productivity in trade is higher in the Soviet Union than in group II countries, the fact might explain the lower Soviet labor share in this industry. A higher level of product per worker (with worker already adjusted for labor quality and hours of work) can be achieved by one or more of the following: (a) more capital per worker and better production techniques; (b) better working arrangements and organization; and (c) higher utilization of capacity, especially of manpower. This last point is an aspect of organization, but is kept separate for reasons that will become clear.

A full investigation of comparative labor productivity involves examining

31. This is confirmed by Tiukov (pp. 3ff.) who says that the introduction of trade services to rural areas will reduce sales per worker. It is also confirmed by comparative figures on the (urban) state retail system and the predominantly rural cooperative network: In the cooperative network, sales per worker were 27,287 rubles in 1959, or only 75 percent of the figure of 36,074 rubles for the state outlets. (These figures do not include restaurants, which have a completely different service coefficient.) The source is *Sovtorg. 1964,* pp. 40-43, 131.

32. "Localism" and its responsibility for low specialization is a well known issue in the Soviet Union, especially during the decentralization era of the late 1950s and early 1960s. See *CDSP,* 14.13:22 (April 25, 1962).

labor productivity, not only in trade but in other industries as well, both in the Soviet Union and in the countries of comparison. We cannot enter upon such an extensive investigation. Instead, we shall concentrate on Soviet trade and make only a few comparisons. In this way at least the direction in which the factors mentioned above work may be estimated.

When measured by sales per worker, labor productivity in Soviet trade is one of the highest in the world, and thus—relative to other industries—clearly higher than in other countries. At the same time, almost all physical performance indicators for Soviet trade under heads (a) and (b) above indicate a very low level of productivity, even compared with other Soviet industries. If the relative productivity variable is going to help explain the gap in trade it must do so through the capacity factor. This is discussed in the next chapter.

Table 25 compares sales per worker in the Soviet Union and the United States in Soviet and US 1955 prices. The comparisons are for all retail sales and for sales in restaurants and in regular retail outlets separately. For the Soviet Union the corresponding figures for urban areas only have also been compiled, in order to isolate the effect of the lower productivity of distribution that should be attributed to the large rural population.[33] We shall consider the geometric averages of the estimates in the two price systems as points of estimation for the ratio of Soviet to United States sales per worker. For all retail sales, sales per worker in the Soviet Union were about three-quarters of those in the United States [column (5), lines 4 and 7]; when catering establishments are excluded the ratio goes up to 85 percent and above (lines 6 and 9). The effect of the catering category on the ratio is double-edged: the Soviet/ United States ratio is lower than for other retail, and the weight of catering in total retail is higher in the Soviet Union. Since the second of these is an assortment effect, the ratio must be corrected for it; the corrected ratio for total retail is about 0.80.[34]

The Soviet Union has a large absolute sales per worker advantage over countries other than the United States. J. B. Jefferys and D. Knee present figures for sales per worker (and per full-time worker) in retailing proper in 18 European countries in 1955 (in US 1955 dollars). The highest figure per full-time worker is almost $14,000 for Norway, but the figures for most developed countries in the list range between $8,000 and $11,000; the figures for the less

---

33. It is assumed that in the United States the problem of rural trade is relatively unimportant.

34. Goldman arrives at somewhat higher Soviet Union/United States ratios of sales per worker. The difference is due to the exchange rates used. [M. I. Goldman, *Soviet Marketing* (Glencoe, Ill., 1963; henceforth Goldman 1963), pp. 180-181, Table 18.]

Table 25. Sales per Worker in Retail Trade, Soviet Union and United States (1955 Prices)

	Rubles[a] (1)	Dollars[a] (2)	USSR ÷ US 1958 Rubles (3)	USSR ÷ US 1958 Dollars (4)	USSR ÷ US 1958 Geometric mean (5)
United States 1958[b]					
1. Total retail	37,672	20,929			
2. Catering establishments	13,734	7,848			
3. Retail proper	43,322	24,068			
Soviet Union					
1959 all areas					
4. Total retail	23,651	17,917	0.63	0.86	0.73
5. Catering establishments	6,498	6,130	0.47	0.78	0.61
6. Retail proper	31,941	23,486	0.74	0.98	0.85
1959 urban areas[c]					
7. Total retail	23,549	17,840	0.63	0.85	0.73
8. Catering establishments	6,215	5,863	0.45	0.75	0.58
9. Retail proper	34,702	25,516	0.80	1.06	0.92
1955 all areas					
10. Total retail	20,158	15,271	0.54	0.73	0.63
11. Catering establishments	6,869	6,480	0.50	0.83	0.64
12. Retail proper	27,120	19,941	0.63	0.83	0.72
1955 urban areas[c]					
13. Total retail	9,537	14,800	0.52	0.71	0.61
14. Catering establishments	6,314	5,957	0.46	0.76	0.59
15. Retail proper	28,451	20,919	0.66	0.87	0.76

[a]Exchange rates (in rubles per $) were as follows:

	Total	Catering	Retail proper
Rubles to $ (Soviet figures)	1.32	1.06	1.36
$ to rubles (US figures)	1.80	1.75	1.80

The rate used to convert the Soviet catering figures in the exchange rate for food (excluding collective-farm market sales).

[b]The current-price dollar figures were converted to 1955 dollars over the following deflators (1958 = 100) 95 (total retail and retail proper) and 93 (catering).

[c]Based on figures for the state-owned trade organizations which do almost all their business in urban areas.

Source: Soviet Union, *Sovtorg. 1964,* pp. 40-44, 131. United States, D. Schwartzman, United States, D. Schwartzman, *The Decline of Service in Retail Trade: An Analysis of the Growth of Sales Per Manhour, 1929-1963* (Pullman, Wash., 1971), p. 207, Table A2-11 (p. 214, Table A2-15 for deflators mentioned in note b).

Exchange rates (see note a) based on Bergson, "The Comparative National Income of the USSR and USA" (preliminary draft; October 1969).

developed countries in southern Europe are between $3,000 and $5,000. The authors conclude that European sales per worker are on the average only 40 percent of those in the United States at comparable prices.[35]

All these figures are for the absolute volume of sales per person. The relative advantage of Soviet retail trade over other Soviet industries, when compared with other countries, is much larger. This also may be illustrated by a comparison with the United States. Average labor productivity in the Soviet Union in 1955 was estimated at between 23 and 46 percent of that in the United States,[36] which means that the *relative* labor productivity of Soviet retail trade is at least one and a half times that in the United States. There are good indications that the advantage is even greater in comparison with less advanced countries. Even a 50 percent labor productivity advantage is as important as the lower tradable goods proportion and can explain the remainder of the trade gap.

Our task would be at an end here were it not that the physical production conditions in Soviet trade fail to support the conclusions that there is a productivity advantage; indeed, they contradict it. The apparent paradox is resolved in the next chapter. Here evidence is presented on the low physical and operational productivity of Soviet trade.

The level of investment in fixed capital and equipment in the Soviet trade industry is very low according to the plan, and the plan itself is seldom more than 50 percent fulfilled.[37] The trade industry is thus short of shops, adequate storage and refrigeration, and transport facilities. Though shortage of stores means that existing ones are fully utilized and thus contributes to one aspect of productivity (see discussion in Chapter 7 below), conditions in existing stores, as well as in storage facilities, are poor and far from efficient.[38] A similar situation exists with equipment and tools. The industry has little loading and

35. J. B. Jefferys and D. Knee, *Retailing in Europe* (London, 1962), pp. 38-41. See also M. Hall, J. Knapp, and C. H. Winsten, *Distribution in Great Britain and North America* (Oxford, 1961), p. 8, Table 2, where the same conclusions are arrived at on the basis of comparison of the United States with Great Britain and Canada.

36. Bergson 1969.

37. In 1959 only 2.1 percent of the fixed capital production stock was in retail trade and only another 1.9 percent in all other commerce branches (*Narkhoz 1959*, p. 67). On the nonfulfillment of construction plans, which are anyway too modest, see A. Struev, "The Trade Branch," *Problems of Economics*, 8.11:17 (March 1966); *CDSP*, 12.20:43 (June 15, 1960); and U.S., Department of Commerce, Joint Publications Research Service, *Translations on Consumer Goods and Domestic Trade* (henceforth JPRS-*Consumer Goods*), the following issues: no. 77 (March 2, 1965), p. 20; no. 129 (August 22, 1966), p. 16; no. 155 (December 2, 1966), pp. 9ff.

38. See also *CDSP*, 10.41:33-34 (November 19, 1958), and 15.36:28 (October 2, 1963); JPRS-*Consumer Goods*, no. 85 (May 4, 1965), p. 28; no. 108 (March 7, 1966), p. 12, and no. 165 (January 11, 1967), p. 1.

unloading equipment, so that much of this work is done by hand. It has been stated that half a million retail workers are fully occupied in shifting goods inside stores.[39] Less than half the stores and restaurants dealing in perishable goods had any kind of refrigeration equipment in 1959.[40] The Soviet statistical agencies keep records of the number of scales, potato peelers, and other similar tools, which is an indication of their scarcity—a scarcity documented throughout the Soviet press.[41] Considering the level of mechanization in Soviet manufacturing, the impression is that the trade industry has been treated unfavorably in this respect.[42] Furthermore, one gets the impression that as a result of this unbalanced investment pattern Soviet trade has less capital per worker than trade in other countries.

A related factor is the burden put on the trade industry by the shortage of packing materials and the small amount of prepackaging at the production stage. The result is large labor inputs in weighing and packing goods delivered at the store in bulk.[43]

The picture is completely different for one component of capital: the stock of goods. The Soviet trade system seems to be one of the best equipped with this type of capital. Let us first examine some of the figures. Retail stocks of goods in the Soviet Union are valued at 92 days of turnover, which is the average of 49 and 136 days for food and nonfood goods, respectively. These figures are much higher than those for the United States in 1960 (41, 22, and 48 days, respectively) and slightly higher than the figures for the United States, the United Kingdom, and Canada in the early 1950s.[44] The contrast between the high level of stocks and the low level of fixed capital is illustrated by the

39. Dikhtiar, p. 45.
40. *Narkhoz 1959*, pp. 691-692. See also V. Morozov, "Development of Commodity Money Relations in the Countryside," *Problems of Economics*, 8.7:32 (November 1965).
41. *Narkhoz 1959*, pp. 692-693. Mechanization in restaurants is also said to be rudimentary; in *Ekonomicheskaia Gazeta*, no. 25 (June 1966), p. 10, we read "Build for us, please, ordinary dependable ham and sausage slicers, meat saws . . . Convenient and small size carts . . ." This is reflected also in *CDSP*, 14.22:28 (June 27, 1962).
42. It may be true that such items as loading equipment are not available in large quantities for Soviet manufacturing either. But in these branches such equipment is marginal, whereas for trade, especially wholesale, it is a basic requirement.
43. See JPRS-*Consumer Goods*, no. 69 (December 6, 1964), p. 17, where it is reported that wine, salt, jam, butter, and the like are still sold in bulk and weighed and wrapped in the store. On the lack of packaging and how it interferes with advanced selling techniques such as self-service, see *CDSP*, 12.24:27 (July 13, 1960); *Sovetskaia Torgovlia*, no. 11 (November 1965), pp. 4-8 and 18-20; and *CDSP* 17.9:28 (March 24, 1965), in which it is stated that packaging is one-fifth as efficient in a store as in a specialized enterprise, and that it accounts for 8 percent of retail labor input.
44. For the Soviet Union, from *Sovtorg. 1964*, p. 112; for the United States, U.S., Department of Commerce, Bureau of the Census, *Statistical Abstract of the United States 1962* (83rd annual edition; Washington, 1962; henceforth U.S., *Abstract*), p. 833; and for Canada and the United Kingdom, Hall et al., p. 27.

following observation. In the Soviet retail industry, the value of stocks is more than four times the value of fixed capital, while in the United States the ratio is only about 40 percent.[45] This picture is only slightly modified when wholesale stocks are included. The volume of wholesale stocks in the Soviet Union is similar to or a little lower than what it is in the United States. The average value of all trade inventories is still about twice as large in the Soviet Union as in the United States.[46]

The conclusion to be drawn after examining the reason for the stock accumulation as well as its results is that in many cases the large volume of stocks is a heavy burden on the retail system and its level of services, and that where stocks do help to improve the service to consumers they are not large enough to offset all the other factors that make for scarcity of goods in the stores.

A large part of the stock consists of unmarketable goods, which do not serve the consumer but increase the congestion in the inadequate storage facilities of the retail and wholesale systems.[47] The goods are unmarketable for several reasons, ranging from low quality to various kinds of inconsistency between supply and demand. Inconsistencies are often local, and on the average for the whole country supply may match demand; sometimes they are general: too much was produced.

The price rigidity in Soviet marketing is one major reason for inability to correct such mistakes simply by price adjustments. Doctrinal conservatism—the belief in the Marxian law of value—and administrative and accounting difficulties in a rigid marketing system are the major explanation for this price rigidity. Unmarketable stocks also build up because little consumer research is carried out and because of the principle of delivery rather than selling that governs the Soviet distribution system at all stages but the last, the retail store where all the delivered and unsold goods end up. This is another example of how higher *measured* productivity in production is achieved at the cost of lower productiv-

45. United States, Schwartzman, p. 65, Table 5-1; Soviet Union, *Narkhoz 1959*, pp. 67, 657.

46. In 1959 wholesale stocks were for 30 days in the Soviet Union (*Sovtorg. 1964*, p. 112), and in the United States (in 1960) for 37 days (U.S., *Abstract 1965*, p. 835). Wholesale stocks constitute less than one quarter of Soviet and almost half of United States total trade stocks. The comparison may be indicative of both the lack of wholesale storage base and the extent to which retail stocks are unmarketable in the Soviet Union.

47. The discussion here is based on M. I. Goldman, "The Reluctant Consumer and Economic Fluctuations in the Soviet Union," *Journal of Political Economy*, 73.4:366-379 (August 1965; henceforth Goldman 1965), and on many articles in the Soviet press: *CDSP*, 10.41:33-34 (November 19, 1958); *CDSP*, 11.32:23 (September 9, 1959); *CDSP*, 14.24:15 (July 11, 1962); *Sovetskaia Torgovlia*, no. 11 (November 1964), pp. 1-5; JPRS-*Consumer Goods*, no. 137 (September 19, 1966), p. 1; A. Struev, "The Trade Branch," pp. 17-20, and A. Struev, "Kazhdi Den-Chastitsa Iubileinogo Goda," *Sovetskaia Torgovlia*, no. 2 (1967), p. 2.

ity in distribution. Finally, goods are unmarketable because of the poor system of information about what is available.

Given the Soviet distribution system, there seems to be good reason for retail stores to be interested in holding higher stocks of marketable goods; it can be summed up as the inefficiency and undependability of wholesale supply, some of which is attributable to the production system. An extreme example is the system of "minimum order sizes" under which a store can order a given good only in indivisible, rather large, quantities. This saves transport and other distribution costs but increases stocks and the spoilage of perishables.[48] The final result is that despite the huge stocks in the retail system the stores have much less of what the consumer wants than is considered standard in the market economies.

It is claimed in many sources, and justifiably so, that the increase in the standard of living during the late 1950s and early 1960s has made the Soviet consumer ready to wait for what he wants and discriminating in his buying; since the industry was not ready for the change, retail (and other) stocks piled up. This is no doubt a sound explanation. One must bear in mind, however, that retail and total stocks were also high in the early 1950s long before the jump in the standard of living. Thus in 1950 the total duration of stocks amounted to 105 days (90 days for food), of which 70 (42 for food) days were in the retail system; the lowest level in the decade occurred in 1957 (94 days), which is still very high. This suggests that the other factors operated all along despite the general shortage of goods, and that they were reinforced when the general shortage disappeared.[49]

In addition to the organizational aspects mentioned in the discussion of the use of capital in trade, the following factors which reduce physical productivity may be noted. The method of selling is inefficient and time-consuming: the consumer can examine the product only with the help and supervision of a salesman, pays at a special cashier's stand, and then goes back to the counter to pick up the item bought.[50] The self-service stores introduced in 1954 were no doubt an improvement, but apparently not a major one. They did not spread rapidly and the definition of self-service became narrower and narrower after a time, and more and more barriers appeared between the consumer and the merchandise. One reason for these complications is the need for and insistence

48. See JPRS-*Consumer Goods,* no. 134 (September 6, 1966), p. 10, and no. 178 (May 17, 1967), pp. 21-25. Under this system, clothing deliveries, for example, can be made only two or three times a year.

49. See Goldman's discussion of this point in Goldman 1965, pp. 373-377. The figures cited are from *Sovtorg. 1964,* pp. 111-112.

50. Goldman 1963, pp. 17-20.

on strict administrative and financial control by the upper agencies and the small confidence given to store managers and salesmen.[51]

Many organizational and other factors reduce transaction size in Soviet retailing, compared with other countries. As stated, the efficiency of retail service is likely to go up with the number of items bought and with the quantity of each bought in one transaction or one visit to a store.[52] The transaction size is likely to be lower in the Soviet Union than in other countries of the same LED, for the following reasons: (a) The stores often run out of particular goods and the consumer is forced to visit more stores or the same store more often for a given volume of goods. (b) Soviet stores are much more specialized than those in the West. Specialization is maintained to simplify the network of links to the wholesalers, since links to many wholesale bases and ministries are difficult to maintain.[53] (c) A smaller proportion of the Soviet population owns refrigerators and few families have cars, both of them prerequisites for buying food in large quantities. As late as 1965 only 11 percent of all Soviet families had refrigerators and only 1 percent owned cars,[54] which is definitely lower than in any country of group II. (d) A lower level of private disposable income means smaller transactions.

Finally, we can apply to the retail system the argument about the disadvantage of being a small unit in a centrally planned economy (see Chapter 9). The average retail store is the smallest accounting unit that operates in the Soviet Union under the social production system and thus suffers the most from the overhead costs of administration, control, directives, and so forth.

In listing the main sources of inefficiency in Soviet trade, I have concentrated on those aspects that seem to me to affect only trade itself or trade more than the rest of the economy. This avoids a discussion of the major sources of inefficiency in the Soviet economy, such as the system of incentives, the training of managers, and the price system, where it is difficult to estimate which industry is hurt most. In some cases the trade industry suffers from inefficiencies in the production sphere, such as the low quality of many products and poor packaging. I think that the relatively poor performance of Soviet trade has been amply demonstrated, despite the lack of hard figures. The next chapter tries to reconcile the low physical productivity and the high level of sales per worker.

51. A. Vakulov, "Za Pliushevim Kanatom," *Ekonomicheskaia Gazeta,* no. 38 (September 1966), pp. 33ff. This is a survey article on the new trade practices and their problems.
52. See the detailed discussion in Schwartzman, chap. 8.
53. See *CDSP,* 17.26:35 (July 21, 1965) and 18.4:29-39 (February 16, 1966); JPRS-*Labor,* no. 120 (August 4, 1966), p. 14.
54. M. I. Goldman, *The Soviet Economy: Myth and Reality* (Englewood Cliffs, N.J., 1968), pp. 53-58. See also below, Table 28, column (7).

7. The Service Gap in Trade: II

The preceding chapter concluded by stating the apparent efficiency paradox of Soviet retail trade. On the one hand, sales per person are exceptionally high, while on the other, most of the evidence points towards low efficiency of operation in the industry: the low level of capital per worker; the heavy burden of abnormally large stocks and the small benefit they confer; and many organizational inefficiencies. One way out of the paradox is to conclude that the amount of services offered by the industry per unit of goods sold is lower than in the countries of comparison. In this chapter the assumption of a rigid trade service coefficient in the retail industry is modified; instead it is assumed that some services can be produced by consumers in their own free time, so that fewer services are offered by the industry. The discussion begins by expanding the model of Chapter 6 to include substitution between market and self-supply of trade services, and the factors that tend to increase or reduce the contribution of each are analyzed. The probable patterns of change with LED of the importance of self-supplied relative to industry-supplied services are also discussed. The third section explores the implications of this new element for the size of the trade industry in the Soviet Union.

The last section deals with the high proportion of sales by catering establishments—a special case of substitution between home and market services.

The Introduction of Self-Supplied FT Services

The only change introduced into the model of the last chapter is that FT services can now come from two sources: the FT industry and self-supply by the household. The decision on how much to buy from each source is assumed to lie with the consumer. It is further assumed that both sources supply the same type of service, so that the choice is made on the basis of cost minimization, that is, a comparison of own cost with the industry's price for the service.

Thus the assumption of a fixed proportion between goods and services is kept, and the total amount of FT units produced is still fully dependent on the amount of commodities bought; but although the overall trade coefficient remains constant, the specific coefficient for the FT industry is variable and is endogenously determined by consumer choice. What are the elements involved in the choice between self-supply and purchase of FT services? Most consumers both buy and produce FT services at the same time, and they very rarely find a corner solution—using only one source—least costly. Few people go to factories to buy, or, at the other extreme, order all their needs by telephone. The conclusion to be drawn is that at least one of the two ways of producing FT services suffers from increasing marginal costs along the relevant range. In what follows it is assumed, for reasons to be specified presently, that it is the FT industry rather than the consumer which suffers from increasing costs.

The conceptual framework of what follows is in the spirit of Gary Becker's introduction of the consumer's time budget into his optimization behavior.[1] Let us define as a unit of FT services the amount of services self-supplied by a household in a unit of time, say one hour, and at a given level of labor productivity (at a given level of technology and capital inputs, such as car or refrigerator). Assume further that, *for a given amount of goods bought,*[2] the housewife's productivity per unit of time is constant as private shopping time increases, and also that the cost attached by the consumer to his shopping time is constant at a rate w_1 assumed for the moment to be equal to the rate of forgone earnings, that is, to the market wage rate. All this gives us a constant-cost self-supply curve for FT services. Though it could be argued that labor productivity or w_1 or both may go up as more time is spent on shopping, the constancy assumption does not look too unrealistic, and it is a helpful working assumption.

The FT industry may be looked upon as producing units of time saved for the consumer. We argue that for a given amount of goods the FT industry offers an increasing-marginal-cost supply curve to the individual household. The productivity of the industry declines as it increases the amount of time saved for the individual consumer, that is, as it approaches him and provides a substitute for an increasing amount of his self-supplied services. This phenomenon is the other side of the well-known increasing-returns-to-scale character of

1. See his "A Theory of the Allocation of Time," *Economic Journal,* 75:493-517 (September 1965).
2. As the amount of goods bought increases, one would expect costs per unit of service to go down. See the discussion below.

the trade industry in general. As the industry comes closer to the consumer, it moves from activities that serve many people at the same time to more specific activities that serve fewer people. Thus wholesaling has a greater advantage over self-supply than retailing, which in turn has a greater advantage over self-supply than home delivery. The same applies to the nongeographical aspects of distance: avoiding successive units of customer waiting time becomes increasingly costly to stores; and it applies also to the size and variety of stocks: the marginal costs of avoiding nonavailability of specific goods increase as successively rarer peculiarities of consumer taste are catered to. The reader will remember that this discussion holds only for a given amount of goods. When the amount of goods increases, one would expect increasing returns, or declining costs per unit of service, for both self-supply and the industry's activities in producing FT services.

The consumer, faced with constant cost for self-supplied and increasing cost for industry-supplied FT services, will decide on the allocation between the two sources by equating the two marginal cost schedules. Denoting by n the proportion of services supplied by the FT industry, the optimization rule for each consumer can be written

(1)
$$MC_1 = \frac{w_1}{x_1} = \frac{w_2}{x_2(n)} = MC_2,$$

where w and x are the labor costs and marginal products respectively of self-supply (subscript 1) and industry (subscript 2) labor.[3] With the existing assumptions and under competition, $w_1 = w_2$. According to our previous dis-

---

3. Using the notation of note 10 in Chap. 6, equation (1) here is obtained as follows:

FT services X are now divided into two different services by source $X_1 + X_2 = X$, where X_1 is self-supplied by the consumer and X_2 is produced by the FT industry. The trade-service coefficient is broken down correspondingly: $a_1 + a_2 = a$. Self-supplied FT services are produced (for a given G) by the production function: $X_1 = L_{X_1} \cdot x_1$, where L_{X_1} is the household's labor input and x_1 its average and marginal product. At some point, x_1 is defined as unity to get X_1 in units of time. The corresponding marginal or average cost of household FT services is $P_1 = w_1/x_1$. The marginal cost function of X_2 is $MC_2 = [w_2/c(G)] \cdot f(X_2/G)$, where $\partial c/\partial G < 0$ (increasing returns with G) and $f'(X_2/G) > 0$ (increasing costs as the share of X_2 increases) and where w_2 is the wage rate and c is the marginal product of labor in the FT industry, for given G and X_2/G.

Assume G = constant. Define $n = X_2/X$ and note that $a = X/G$, so that $X_2/G = n \cdot a$; then
$$MC_2 = \frac{w_2}{c} \cdot f(n \cdot a). \qquad\qquad [f'(n) > 0]$$

Assuming that all the variables are independent of changes in a, we get $MC_2 = \frac{w_2}{x_2}(n)$, where $x_2(n) = c/f(n)$.

cussion, x_2 declines with n or MC_2 increases with n. The equilibrium condition of equation (1) can also be written

$$(1') \qquad\qquad \frac{w_1}{w_2} \quad \frac{x_1}{x_2(n)},$$

that is, the wage rates are equated with the rate of the marginal labor products of the two activities. In both cases n is determined for given values of the other parameters (and for given amounts of goods and hence given total amounts of services). The determination of n is presented in Figure 1 in two ways corresponding to equations (1) and (1'). In both figures n is plotted on the horizontal axis. On the vertical axis we have marginal costs in Figure 1A and relative wage rates and relative marginal products of labor in Figure 1B. An initial equilibrium is achieved at the equivalent points F_a in both figures where $n = n_0$. For a given amount of goods bought, and thus of services supplied, On_0 and n_0O' represent both the proportion and the amount of services supplied by the industry and the household.

One point regarding the equilibrium condition remains to be cleared up. According to equations (1) and (1') and the diagrams, the individual consumer appears as a monopsonist in the market for FT services; that is, he can buy less services at a lower price. If this were the whole story, then he should equate his own cost, not with MC_2 but with its marginal factor cost curve. This is not so, since it is argued that the consumer is a perfectly discriminating monopsonist who pays successively higher prices for successive units of the industry's services, for each unit its marginal cost. In everyday terms, the commercial markup added to the factory price of the good is the cumulative sum of the costs per unit of FT services from the factory to the final commercial stage used by the consumer.[4] In Figure 1A his total payments to the industry consist of the integral of MC_2 from zero to n_0 and not the rectangle $n_0(w_1/x_1)$. This is so because at any moment of time there are (competitive) markets for all (or many) levels of n and, presumably, also competition within any level.[5] Thus one can draw up an average price schedule for the industry's services. As seen in Figure 1A, schedule P_2 is below MC_2 and at n_0 the average price per unit of time saved paid by the consumer is P_a lower than the marginal cost, F_a.

4. $P_2 = (1/n) \cdot \int_0^n MC_2 dn = MC_2 \cdot [1/(1 + 1/\eta)]$, where η is the elasticity of P_2 and is positive.

5. Another way of looking at the matter is to define a separate type or quality of service for every distance from the consumer. In such a case the higher price is paid only for the higher quality service units while lower prices are paid for the lower quality, more distant, service units.

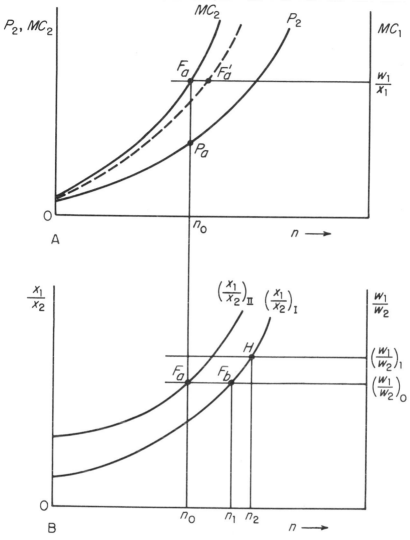

Figure 1. Market and Private Supply of Final Trade Services, the Determination of n ($0 < n < 1$)

Two of the assumptions made above should be examined: the first is whether in real life a marginal solution to this problem may be expected, since the indivisibilities in the labor market are so important and the time on shopping so small, relatively. My answer to this is qualified but tends to the affirmative, especially when the model is applied to national economies and to the long run. I shall adduce only two arguments to support this view. One is the well-known proposition that the decision on how much to work has much more flexibility than the organizational, short-run appearance of the labor market may indicate. This is especially true when there are long-run considerations and when the relevant decision unit is the household, husband and wife. Second, even if the household is irrational or uninformed and tends to ignore opportunities for small gains in its well-being, or if it is not possible to make small changes in working time, the trade industry is rational and for it the gains as well as the changes are large. In the long run the industry is bound to offer households a deal from which both sides will benefit, and all will move towards equilibrium.

The second assumption we have made is that w_1 is equal to the market wage rate. This seems to be even less realistic than the first assumption. It is usually assumed for a variety of reasons that w_1 will be lower than w_2. One reason is the indivisibility of labor units in the market mentioned above. Another is that the division of labor in the family tends to assign household tasks to those members of the family who can earn least by going out to work. In particular, the lack of job opportunities for women (genuine or by social convention) and especially the lack of part-time jobs may reduce w_1 for the family. Moreover, w_1 may be lower because some other tasks can be accomplished simultaneously with shopping or because shopping is more fun than work. Finally, w_1 may be lower if shopping has less disutility than work.

Compared with our initial equilibrium points, a lower w_1 will tend to reduce n and will also make x_1 smaller than x_2, but the basic properties of the model do not change. The crucial aspect of this discussion is how sensitive w_1 is to changes in w_2. In particular, is the elasticity of w_1 with respect to changes in w_2 smaller than, equal to, or greater than unity? If it is unity, then when w_2 changes, the ratio w_1/w_2 remains constant and in this respect there is no departure from our second assumption. If, however, the elasticity is less than unity, w_1/w_2 will go down when the wage rate goes up; thus (all other factors being equal) a decline in n, which will be steepest in the extreme case where w_1, is said to be completely independent of w_2. If the elasticity is greater than unity, w_1/w_2 will increase and cause an increase in n.

In applying the model to whole economies rather than to the single household it is assumed that the household is representative in all relevant aspects. The data necessary to analyze the pattern of changes in n over the process of economic development are not available. For the same reason the Soviet Union will be compared mainly with group I countries. We shall try to infer something about what happens to n over the group II to group I income range and thus get some idea of the outcome of the Soviet comparison with group II; this attempt is made in general terms.

The most commonly accepted pattern of change is that technology and labor productivity advance most in the nonservice industries and least in household operation, with service industries in between. If this is so then x_2 will increase more than x_1, x_1/x_2 will go down, and the curve $(x_1/x_2)_{II}$ will shift rightward and down to curve $(x_1/x_2)_I$. Assuming that w_1/w_2 stays constant, a larger $n = n_1$ is determined at the equilibrium point F_b (Figure 1B). If, however, the elasticity of w_1 with respect *to* w_2 is greater than unity, then w_1/w_2 will also rise, pushing the equilibrium point further to the right to point H with a still higher $n = n_2$.

That the elasticity of w_1 with respect to w_2 is greater than unity may be argued from the fact that, especially at high levels of development, a marked increase takes place in the number of job opportunities for women (including part-time) accompanied by a relaxation of the social inhibition against women working. This, with an increase in the flexibility of the labor market, may raise the calculated alternative cost of private household work by more than the increase in the real wage as measured in the market.

Each of these points can be debated and challenged as regards trade, particularly its retail section. It may be argued that productivity grows no more slowly in household shopping than in the retail industry. The introduction of refrigeration and cars to help household shopping may indeed have increased the private technology to a great extent. On the market services side, part of what seems to be an increase in productivity may be only a reduction in the amount of services provided by the industry. An example is the decline, with the development process, in the number of small neighborhood stores. Though usually measured as an increase in productivity through the elimination of excess capacity, it may be that what is actually happening is a pattern of getting away from the consumer.[6] If all this is important enough, then the rightward shift in the x_1/x_2 curve with the level of development becomes milder and may disappear altogether. There is thus no clear-cut answer to the question whether the level of n increases or declines with development. We shall return later to the discussion of how relative productivities of labor change with per capita income.

6. See the discussion of this point in Schwartzman, chap. 6, and Denison 1967, chap. 17. Shop owerns who are willing to operate at less than the market rate of monetary compensation provide extra services for their customers. We discuss the point further, below.

Theoretically, the value of n for a given country can also be estimated from information on the labor inputs invested in X_1 and X_2 and from their relative *average* labor productivities:

$$(2) \qquad m = \frac{n}{1-n} = \frac{X_2}{X_1} = \frac{L_{X_2}}{L_{X_1}} \cdot \frac{\bar{x}_2}{x_1},$$

where $\bar{x}_2$ is the average product per worker in the trade industry (and is greater than x_2 as the latter declines over n),[7] and m is the ratio of market to self-supplied trade outputs. Empirically, what we can get is data on the labor inputs in X_1 and X_2 for a few countries. There are no estimates of the productivity elements.

Using the descriptive definition of n in equation (2) and the behavior model described earlier in this chapter, we shall try to estimate the differences in the value of n between the Soviet Union and countries of group II.

The Share of Trade in the Supply of Final Services in the Soviet Union

This section demonstrates that the proportion of commercial services supplied by the trade industry is lower in the Soviet Union than in most other countries. An attempt is also made to measure the effect of this factor on the size of the industry and to discuss contributory policies and factors.

The main point of the first part of the demonstration is to show that the high rate of sales per worker in Soviet trade results from high capacity utilization of the trade labor force, which amounts to bringing trade services to a point much further away from the consumer than in other countries.

Compared with other countries, the Soviet Union operates a much smaller number of stores relative to the size and density of the population. This permits the Soviet Union to have larger stores, on the average, than other countries. This is true when size is defined by the number of workers per store, and even more so when it is defined by volume of sales.

As each store serves more consumers, it is they who do all the waiting while the sales clerks are kept constantly busy, never waiting for customers and never having enough time for those being served. To the small number of larger stores one could add the "saving" enjoyed by the trade system on stockkeeping

---

7. See note 4 in this chapter and note that $\bar{x}_2 = w_2/P_2$ and $x_2 = w_2/MC_2$.

(whose service value is, despite the waste, still much below market economy standards), on opening hours (which are usually for one shift), and possibly also on specialization insofar as the gain in administrative simplicity offsets the loss due to the decline in transaction size. This full capacity operation (mainly full capacity of manpower) offsets all the inefficiencies in the performance of the service to raise sales per person to such high levels. In trade and some other service industries, higher utilization of labor capacity implies less service.

Table 26 presents figures for the Soviet Union and three group I countries on the number of stores per 10,000 inhabitants [column (1)] and on the average size of store by employment [column (2)]. The Soviet figure for stores per 10,000 inhabitants is in no case higher than a third of the corresponding numbers in the other countries and in most cases it is lower. This is less true of catering (see the section on catering below). It is more than likely that the difference between the Soviet Union and group III countries is even greater, since in less developed countries we would expect to find more (and smaller) stores, mainly as the result of a lower technical level (the fact that consumers lack refrigerators and cars and that the stores lack self-service methods and equipment) and a lower degree of population concentration (smaller cities). When only urban areas are compared, these observations hold almost to the same degree. The relevant Soviet data are given in the second line of the table;

Table 26. Number and Size of Retail Stores, Selected Countries and Years

	All retail stores		Catering establishments	
Country	*Number per 10,000 population* *(1)*	*Size in workers per store* *(2)*	*Number per 10,000 population* *(3)*	*Size in workers per store* *(4)*
Soviet Union (1959)				
Total	26	3.8	7	7.0
Urban[a]	26	5.3	10	8.4
Rural[a]	26	2.6	3	4.2
United States				
1929	104	3.6	11	4.4
1958	82	4.9	20	5.0
Canada (1951)	92	..	9	..
United Kingdom (1950)	118	3.8	10	..

[a]Urban figures for number of workers are based on the state-owned system, and rural figures on the cooperative system.
Source: Soviet Union—*Narkhoz 1959,* pp. 682-689 (number of stores); *Sovtorg. 1964,* p. 131 (number of workers); *Census 1959,* p. 13, Table 1 (population).
 United States—Schwartzman, p. 204, Table A2-8, and p. 207, Table A2-10.
 United Kingdom and Canada—M. Hall, J. Knapp, and C.H. Winsten, *Distribution in Great Britain and North America* (Oxford, 1961), pp. 14, 22, 72.

the urban data for the other countries are not much different from their overall figures. Finally, there is little to suggest that urban population is more concentrated in the Soviet Union than elsewhere.

The other side of the picture is presented in column (2) of the table, which shows that the size of store (measured by number of workers) is a little larger in the Soviet Union than in the other countries. In this way the stores can maintain high levels of "efficiency."

For the Soviet consumer, fewer stores means that he has to travel further for his shopping; more people (as many as three to four times more) per store and shorter hours mean having to wait in line; specialized stores means having to go to two or three stores before all the basic foods can be purchased, and carelessness in the supply system means that the consumer has to make several trips to any one store before he is successful. The problem is aggravated by the fact that the Soviet consumer has less household equipment than his counterpart in other countries, where stores are nearer and queuing is infrequent—the most important missing item being the refrigerator.

It is not surprising that all these are a subject of constant complaint in countless letters and articles.[8] All of them can be summarized in one sentence: shopping takes too much time—time that could have been devoted to more productive or enjoyable matters.

That the Soviet value of n (that is, the proportion of commercial services supplied by trade) is smaller than in other countries of the same LED can be demonstrated and explained by the behavior model. Using equation ($1'$), it is assumed that the curves $(x_1/x_2)_0$ and $(w_1/w_2)_0$ [Figure 2, of the Figure 1B type] describe the situation in a country of the same LED (in terms of GNP per capita for the time being) as the Soviet Union. The point of equilibrium is N_0 and the equilibrium level of n is n_0. I believe that the distribution of commercial services in the Soviet Union between market and self-supply (n_{su}) differs from that of other countries for several reasons. Lower relative productivity in producing market retail services: the discussion in the preceding chapter leads to the conclusion that productivity of labor in trade relative to that in

8. Many of these complaints appear in the sources cited in Chap. 6. There are specific references to the connection between the inefficiencies of the trade system and consumer time in, inter alia, *CDSP*, 10.41:45 (November 19, 1958); *CDSP*, 17.19:30-31 (June 2, 1965); *CDSP*, 18.28:15 (August 10, 1966)—this source presents letters grouped by the type of complaint; *CDSP*, 18.4:29-30 (February 16, 1966)—from *Pravda* on standing in line and on overspecialization of stores. The last point and others are also referred to in JPRS-*Labor*, no. 120 (August 4, 1966), p. 14. See also G. A. Prudenski, "Opit Ekonomiko-Sotsiologicheskikh Issledovani," *Ekonomicheskaia Gazeta*, no. 2 (1966), p. 10; and G. S. Petrosian, *Vnerabochee Vremia Trudiashchikhsia v SSSR* (Moscow, 1965), p. 37.

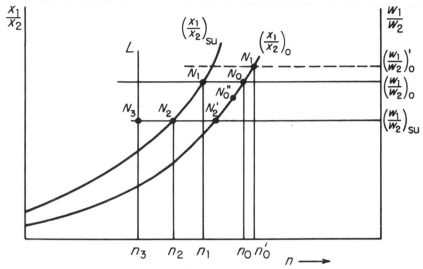

Figure 2. The Determination of n, the Soviet Union and a Normal Country

the household is lower in the Soviet Union than in the normal country for every level of n. That is, $(x_1/x_2)_i$ is lower than $(x_1/x_2)_{su}$. True, both x_1 and x_2 are lower in the Soviet Union than in the control country, but since x_1 depends more on the services of simple labor and x_2 on capital and organization, it appears that the shortage of capital in trade and households and the organizational weaknesses bear only on the trade industry. However, I do not think that this is quantitatively very important. In the diagram the difference is shown by a higher Soviet labor productivity curve $(x_1/x_2)_{su}$. If this were the only difference between the countries, the Soviet equilibrium point would be N_1 and the value of n would be $n_1 < n_0$.

Policy factors seem to be much more important. Two different, not exclusive, policy measures applied in the Soviet Union reduce the value of n. One is the tax system—in the most general sense of the term—which is the principal tool for resource allocation between investment (and other government uses) and private consumption, and the other is a physical constraint on the size of the trade industry. Though both are used, it is not entirely clear which of them is the operative constraint on trade.

The tax and resource-allocation system: The Soviet tax system has two features of interest to us here. The first is that the amount of tax is a higher proportion of GNP than in any other country. After taxes the Soviet citizen is left with less than half the GNP, which is some 15-20 percentage points less than what is left as personal (after-tax) income in other countries.[9] The second is that most of the taxes are levied *ad valorem* on most consumer commodities and services.[10] Disregarding the different rates on different commodities, the generality of the tax makes it in the aggregate very similar in its effect to a wage tax (or income tax) at a much higher rate than in other countries.

The total income effect of the tax is introduced in the explanation of the low proportion of tradable goods in the Soviet Union. It can also explain the much higher labor force participation rate, especially the high urban and female rates. More precisely, and in line with the model of this chapter, the strong income effect (compared with other countries of the same LED) induces the Soviet family to spend more time on work, both in the market and at home, as opposed to leisure. The substitution effect of a lower wage makes them spend a higher *proportion* of the total working time in self-supply of one kind or another and, high as this proportion is, it still leaves the amount of paid work offered higher than in other countries. Though we cannot evaluate the total private/market substitution in all services and goods in which it might appear, we think that it does explain the high proportion of self-supplied commercial services.

In terms of Figure 2, the chief effect of the tax system is to reduce the value of w_1 while keeping the value of w_2 [curve $(w_1/w_2)_{su}$], the wage paid in the economy, untouched. The extent of this change depends, of course, on what is assumed about the sensitivity of w_1 to different levels of wages as well as on the differential in the tax rate between the normal country and the Soviet Union. Unless it is claimed that there is no connection between the two in either country, then the Soviet w_1/w_2 ratio will be lower. The equilibrium point will be N_2 and the value of n_2 below n_0 and n_1.

Given the structure and size of the tax this hypothesis states that the retail trade sector is the "right" size. Under these conditions people would buy no more commercial services than they do even if they were available, since there would in this case be a higher marginal cost. The complaints mentioned above about the scarcity of trade services must be interpreted as representing aspirations for a better life—but not market purchasing power.

Quantity restriction: The second possibility is that the planned size of the retail industry is below what is needed for equilibrium at point N. In such a case n is fully determined by this physical restriction, and consumers must

9. See pp. 87-88 above.
10. These taxes are known as profit and turnover taxes in the Soviet Union.

apply the rest of the commercial services needed to get their goods home. This is an additional tax on tradable goods and it differs from the turnover tax only in that it is imposed directly on free time and not indirectly through income, and that it is not imposed on services not purchased through the retail system. From the point of view of resource allocation this type of physical restriction is thus very similar to the turnover tax.

In the diagram we assume that the quantitative restriction and not the tax is the operative constraint, thus keeping the level of n at n_3, which is the lowest of all and is achieved by the constraint L with equilibrium at point N_3. If this is not the effective constraint, N_2 will remain the equilibrium point. It is difficult to determine which is the effective restriction, though I tend to think that it is the physical constraint.

Under either hypothesis there is a situation in which women are induced to work more than in the normal country, not by providing them with more commercial services, but by cutting wage rates, thereby creating a situation in which the household both works more and uses more of its free time for self-supply than in the normal country.

A question arises as to whether either the tax system or the physical constraint really achieve the planners' objective function, which is, we assume, maximizing the labor force (in terms of the number of workers) in the "productive" sector of the economy. The specific question here is whether the number of persons who can join the labor force when more services are provided through the market is greater than the number of persons needed to expand the trade industry. If all working time invested above the normal level of self-supplied services—between n_3 and n_1, at least—can be diverted into paid work, then, as is clear from the diagram, only part of it need be engaged in providing the same amount of services.[11] The rationalization for not allowing part-time work could be that the income effect (on a backward-bending supply for labor) would absorb part of the substitution towards market production (that is, paid work in the economy) so that some of the additional income created in the process would be devoted to more leisure; a second reason could be the high price of capital, which is partly responsible for the higher labor productivity in trade and makes the price of the substitution too high. These explanations assume that we start from equilibrium in all the markets, given, of course, the tax level.

Other explanations may be based on nonequilibrium initial situations. The

11. If $(w_1/w_2)_0 \leqslant 1$, then any private work to the left of n_1 is carried out with definitely lower productivity than the potential market production in this range.

Soviet household, or the Soviet woman, works more than she really likes to.[12] This situation may result from the fact that hardly anyone is permitted to work part-time in the Soviet Union, including women. If the large majority of women choose full-time work, when faced with the choice of full-time or no work at all, then an increase in the amount of available services only brings them closer to the optimum position without any change in their readiness to work more. If, however, there are enough women who decide not to work but are close to deciding to do so, then the inflow of new labor resulting from more services may achieve what the planners are after. The only indication on this score is a statement by M. Sonin that about 7 percent of working women would have preferred to work part-time.[13] Had they been permitted to do so, making up the resulting loss in working time would, according to his calculations, have required 25 percent of nonworking women to take up part-time work. Sonin concludes that this condition could easily be met.

It is also possible that it is not the lack of commercial services that is the immediate obstacle preventing more women from going to work. Though commercial services are mentioned in every discussion on why more women do not work, the main attack seems to be on the shortage of preschool facilities for children. If this is the operative constraint, then there is no point in trying to alleviate the situation in other services first.

Finally, there is always the possibility that the planners have failed to maximize what they are presumably trying to maximize. Some of this may be explained by the ideological stigma attached to the trade industry. Whether or not this stigma is important, the fact remains that commonly only a small proportion of the construction plans approved for trade is implemented.[14]

The larger n of market economies can also be explained by the existence of excess capacity in the retail trade industry, which results in underpriced retail services; this is well documented in the literature.[15] The retail industries which suffer from excess capacity typically consist of many small individually owned and operated corner stores. For several reasons these small proprietors are willing to operate their business for a smaller monetary return (to labor or capital) than they could command elsewhere in the economy. In so far as this willingness is connected with the form of ownership such excess capacity can-

---

12. "Likes" in the economic sense of optimization under given conditions.

13. M. Sonin, *Aktualnie Problemi Ispolzovania Rabochei Sili v SSSR* (Moscow, 1965), pp. 140-153.

14. See note 37 in Chap. 6.

15. See, for example, Schwartzman, chap. 6, pp. 71-78, and Denison 1966, chap. 17, pp. 4-7.

not arise in the Soviet Union, where private ownership of means of production was abolished long ago.

In our model lower returns for labor means lower w_2, so that the supply of marketed retail services is shifted to the right and downwards in Figure 1A (broken line) or the w_1/w_2 curve is shifted upwards to $(w_1/w_n)_0'$ in Figure 2. In both cases the result is an increase in the proportion of purchased services, n, as these services become cheaper (for every level of n). Assuming now that our original n_0 describes a normal market-economy case but *without* excess capacity we get a normal case *with* excess capacity at equilibrium points F_a' and N_0' in Figures 1A and 2 respectively. If we now compare (Figure 2) n_0' with n_2 or n_3—those of the Soviet Union—we see that part of the difference is explained by what one may preliminarily describe as a nonoptimum situation—or waste—in the market economies.[16]

The lower physical productivity of these small stores, expressed in a lower level of sales per worker or algebraically in higher x_1/x_2, is the result of the higher level of n, which is in turn the result of lower w_2 and not in itself an expression of excess capacity.

Two explanations are usually advanced for the willingness of small proprietors to be undercompensated. One is that their independent status as self-employed generates nonmonetary benefits that are lost if they become employees. A list of such benefits usually includes higher social status, more personal freedom, avoidance of supervision, and more self-expression. Though the benefits are nonmonetary there is no excess capacity or suboptimality from either the efficiency or the welfare point of view. To the extent that there is such nonmonetary compensation, the consumer in the market economy enjoys the external benefit of a private ownership system, benefits from which his Soviet counterpart is barred. The effect of this factor on the relative sizes of n and on the Soviet trade gap is calculated at the end of this section.

The second factor or group of factors explains the excess capacity as a result of barriers that prevent the movement of people and capital into better-paying activities. These barriers may be lack of information or its high cost, the real or psychic costs associated with the change in status, or the immobility of labor caused by the fear of unemployment. In some cases employment in the retail trade is an intermediate step between even less remunerative agricultural occu-

---

16. Moving from N_0 to N'_0 does not mean that the difference itself has increased. An alternative presentation that emphasizes this point would be to move left of N_0 to N''_0—a point that would describe a normal case without excess capacity while N_0 describes the normal case with excess capacity.

pations and industrial or other higher paid urban employment. Like the other immobilities described, this last phenomenon (which I have called bulging) cannot occur in the Soviet Union because people are not free to move to the cities and open small private businesses. Whatever the reason, if such immobility exists, the excess capacity in the trade industry is "real" and the short-run situation at least is suboptimal. Any increase in n due to this factor should be interpreted as a misallocation of resources.

Although the model can demonstrate and explain the lower Soviet n, it can be of only limited help in trying to measure the difference. The most productive way of doing this is to use equation (2) above. We first compare labor and time inputs in trade and in privately supplied commercial services and then estimate relative productivities. To avoid the direct comparison of labor inputs and private time we first compare ratios of labor inputs of the same kind between pairs of countries in the following way:

In accordance with equation (2) we can write:

$$(3) \qquad\qquad \frac{m_i}{m_{su}} = \frac{\lambda_{2,i}}{\lambda_{1,i}} \cdot \frac{\delta_i}{\delta_{su}}$$

where
$$\lambda_{2,i} = \frac{L_{X_{2,i}}}{L_{X_{2,su}}}; x_{1,i} = \frac{L_{X_{1,i}}}{L_{X_{1,su}}}; \text{ and } \delta_i : \frac{\bar{x}_{2,i}}{x_{1,i}},$$

the industry-home productivity ratio; i is for country. λ_2 and λ_1 are ratios of trade labor inputs and private time inputs respectively; the ratio between them provides the labor input component of the m_i/m_{su} ratio while δ_i/δ_{su} is its productivity component.

For compiling λ_2, we use the labor force shares in the trade industry used all along. The data for λ_1 ratios are included in time budget studies of households.

There is apparently much more interest in time budgets in the Soviet Union than in the West. One result of this interest is many studies of how people spend their time in the Soviet Union (starting from the early 1920s), mainly for the 1959-1965 period.[17] Table 27 summarizes the findings on shopping time of some of the most important recent studies.

17. Complete lists of the Soviet publications in this field are given by Dodge, p. 92, and M. Yanowitch, "Soviet Patterns of Time Use and Concepts of Leisure," *Soviet Studies* 15:17-37 (July 1963). More recent studies are V. D. Patrushev, *Vremia Kak Ekonomicheskaia Kategoria* (Moscow, 1966), and G. A. Prudenski, "Biudzhet Vnerabochego Vremini," *Ekonomicheskaia Gazeta,* no. 17 (April 1967), pp. 6-7. See also Sonin 1965, chap. 5.

Table 27. Shopping Time in the Soviet Union, Selected Data (Hours per Day)

Locality	(2) + (3) (1)	Men (2)	Women (3)
1. Twelve cities[a] (circa 1960)	0.93[b]	..	..
2. Krasnoyarsk (1960)			
a. Source (1)			
Working days	1.00	0.42	0.58
Nonworking days	1.80	0.40	1.40
Average day	1.13	0.42	0.70
b. Source (2)			
8-hour working day	1.09	0.37	0.72
7-hour working day	1.28	0.56	0.72
6-hour working day	1.08	0.41	0.67
3. Norilsk (1960) 7-hour working day	1.36	0.51	0.85
4. Novosibirsk (1960)			
Working days	1.03	0.43	0.60
Nonworking days	1.63	0.68	0.95
Average day	1.11	0.47	0.65
5. Yerevan (1960)			
Working days	1.40	0.65	0.75
Nonworking days	1.80	0.77	1.03
Average day	1.46	0.67	0.79
6. Krasnoyarsk krai[c] (1959)	1.05	0.35	0.70
7. Krasnoyarsk krai, Xacckaya oblast[c]	0.84	0.28	0.56
8. Krasnoyarsk krai, other rayoni[c]	0.62	0.18	0.44
9. Pskov (1965)[d]			
Working days	0.65	0.17	0.48
Nonworking days	1.0	0.4	0.6
Average day	0.7	0.2	0.5

[a]Includes the following cities (1959 population in thousands in parentheses): Moscow (5,046), Kolomna (100), Yerevan (509), Tbilisi (695), Sverdlovsk (778), Novosibirsk (886), Krasnoyarsk (412), Norilsk (109), Novokuznets (377), Omsk (581), Kastroma (172); the twelfth city is not specified.
The average appears to have been produced by pooling all budgets without ascribing specific weights to the cities.

[b]Actual time spent by average person (and not the sum of men's and women's shopping time).

[c]Krai, oblast, and rayon are administrative district subdivisions (in descending order of magnitude).

[d]The 1959 population of Pskov was 81,000. The source gives only the separate figures for men and women for working and nonworking days; for the average day, the source gives an average per person of 0.4–double this amount compares with the 0.7 computed as the sum of men's and women's average time.

Source: Twelve cities, Krasnoyarsk (a), Novosibirsk, and Yerevan from source (1). Krasnoyarsk (b) from source (2). Norilsk and Krasnoyarsk krai (lines 6, 7, 8) from source (3). Pskov from source (4).

(1) G. S. Petrosian, Vnerabochee Vremia Trudiashchikhsia v SSSR (Moscow, 1965), pp. 94-96, 141.

(2) V. D. Patrushev, Intensivnoct Truda Pri Sotsializme (Moscow, 1963), pp. 116-117, 108-109.

(3) V. D. Patrushev, Vremia Kak Ekonomicheskaia Kategoria (Moscow, 1966), pp. 215-217.

(4) A. Szalai et al., "Multinational Comparative Social Research," American Behavioral Scientist, Vol. 10 (Appendix to no. 4, December 1966), Tables III.2, III.3, III.5, and III.6.

The variable we are most interested in is the average shopping time per family, and we compute it as the sum of the reported shopping times of employed men and employed women. Only one source deals with nonworking women (Pskov, 1965), and reports that they spend more time shopping than employed women.[18] We do not know to what extent this is compensated for by the husband doing less shopping. Also, we have no data on shopping time of other nonworking members of the family. Some of the data are for working days only and some include Sundays and days off; such figures are higher, since it is customary to shop on Sundays in the Soviet Union.

The data show that an urban family with husband and wife working spends at least one hour daily on shopping. If we take the line 1 figure as the most representative and add to it about 10 percent to account for Sunday shopping and an allowance for the longer shopping time of nonworking women, we get a figure of a little over one hour. There are differences between the cities listed, but except for Pskov the unadjusted figures are all above one hour. The Pskov figure is probably lower because travelling for shopping purposes is not included; it is included in the other cases—or so we assume. Prudenski has stated as recently as 1967 that travelling to the place of service takes about one-third of total shopping time.[19] If we add this much to the Pskov figure we come very close to one hour. The difference between the Pskov figure and the others might also be due to specific conditions in Pskov, or to an improvement in trade services from 1959-60 to 1965; but this is not likely.

The time devoted to shopping in rural areas is apparently less than in the cities, as can be seen in lines 6-8 of the table, which represent predominantly rural populations. This is, of course, the result of lower dependence on shopping and not of better services.

Table 28 presents an international comparison of shopping time in several West European countries, the United States, and the Soviet Union. Though the data come from separate country studies, they were collected according to preagreed definitions and conventions so that definitional comparability should be quite good.[20]

The Soviet figures for total population are in line with the Western European and below the United States figures [column (1)]. The figures are weighted averages of three groups of shoppers: working men, working women, and non-

---

18. In 1965 a nonworking woman in Pskov spent on the average 0.1 hour more per day on shopping than a working woman. [A. Szalai et al., Appendix to "Multinational Comparative Social Research," *American Behavioral Scientist,* vol. 10 (Appendix to no. 4, December 1966), Table III-4.]

19. Prudenski 1967, p. 6.

20. For a description of the preparations for this international undertaking, as well as for the definitions used and other details, see Szalai et al.

Table 28. Shopping Time and Other Indicators, Selected Countries

Country	Shopping time (hours per day)				travel[a] (2)+(3)	Nonwork (hours per day)	Percent households with cars
	Total popu- lation	Employed		Non- employed women			
		Men	Women				
	(1)	(2)	(3)	(4)	(5)	(6)	(7)
United States							
All cities	0.5	0.4	0.5	0.7	0.45	0.8	92
Jackson, Michigan	0.6	0.4	0.7	0.8	0.55	0.9	98
West Germany							
All cities	0.4	0.1	0.4	0.8	0.25	0.3	42
Osnabrück	0.5	0.2	0.5	0.9	0.35	0.4	46
France	0.4	0.2	0.4	0.7	0.30	0.5	57
Belgium	0.3	0.1	0.3	0.6	0.20	0.5	66
Soviet Russia							
Pskov	0.4	0.2	0.5	0.6	0.35	0.8	2

[a]Total population.
Source: Szalai et al. (Appendix), Table I [for column (7)], Tables III.1 to III.4 (other columns).

working women. The last clearly shop more than the other two.[21] The proportion of nonworking women is much lower in the Soviet Union than in any of the countries of comparison; in the Soviet sample, only 11 percent of women do not work, compared with no less than 55 percent in the other countries.[22] A sort of standardization for this factor is carried out in column (5), where it is assumed that, had she worked, a nonworking woman would shop the same amount of time as a working woman, and that the average shopping time for each partner in a family where both husband and wife work is the simple average of the figures in columns (2) and (3). Standardized in this way, the figure for the Soviet Union is higher than those for Belgium, France, and the all-cities average for West Germany, though it is lower than the figure for the United States.

Adding travelling time probably means that the Soviet figure would gain somewhat compared with the other countries. This conclusion is based on the exceptionally high Soviet figure for travelling time for all purposes except work [double the figures in Western Europe, see column (6)], and on the assumption that probably less travel in the Soviet Union is for pleasure and more for nonwork business, shopping included. Taking this into account, the Soviet figure might reach the all-cities figure for the United States. The reader should

21. Szalai et al., Appendix, Table I.
22. It can be assumed that the alternative cost of self-supply, w_1, will be lower for nonworking than for working women.

bear in mind that Soviet shopping time is underestimated in the calculations that follow.

Even without precise measurement, one can see the contrast between this comparison and the comparison of labor inputs in retail trade. Although the Soviet labor share of retail trade is less than half the figure for countries in the same income group and about a third of the figure for most group I countries (including those for which we have time budget comparisons), private time inputs in shopping are higher than in Western Europe and very close to those of the United States. If there are no marked offsetting differences in the labor-productivity ratios between the Soviet Union and the countries of comparison (the δ ratios), the size of n in the Soviet Union is much smaller than in those countries. [See equations (2) and (3).]

The labor input ratios λ_1 and λ_2 and the ratios between them are shown in Table 29. The λ_2 ratios are based on the proportion of trade workers in the total population of each country. This is done in order to make the λ_2 ratios

Table 29. Ratios of Labor Inputs in Trade (λ_2) and Private Shopping (λ_1), Selected Countries to Soviet Union[a]

	United States[b]	West Germany	France	Belgium	Average, four countries
Ratios for trade (λ_2)					
1. Total trade	3.0	2.6	2.2	2.3	2.5
2. Retail and wholesale	3.3	(2.9)	2.4	2.5	2.8
3. Retail only	4.1	(3.1)	(2.7)	(2.7)	(3.1)
4. Private shopping ratios (λ_1)[c]	1.4	1.1	1.1	0.9	1.1
λ_2/λ_1					
5. Trade (line 1 ÷ line 4)	2.1	2.4	2.0	2.6	2.3
6. Retail and whole-sale (line 2 ÷ line 4)	2.4	2.6	2.2	2.8	2.5
7. Retail only (line 3 ÷ line 4)	2.9	2.8	2.5	3.0	2.8

[a]Figures in parentheses are based on an arbitrary estimate of the labor force share of retail.
[b]Calculations are based on the "all cities" figure (see Table 28).
[c]Hours per adult per day.
Source: Labor inputs in trade, Table 9, and source of Tables 2 and 8. Private shopping time, Table 28, column (1). The Soviet figures are deflated by 10 percent as explained in the text.

conform with those of shopping time λ_1.[23] We present three alternative λ_2 ratios based respectively on the number of workers in total trade, in retailing and wholesaling, and in retailing alone. Although the first figure is based on better data, the latter two are upper and lower limits for final trade services *less* catering and thus correspond better to the shopping-time data, which do not include time spent in restaurants. The implications of the larger proportion of workers in Soviet catering services are discussed separately in the next section. The λ_1 ratios are based on average shopping time for the urban population [the figures in column (1), Table 28] [24] but corrected so as to represent the average shopping time for the total Soviet population rather than the urban population only. The Pskov shopping time of 0.4 hours per adult was deflated by 10 percent to give 0.36, according to the data of Table 27. The shopping-time data of other countries were not corrected in this manner because of lack of data and the presumption that, with a small proportion of rural population, the effect would be smaller than in the Soviet Union. If there is a bias here, it is to underestimate the relative importance of shopping time in the Soviet Union.

A related question that arises is how far to correct the Soviet data, both L_{X_2} and L_{X_1}, for factors that have already been found to explain some of the trade gaps. It can be assumed that most exogenous factors that explain a smaller trade industry explain also smaller shopping-time inputs (the obvious example is the smaller TGS), so that no such correction need be made. This conclusion is reinforced in view of the large Soviet rural population proportion. Lines 5-7 present ratios of the form λ_2/λ_1 based on the different λ_2 definitions. Finally, to the comparisons with the four group I countries we add (in the last column) computations based on averages for these four countries. The description of the results refers to this column, although the variance of the ratios around the averages is sometimes substantial.

The average figures come to 2.3-2.8 with relatively little variation between the countries. These ratios demonstrate that other countries invest between two and a half and three times more labor in trade than in private shopping, compared with the Soviet Union.

Equation (3) above shows that only a productivity ratio (δ_i/δ_{su}) of about 0.4 (the reciprocal of the λ ratio) can make the m_i/m_{su} ratio equal to unity. In other words, for this to happen, the difference in labor productivity between

---

23. Even so, there remains a small difference that could bias the results: in private shopping time the ratio is in terms of adult and not of total population. We ignore this bias.

24. If the figures adjusted for nonworking women were used [as in Table 28, column (5)], the λ_1 ratios would be lower, of course, since they show relatively higher Soviet shopping time.

trade labor and private shopping labor in the Soviet Union must be two and a half to three times as large as in other countries; this is very unlikely.[25] Nor can the very small difference in n values between group I and group II countries explain more than a small part of the difference in the m values.[26] On the basis of fairly tough but plausible assumptions about orders of magnitude I conclude that the trade/private output ratio in the Soviet Union is by no means much higher than half of that in group II countries.

Estimating the quantitative effect of the lower Soviet n proportion from the ratios of labor inputs estimated in the last section requires two more steps, both of them involving arbitrary assumptions.

The first step is to derive estimates for L_{X_2}/L_{X_1} for at least one country in order to be able to convert the m_i/m_{su} into n_i/n_{su} ratios or, in other words, in order to get an indication of the relative importance of private shopping in the total amount of labor invested in commercial services.[27] A direct but crude estimate of labor inputs in the United States and the Soviet Union, on the basis of retail trade, shows that $(L_{X_2}/L_{X_1})_{us}$ = 0.85 and $(L_{X_2}/L_{X_1})_{su}$ = 0.30,[28] and their ratio is 2.9, the same as we get for the corresponding figures in Table 29.

Second, a figure is required for the average productivity of trade workers relative to private shoppers in any one country to enable us to convert ratios of n into a quantitative effect on the size of the trade industry.

Making several plausible assumptions about δ_1 (of group I), δ_{su} and m_I/m_{II}, we get a set of estimates of the effect that the lower Soviet n has on the size of

25. As can be seen with the help of Figure 2:
(a) for a given value of n $(x_1/x_2)_{su} > (x_1/x_2)_0$ and thus $\delta_1/\delta_{su} > 1$; but
(b) for equilibrium of $n_{su} < n_0$ when both are on *the same* x_1/x_2 curve (compare points N_0 and N_2) $(x_1/x_2)_{su} < x_1/x 2)_0$ because $(w_1/w_2)_{su} < (w_1/w_2)_0$ and therefore δ_i/δ_{su} II < 1 and offsets part of the difference in the labor input ratio. For this to be true n_{su} must be smaller than n_0 and thus δ_i/δ_{su} cannot entirely offset the effects of the λ_2/λ_1 ratios.
(c) When the $(x_1/x_2)_{su}$ curve is to the left of $(x_1/x_2)_0$ we have in equilibrium (such as at N_0 and N_2) a combined effect of (a) and (b) above with an even smaller offsetting effect, if any.
26. See Figure 1 and the accompanying discussion.
27. From the definition of n and m (pp. 101, 106 above) it can be seen that there is more than one possible value n_i/n_j for every given value of m_i/m_j.
28. United States: L_{X_2} is about 8.3 million workers in retail trade (1960, from Table 9 above). L_{X_1} is about 9.7 million in full-time equivalent; the figure is computed as follows: total annual shopping time is computed for the adult (20+) population of 111 million assuming 0.5 hours shopping per day; the result is converted to full-time equivalents assuming fifty 40-hour weeks per year.
Soviet Union: L_{X_2} is about 2.4 million workers in retail (1959, see Table 7). L_{X_1} is 9.2 million full-time equivalent; computed as for the United States, for an adult population of 131 million and a daily shopping time of 0.36 hours.

its retail industry. According to these estimates the Soviet retail trade would have been larger by between 22 and 43 percent if it had supplied the same proportion of retail services as are supplied in the countries of comparison. The most reasonable set of assumptions yields a rate near the upper end of this range.[29]

What does excess capacity in other countries contribute to the Soviet trade gap and to the differences found in the *n* values? To answer this let us first estimate the probable loss in production caused to the trade industry in market economies by the existence of self-employed workers.

Data and some calculations are presented in Table 30. The first line gives the proportion of self-employed (not including employers) in the commercial sector in groups of countries. The next two lines show the loss of product (actually sales) due to excess capacity based on two extreme assumptions: (a) that sales per independent proprietor are only 60 percent of sales per person in a small store operated by employees, and (b) that the proportion is 80 percent. The lower estimate is based on United States data for 1939 sales ratios between independent stores and stores with two or three employees. In the United States, 1939 came at the end of ten years of depression, a situation that tends to keep people in independent retailing or push them into it, even when their money income is very low. The higher limit is based on data of the same kind for the United States in 1963 and Great Britain in 1950.[30] The sales ratios are

---

29. Below are the assumptions producing the estimates of 22, 35, and 43 percent increases of the Soviet final retail trade industry and the corresponding *n* values for group II countries and the Soviet Union.

Effect	n_I	n_{su}	δ_I	δ_{su}	$\dfrac{m_{II}}{m_I}$	$\left(\dfrac{L_{X_2}}{L_{X_1}}\right)_I$	$\left(\dfrac{L_{X_2}}{L_{X_1}}\right)_{su}$
0.22	0.67	0.55	3.0	4.0	0.8	0.85	0.3
0.35	0.58	0.43	2.0	2.5	0.8	0.85	0.3
0.43	0.50	0.35	1.5	1.8	0.8	0.85	0.3

when $m_i = \delta_i \cdot \dfrac{L_{X_2}}{L_{X_1}}$ and $n_i = \dfrac{m_i}{m_i + 1}$.

The use of retail trade data for the computation is justified by the fact that according to the Soviet figures only 15 percent of wholesale is engaged in servicing the retail industry.

30. The United States 1939 figures giving the lower limit are: sales per employed person in independent stores were 70 and 64 percent of sales in stores with two and three employees, respectively (total retail); the corresponding figures for food stores were 60 and 53 percent, respectively, and 60 and 56 percent in clothing stores (Schwartzman, p. 93, Table 6-8). The figures giving the upper limit are United States (1963, in the same order): 85, 82, 87, 85, 80, and 75 percent; Great Britain (1950): sales per person in independent groceries with no or one employee, 82 and /0 percent of sales in groceries with two and three employees, respectively (Hall et al., p. 70).

Table 30. The Effect of Excess Capacity on Trade Productivity in Market Economies, by Country Group, circa 1960

	Country group		
	I	II	III
Percent of self-employed in C labor force	8.7	24.4	38.4
Loss of C product[a] (percent)			
Assumption (i)	3.5	9.8	15.4
Assumption (ii)	1.7	4.9	7.7
Loss of retail product[b] (percent)			
Assumption (i)	7.0	19.6	30.8
Assumption (ii)	3.5	9.8	15.4

[a] Assumption (i) is that sales per independent are 60 percent of sales per employed person; assumption (ii) is that this ratio is 80 percent.
[b] Assuming that retail employs half the labor of the C sector, and that all the self-employed are concentrated in retail.
Assumption (i) and (ii) as in note a.
Source: Issues of UN, Demographic Yearbook for the early 1960s.

not likely to be much outside our limits. It can be assumed that in general they are closer to the lower limit because status effects and barriers in mobility seem to be stronger in less developed countries. In the United States, the special conditions of 1939 combined with an exceptionally high entrepreneurial spirit seem to push the ratios to quite a low level. The average loss in product due to this factor is accordingly estimated at between 5 and 10 percent for group II countries. Assuming (on the basis of Table 9) that retail trade employs about half the labor of the C sector and that all the independents belong to retail, the loss of product to this industry is estimated at between 10 and 20 percent. Alternatively, the consolidation of small stores with one self-employed owner into larger stores with a few employees could save between 10 and 20 percent of the labor inputs in these industries and thus reduce the basic trade gap of the Soviet Union by 1 to 2 percentage points.

This estimate is much higher than the contribution of the excess capacity factor. First, part, and maybe a considerable part, of the computed loss in product results from scale effects included in the calculations, some of which exist also in the Soviet Union between small and larger stores.[31] Second, we have seen that only part of the monetary excess capacity is real; the rest is eliminated when nonmonetary benefits are taken into account. Finally, some of the difference in productivity is due to the lower quality of self-employed

31. Some of the data presented by Hall et al. show quite large differences in sales per employee between independent stores and stores of the same size belonging to chains. This may indicate that the scale effect is unimportant. However, scale effects may still be operative in the area of stocks, supply system, credit, information, advertising, and the like. See Hall et al., pp. 69-70.

workers and their family members, a factor that is already accounted for in the discussion of Chapter 5. Without trying to estimate how much each of these elements contributes to the productivity loss found in Table 30 we must assume that the pure excess-capacity factor is only a part of the explanation and probably not a major one.

Catering

In the catering subsector of trade there is more substitution of household services by the market in the Soviet Union than in other countries of the same LED. Our rough estimates indicate that as many as 375,000 workers, or more than one-third of the Soviet catering labor force actually replace housewives beyond the standard in other countries. This cannot be considered a very great achievement when one takes into account that the development of public catering is supposed to be one of the main ways of relieving "millions of women from tiresome housework"—a professed Soviet social goal.[32]

We estimate the effect of this substitution on the size of catering by: (a) estimating the differences between the Soviet Union and other countries in the proportions of retail goods channeled through restaurants, and (b) estimating the difference in trade coefficients between catering and retail proper.

The Soviet Union sells between 2 to 3 percentage points more of total retail goods through catering establishments than the United States (in constant prices, panel A of Table 31). The difference goes up to 3 to 5 percentage points when only the urban areas in the Soviet Union are included. The differences are estimated on the basis of exchange rates which discriminate between food and nonfood prices but which do not take into account other differences between United States and Soviet relative service prices (see notes to Table 31). Since relative Soviet service prices are much lower, including this element in the constant price comparison will increase the differences between the Soviet and United States figures. From a few observations on labor force shares of catering in the United States and other countries, it may be concluded that the proportion of tradable goods channeled through this industry is lower in group II countries than in the United States, so that differences between the Soviet Union and group II are greater. Taking these points together, the conclusion is that a proportion of total retail sales made through catering and drinking places of 10 percent for the Soviet Union and 5 percent for group II countries is plausible and that the differences between them are definitely not overstated. For the urban population the differences are presumably even higher.

32. Dikhtiar, p. 50.

Table 31. Catering Sales as Percent of Retail Sales, Soviet Union (1959) and United States (1958), 1955 Prices[a]

	Rubles		Dollars	
	Soviet Union	United States	Soviet Union	United States
A. Total sales (billions)				
Total population				
1. Retail	71.9	332.1	54.5	184.5
2. Catering	6.4	23.6	6.1	13.5
3. Catering as percent of retail	8.9	7.1	11.2	7.3
Urban population (billion)				
4. Retail	49.8		36.6	
5. Catering	5.1	b	4.9	b
6. Catering as percent of retail	10.2		13.4	
B. Sales-per-worker ratios (percent)				
Total population				
7. Catering as percent of retail excluding catering	20.3	31.7	26.1	32.6
8. Catering as percent of food sales	23.3[c]	25.0	23.3[c]	25.0
Urban population				
9. Catering as percent of retail excluding catering	17.9		23.0	
10. Catering as percent of food sales	20.6[c]	b	20.6[c]	b

[a]Exchange rates as for Table 25, except for catering and food, to both of which the food exchange rate was applied.

[b]The United States urban figures are assumed to be negligibly different from the total figures.

[c]Based on sales per worker in state-owned stores in the last quarter of 1961.

Source: Table 25 and its source. The figures referred to are from *Sovtorg. 1964*, pp. 220-221.

Panel B of Table 31 shows the ratio of sales per worker in restaurants to ordinary retail trade and in food retailing for the Soviet Union and the United States. On the basis of all retail sales, sales per persons in catering (compared with total retail) are considerably lower in the Soviet Union than in the United States (lines 7 and 9). Compared with food sales, the ratios in the two countries are very close to each other (lines 8 and 10). The two sets of ratios differ because in the United States per worker sales of food are much higher than those of nonfood, while the opposite is true for the Soviet Union.

As in all other trade sectors, so also here, sales per worker differ because of differences in either productivity or the amount of service offered. The ratio of sales per worker, which includes both elements, is a measure of the burden on the economy, specifically on the trade labor force, of the additional catering services. The benefit derived from this by housewives, however, should be estimated from pure trade coefficient ratios, that is, the sales per worker ratios adjusted for differences in relative productivity.

In the Soviet case, the pattern found for retail stores exists here also: a very low productivity in performance that is compensated for by very low trade coefficients. Almost everything that has been said with regard to the low productivity in the performance of retail trade is true also here. With regard to the low trade coefficients, this is apparent in several other ways: more than 90 percent of the eating and drinking places in the Soviet Union are run in the form of cafeteria and self-service establishments;[33] more than 50 percent of the sales are in the form of take-home rather than on-the-premises consumption;[34] opening hours are restricted in most places to rush hours in which much time is wasted by the customers standing in line; and, finally, the menus are usually very restricted.[35]

We estimate the additional burden on the Soviet trade industry using the sales ratios for food sales, which happen to be also about midway between the Soviet and United States ratios for retail and trade as a whole. It is thus assumed that the trade coefficient in eating and drinking places is four times as large as in food retailing.

Combining the assumptions made above we find that if the proportion of sales through eating and drinking places in the Soviet Union were 5 percent of all retail sales (as in the normal country), instead of 10 percent, then half of the catering labor force could be released, and a quarter of the released workers would be able to sell, through the regular retail outlets, what is sold by all of them in the eating and drinking sector. The potential saving amounts to 3/8 of all catering workers in the Soviet Union—about 375,000 workers. It is not clear exactly how much of this difference should be attributed to the differential in relative productivity, but I tend to assume that most of it is derived from a real difference in the *amount* of the services supplied. This aspect of the Soviet retail system compensates for only part of the substitution in the opposite direction found in the previous sections. In terms of explaining the gap in the trade industry, this factor *adds* to the gap that is to be explained. About 10 percent of all workers in final trade services in the Soviet Union are performing an extra service that is not performed in the countries that constitute our standard of comparison.

The contributions of the various factors that explain the gap in final trade

33. *Sovtorg. 1964*, p. 245.
34. *Narkhoz 1959*, p. 655; *Sovtorg. 1964*, p. 100.
35. See for example, JPRS-*Consumer Goods*, 69 (December 4, 1964), pp. 32, 36, and Dikhtiar, pp. 49-50.

service may now be summarized. The FT gap of between 4 and 5.5 points that remained to be explained at the beginning of Chapter 6 is further increased by up to half a point by the excess in catering services. The remaining gap is fully explained by (a) the lower proportion of tradable goods in the Soviet national product and (b) the higher "productivity" as measured by relative sales per worker. Of these two factors, the second is somewhat more important (Chapter 6).

From two-thirds to the whole of the sales-per-worker, or "productivity" advantage is attributable to the fact that the trade industry offers fewer services with the goods it sells; the extra service burden is carried by the consumer (Chapter 7). The rest, if any, of the "productivity" advantage is achieved mainly through a low level of product diversification and to a lesser extent by savings in other elements of the service coefficient, partly offset by the lower operational productivity (pp. 94-98) of the system. In fact, it is doubtful if a residual of significant magnitude really remains.

Part, and, I assume, a rather small part, of the extra services offered by the trade industry in the normal country is due to the excess-capacity factor and could be considered to stem from inefficiency in the market economy, rather than in the Soviet Union. Another small part of the excess burden placed on the Soviet consumer by the retail industry is compensated for by providing more catering services.

8. The Effects of the
Socialist Economic System:
Empirical Tests

Up to now we have tried to account for the gaps in the Soviet service industries in terms of specific, seemingly unrelated factors. At this point, the next step is to look for a synthesis or a common denominator of all or most of the factors explaining the service gaps: my argument is that the socialist economic system is such a common denominator. The hypothesis is tested empirically in this chapter, while the next contains a systematic analysis of the relation between the characteristics of the socialist system and the industrial structure of the economy.

For our purposes the relevant characteristics of the socialist economic system prevailing in the Soviet Bloc are: (a) state ownership of the means of production; (b) determination by the state of the rates and direction of economic growth; (c) centralized economic planning and organization; and (d) adherence to a few "Marxian" ideological norms (to be specified later).[1]

An Empirical Test

The effect of the socialist economic system on service shares is estimated in the following way. To the original sample of countries included in the regression of Chapter 2, we add seven socialist countries of Eastern Europe.[2] To the list of development variables a dummy variable called "being a socialist country" (Sc)

1. This is a more restrictive definition than that of B. N. Ward, which covers only the first two points [B. N. Ward, *The Socialist Economy: A Study of Organizational Alternatives* (Berkeley, Calif., 1967), p. 7].
2. Bulgaria, Czechoslovakia, East Germany, Hungary, Poland, Romania, and Yugoslavia. It is not entirely clear whether Yugoslavia belongs among the socialist countries. It certainly does not have centralized economic planning and organization. The country is nevertheless included on the grounds of its other characteristics and taking into account that any deviations from the socialist pattern can have only a slight effect on the quantitative and almost no effect on the qualitative results.

is added and the original equations are then re-estimated with the additional variable.[3] This procedure amounts to assuming that socialist countries have the same basic pattern of differences in industrial labor force structure as market economies and only the *level* of the various shares differs by a constant at each development level. This constant difference is estimated by the coefficient of the dummy variable.

As in Chapter 2, the discussion of the general regression results is followed by an estimate of the difference between the normal and actual service shares for the Soviet Union. The regression results are presented in Table 32, with $\bar{R}^2$ in columns (1)-(3) and the Soviet service gaps in columns (6)-(8). The results are for three sets of equations: the original equations estimated for nonsocialist countries [columns (1) and (6)], the same equations but with the observations of the socialist countries included [columns (2) and (7)]; these two serve as a control group for the third set of equations, which differ from the others in that they include *Sc* as an additional variable.

From the corresponding values of $\bar{R}^2$ for the different sets of regressions it can be seen that when the socialist countries are added to the sample $\bar{R}^2$ values decline [compare column (1) with column (2)], though the importance of this statistic should not be stretched too far. This is an indication that the seven additional observations do not fit very well among the other countries with respect to the relation between the service shares and the LED variables. The increase in $\bar{R}^2$ when *Sc* is added to the regressions [compare column (3) with column (2)], as well as the high significance level of the *Sc* coefficients, indicates that "being a socialist country" may be the factor that makes this group differ from the patterns established by the nonsocialist countries. It is interesting to note that the differences between correlation coefficients diminish as we move from the equations with only the GNP per capita representing the LED to the more complex equation (from line 1 to line 4 for the S sector).

The coefficients of the dummy variable *Sc* [column (4)], indicate that "being a socialist country" produces lower service shares for the S sector as well as for C and OS and that this is true whatever definition of LED is used. The coefficients (b_{Sc}) measure (statistical errors apart, of course) by how much the service shares should be lower in socialist countries at each level of development. Thus, when the level of economic development is defined by log y alone the socialist service shares are at each level of economic development lower than in market economies by 15.0, 7.0, and 8.0 percentage points for the S, C, and OS sectors respectively. As the other development variables are added, the negative *Sc* coefficients of each service sector decline until they reach their

3. The *Sc* variable has the value 1 for socialist countries and 0 for nonsocialist countries.

lower values of 8.0, 5.9, and 2.3 percent for the three sectors respectively (the C coefficient here does not differ significantly from zero, even at the 5 percent confidence level).

These results indicate a measure of substitutability between "being a socialist country" and the other development variables, that is, the level of urbanization and the labor force participation rate. More specifically, it may be that socialist countries have a growth strategy that results in a distinctly different LED structure, that is, a higher level of GNP per capita achieved at a relatively low level of urbanization and to some extent by the employment of a higher proportion of the population, all compared with other countries. Thus, when LED is measured by the income variable alone the difference is larger than when LED is measured by all three variables. The reader may recall the discussion of the various definitions of economic development in Chapter 2, and of whether differences in growth strategies should be considered as different levels of development or should be attributed to other factors affecting the development variables. Whatever view one takes, what may be called the growth strategy of the socialist countries does affect their relative levels of y, RU, and PR vis-à-vis the nonsocialist countries.

The same thing can also be seen when the various socialist countries are ranked among the other countries by level of economic development, as defined by the size of the S shares estimated from the regressions. With one exception the rank of all seven socialist countries moves down as PR and RU are added to the LED definition (Table 33). This means that the level of urbanization was below and the labor force participation rate was above that of other countries of comparable income per capita.[4]

The particular relation between y, PR, and RU results from various elements of the growth strategy of the socialist countries represented here, as well as those of the Soviet Union. First is the declared policy of inducing as many women as possible to enter the labor force in rural and, even more important, urban areas. This is the principal part of a general policy, executed mainly by means of wage determination, of increasing labor force participation. Second is a growth strategy based on the rapid development of the industrial sector, preferably heavy industry, which means in practice that the bulk of capital resources is allocated to heavy industry to the neglect of technological changes in agriculture. This results in a relatively capital-intensive and modern industry sector and a lag in the labor-intensive agricultural sector for any given level of

---

4. According to UN, *Demographic Yearbook 1963*, Table 18, the women's participation rates of Bulgaria, Poland, and Romania are the highest in the world. The figures for Hungary and Yugoslavia, though more in line with other European countries, are still on the high side at 30 percent. There are no data on Czechoslovakia in this source.

Table 32. *The Effects of "Socialist Economic System" on the Service Gaps of the Soviet Union*[a]

Dependent variable	Independent variable	$\bar{R}^2$[b] Nonsocialist countries (1)	$\bar{R}^2$[b] All countries[c] Without Sc (2)	$\bar{R}^2$[b] All countries[c] With Sc (3)	b_{Sc}[d] (4)	Estimated shares[e] (percent) (5)	Soviet services gaps[f] (percentage points) Nonsocialist countries (6)	Soviet services gaps[f] (percentage points) All countries[c] Without Sc (7)	Soviet services gaps[f] (percentage points) All countries[c] With Sc (8)
S 1.	log y	0.65	0.42	0.68	−15.0 (2.4)	21.1	14.9	12.0	0.0
2.	log y, PR	0.74	0.70	0.77	−9.2 (2.4)	20.6	8.5	4.3	−0.5
3.	log y, RU	0.71	0.61	0.76	−11.9 (2.2)	21.0	12.0	8.1	−0.1
4.	log y, PR, RU	0.77	0.76	0.81	−8.0 (2.2)	20.6	7.5	3.5	−0.5
C 5.	log y	0.67	0.44	0.72	−7.0 (1.0)	7.6	9.6	8.2	2.6
6.	log y, PR	0.68	0.59	0.72	−6.0 (1.2)	7.5	8.5	5.6	2.5
7.	log y, RU	0.68	0.53	0.73	−6.4 (1.1)	7.6	9.0	7.0	2.6
8.	log y, PR, RU	0.68	0.61	0.73	−5.9 (1.2)	7.5	8.3	5.4	2.5
OS 9.	log y	0.43	0.30	0.48	−8.0 (1.9)	13.5	5.3	3.8	−2.6
10.	log y, PR	0.59	0.61	0.63	−3.2 (1.9)	13.1	0.0	−1.4	−3.0

11.	log y, RU	0.54	0.52	0.59	− 5.6 (1.8)	13.4	3.0	1.2	− 2.7
12.	log y, PR, RU	0.64	0.68	0.69	− 2.3 (1.8)	13.1	− 0.8	− 1.9	− 3.0

[a] LF(a) data.

[b] All coefficients are significant at the 1 percent level, except for 0.30 in column (2), line 9.

[c] In addition to the 43 countries included in the regression of column (1), includes also Bulgaria, Czechoslovakia, East Germany, Hungary, Poland, Romania, and Yugoslavia. For these, labor force industrial distribution is from sources (1), (2), and (3), listed below; in a few cases figures from the last two sources were adjusted in order to make the distribution more consistent with the rest of our figures. GNP per capita (y) (shown in part B of Appendix Table A-1 below) is based on source (5)—figures for 1964 (in 1963 US dollars) from Table 1 of the source were converted to 1961 data (in 1960 US dollars) using the 1961-1964 growth rates in Table 4 of the source and assuming arbitrarily that in all seven countries population grew at 1 percent annually; conversion to 1960 US dollars was by means of the implicit price index for the GNP of the United States from source (6).

[d] Numbers in parentheses are the standard errors of the coefficient.

[e] Estimated from the regression of column (3), i.e., including *Sc* in addition to the variables listed in the stub.

[f] Estimated *less* actual share (as in Table 8), i.e., the minus sign indicates an *excess* over the norm.

Source: Labor force data for the socialist countries—(1) ILO, *Year Book of Labour Statistics 1965* (Geneva, 1965), Table 2a (Hungary, 1960; Poland, 1960; Romania, 1956; Yugoslavia, 1960).

(2) Zora Prochazka, *The Labor Force of Bulgaria,* U.S., Department of Commerce, Bureau of the Census, Foreign Demographic Analysis Division Publication Series P-90, no. 16 (Washington, 1962), p. 36, Table A-5, and p. 37, Table A-6 (Bulgaria, 1959).

(3) J. N. Ypsilantis, *The Labor Force of Czechoslovakia,* U.S., Department of Commerce, Bureau of the Census, Foreign Demographic Analysis Division Publication Series P-90, no. 13 (Washington, 1960), Appendix Tables and *passim* (Czechoslovakia, 1958).

(4) Samuel Baum and Jerry W. Combs, Jr. *The Labor Force of the Soviet Zone of Germany and the Soviet Sector of Berlin.* U.S., Department of Commerce, Bureau of the Census. Foreign Demographic Analysis Division Publication Series P-90, no. 11 (Washington, 1959).

(5) *New Directions,* p. 877, Table 1 and p. 880, Table 4. The derivation of the figures is explained in Appendix A, pp. 911-912.

(6) U.S., Department of Commerce, *Survey of Current Business,* 46-7: 37 (July 1966), Table 78.

Other data—column (1), Table 2; column (6), Table 8; columns (7) and (8), estimated share from worksheets [for column (7)] and column (5) [for column (8)], actual share from Table 8.

Table 33. The LED Ranking of Seven Socialist Countries[a]

Country	y	y, PR	y, RU	y, PR, RU
Czechoslovakia	9	13	18	18
East Germany	11	21	8	15
Hungary	16	26	26	33
Poland	20	28	21	30
Bulgaria	22	46	30	44
Romania	23	49	34	48
Yugoslavia	25	38	39	43

[a]Rank out of 50 countries.
Source: See source to Table 32.

GNP per capita. The combination of these two major policies enables the socialist countries to achieve growth, at least for some time, with a smaller rural-to-urban population movement than in other countries—the deficit in urban labor needed for industrialization is made up partly by enlisting all adults who move to the cities into the labor force and partly by employing relatively more capital-intensive techniques.

This growth strategy is confirmed also by regression results for the A and M shares in socialist countries. When compared with normal A shares in nonsocialist countries, all but one or two of the seven socialist countries show substantially higher A shares. The exceptions are East Germany, consistently, and Hungary. These large positive gaps in the A sector of the socialist countries are "translated" into a rather large regression coefficient for being a socialist country in the analysis that includes socialist countries. Socialist countries employ 6-16 percentage points more of their labor force in agriculture, the range being produced by the other development variables included in the equations.

There is no definite socialist pattern of gaps with respect to M labor shares, a finding which, though inconclusive, is perfectly consistent with the growth strategy described above. The M shares are below normal in five out of the eight socialist countries and above normal in the other three. Likewise the set of b_{Sc} coefficients for the M equations is neither consistent with regard to sign nor significantly different from zero. This is to my mind a result of the two conflicting effects of the socialist growth strategy on the M shares. On the one hand, the development included in M is stressed and, on the other, labor-saving techniques are used, especially in heavy manufacturing.

Before going on to compare Soviet with Eastern European service and other gaps, one must list at least some of the other possible interpretations of the findings. The first and most important is the possibility that what we have called the *Sc* effect is a manifestation not only of the economic system of the countries involved but also of their economic history;[5] since they are all in the same geographical region on the borders of the much more advanced Western European countries, they may have developed a different pattern of industrial structure for given levels of income or LED. This may indeed be part of the explanation. For one thing, in 1960 (to which our data refer) these countries had been socialist for only 12 to 15 years. A full analysis of this question involves a detailed investigation into the historical trends and dynamic aspects of each one of these countries, a task that is definitely outside the scope of this study. But the possibility is a warning to take the results of the present analysis with some reservations.[6]

Second, there is the possibility that the income estimates used for the socialist countries are biased upward (see notes to Table 32) and that the other development variables simply correct the bias. We have tried to minimize the bias by choosing, of the two available sets of figures, the one that gives the lower estimates.[7]

We turn now to the comparison of the actual Soviet service shares with those estimated by the different equations, including the variable of being a socialist country (Table 32). First, the service shares estimated by any equation including Sc are almost the same in each sector regardless of which of the development variables are included in the equations. Thus, the estimated S share is about 21 percent with 7½ percent for C, and 13-13½ percent for OS. According to the estimate, the actual level of urbanization and the labor force participation rate in the Soviet Union are almost exactly what one would expect given its GNP per capita and that it is a socialist country.

There is a similar finding for the service gaps. Again the newly estimated gaps [column (8)] are compared with the original gaps [column (6)] and also with the gaps that result from the regressions based on all countries but without Sc [column (7)]. The most important and interesting result is that when Sc is added to the equations—and it does not matter to which—the estimated Soviet

5. The low A and high M shares of East Germany and Hungary and the high M share in Czechoslovakia may be the result of their presocialist development.

6. An important additional source for students of these matters is the new volume of studies on Eastern Europe: U.S., Congress, Joint Economic Committee, *Economic Developments in Countries of Eastern Europe* (Washington, D.C., 1970).

7. The figures of F. L. Pryor and G. J. Staller, "The Dollar Values of the Gross National Products in Eastern Europe 1955" *Economics of Planning,* 6.1:1-26 (1966), are considerably higher than ours: in general their 1955 figures were higher than our 1961 figures (both in 1960 dollars).

The income per capita coefficient estimated in the regression is not very large anyway, and an error of $100 in the income level has only a small effect compared with the differences in service shares involved here. For example, changing income by $100 in the regression of S on y and Sc will change the S share by only 0.8 percentage points.

S share comes to within 1 to 2 percentage points of the actual share. The findings are slightly different for the C and OS shares. In the C sector we still find a 2½ percent gap and in OS an excess of around 3 percent. If significant, this is accounted for by specific Soviet conditions. Comparison of columns (6) and (8), indicates that when *Sc* and the observations for socialist countries are added to the equations, the *Sc* factor at each stage explains the Soviet gap not accounted for by the other variables. This suggests a close connection between *Sc* on the one hand and *RU* and *PR* on the other. Thus for the Soviet Union, as for socialist countries generally, the level of urbanization and the rate of participation in the labor force in relation to GNP per capita are in large measure the outcome of the growth strategy of a socialist economy. Being a socialist country also explains more than half of the original Soviet positive A deviation but almost none of its relatively small M gap. Even compared with the group of socialist countries the Soviet Union still has somewhat higher A and *lower* M shares.

A Second Test: The Historical Record

To what extent are the findings and conclusions related to the situation in 1959 applicable to historical developments in the Soviet industrial structure? In this connection it is interesting to find out, first, to what extent the service gap picture is repeated at earlier and later dates and, second, whether such gaps as appear can be explained by the same list of factors. In particular, one would like to know whether the socialist economic system alone can explain away the entire S gap during the existence of the Soviet regime. Such an investigation can serve as a supplementary test of the hypothesis about the relation between economic system and industrial structure suggested in the preceding section. At the same time, we can take a brief glance at the forces acting on the industrial structure of a socialist country in a period of rapid economic growth. These questions are tackled by comparing the observed industrial structure and changes in it during the years 1926-1965 with projected structures and changes produced by the international cross-section regressions, taking into account the changes in the Soviet LED variables.

A short discussion of the applicability and meaning of the comparison of a historical record with an international cross-section analysis is warranted. The specific question is to what extent one should expect to find that the pattern of change of the industrial structure and the S shares estimated from a sample of countries at one point of time is similar to that of a normal country over time.

The usual statistical problem that arises when cross-section and historical data are compared does not arise here; both consist of the same kind of data, that is, single-year observations based on national accounts. The theoretical, or maybe empirical, problem still exists: does the partial derivative (keeping LED constant) of changes in the S shares with respect to historical time differ from zero? In principle of course, one could conceive of any result. In a recent book, Simon Kuznets extensively discusses this issue of comparing cross-country and historical patterns of industrial structure and supplies a good deal of empirical evidence on, inter alia, changes in labor shares since the beginning of the present century.[8] Though his findings are not conclusive, they do show that over the period up to World War II—and for reasonably developed countries (above $500 per capita) up to 1960—the historical pattern of change in the labor shares was more dynamic than indicated by a cross-country analysis at both the beginning and end of the periods covered; that is, the S and M shares rose more and the A share declined more over time than indicated by a cross-country analysis. Other empirical evidence to this effect is included in studies by P. Temin[9] (1967) and Hollis Chenery and Lance Taylor (1968). The first study shows that over the last half century the patterns of change of the A and M shares in the national income of nine countries were very similar to the cross-section patterns, while the second, which in the main reinforces these conclusions, indicates a somewhat larger historical increase in the S share (also in GNP) since World War II. On the assumption that the relative labor productivity of services lags behind the average for the economy, the historical increase in the labor share may be even larger.

Various factors could have increased the consumption of services over the last half century or so, even at constant levels of development. Thus, the consumption of some private services, such as recreation, and even more of public services, such as health, education, and government, appears to be increasing. This seems to be true for both leading and less developed countries. Public and possibly also government services apparently receive much higher priorities today in many development-oriented countries which appreciate the potentialities of these services for the development process. In addition, it is today much easier to imitate the technology as well as the consumption patterns of advanced countries owing to improved international communications, an imitation that may shift the industrial structure to a more advanced level—at

---

8. Simon Kuznets, *Economic Growth of Nations: Total Output and Production Structure* (Cambridge, Mass., 1971), pp. 174-198 and 275-288.

9. P. Temin, "A Time-Series Test of Patterns of Industrial Growth," *Economic Development and Cultural Change,* 15.2:174-182 (part 1, January 1967).

a lower LED. All these affect both the level and slope of the regression lines of the S share on LED.

Figure 3 illustrates what could be expected if the S share increases more in the historical series: the *H* curve represents the historical trend of a country from, say, 50 years ago (t_0) to 1960 (t_1) and the *T* curves represent the cross-country pattern at periods t_0 and t_1. If a strong demonstration effect exists, then the slope of T_1 may be more moderate than that of T_0.

On the basis of the above evidence one would expect the cross-sectional regression to project *at least* the actual increase in the S share that took place in a typical country over time;[10] indeed, it would not be surprising if the historical trend were to show larger increases in the S sector over time, or if the cross-section regression for 1960 were to overestimate the S shares of previous years. Finally, it is plausible to assume that countries whose structure is out of equilibrium for some temporary reason tend to converge to the normal pattern over time; this assumption is to some extent borne out by Chenery and Taylor (pp. 401-403).

With these observations in mind the levels of the various S shares in the

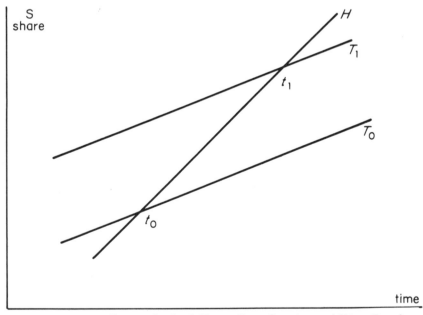

Figure 3. Changes in the S Share: Cross-Country and Time Trend

10. Kuznets 1971, p. 177.

Soviet Union are projected over the period 1926-1965 on the basis of the regression estimates of normal patterns. The actual Soviet shares are shown in Table 34, and the levels of the independent variables are shown in Table 35. The comparison is for five selected years in the period 1926-1965. Table 36 compares the estimated with actual labor shares and shows the derivation of the gaps. Table 37 compares estimated with actual *changes* in the shares, and the

Table 34. Labor Force Distribution,[a] by Main Sector, Selected Years, 1926-1965 (Percent)

Year	S (1)	C (2)	OS (3)	A (4)	M (5)
1926	5.4	1.4	4.0	86.9	7.7
1939	17.5	4.4	13.0	54.8	27.7
1950	20.7	4.3	16.4	51.1	28.2
1959	21.1	5.0	16.1	44.8	34.1
1965	24.8	5.8	19.0	35.8	39.4

[a]LF(a).

Source: 1926–Source of Appendix Table E-2.
1939–*Census 1959,* pp. 98-99, Table 31, p. 110, Table 34, and Appendix Table E-1 below.
1950–*New Directions,* pp. 746, 770.
1959–Table 8 and its source.
1965–*New Directions,* pp. 772, Table A-1 and *Narkhoz 1965,* pp. 555, 558-562.

Table 35. Values of Soviet Independent Variables, Selected Years, 1926-1965

Year	y^a ($)	$\log_e y$	Percent PR	RU
1926	200	5.3	56.2	82.1
1939	500	6.2	51.0	67.0
1950	670	6.5	52.0[b]	60.5
1959	1000	6.9	52.0[b]	52.2
1965	1300	7.2	52.0[b]	46.2

[a]Computed by applying volume charges to the 1959 figure of $1000 (in 1960 US dollars). The figures for *y* are at best crude approximations and may be a source of error.
[b]The rate was very similar in all three years, and the 1959 value was therefore used for all three.
Source: y–based on A. Bergson, *The Real National Income of Soviet Russia since 1928* (Cambridge, Mass., 1961), p. 225, Table 55 [1928 (for 1926) 1939, 1950], and *New Directions,* p. 105, Table 2 (1965). Population data are from *Narkhoz 1965,* p. 7.
PR–*Census 1926,* vol. 34, p. 2, Table 1 (for 1926); *Census 1959,* p. 99, Table 31 (for 1939); 1950, 1965, see note b.
RU–*Census 1926,* vol. 34, p. 3, Table 1 (1926); *Census 1959,* p. 13 (1939); *Narkhoz 1965,* p. 7 (1950, 1965).
For the sources of the 1959 data see Chap. 3, notes 7 and 8.

Table 36. *The Soviet Deviation from the Estimated Share, Selected Years, 1926-1965 (Percent)*

Independent variable	S		C		OS		A		M	
	Estimated share	Deviation: estimated minus actual share	Estimated share	Deviation: estimated minus actual share	Estimated share	Deviation: estimated minus actual share	Estimated share	Deviation: estimated minus actual share	Estimated share	Deviation: estimated minus actual share
1926										
log y	22.9	17.5	8.5	7.1	14.4	10.4	55.9	− 31.0	21.3	13.6
log y, PR	12.1	6.7	6.6	5.2	5.5	1.5	69.2	− 17.7	18.6	10.9
log y, RU	19.0	13.6	7.7	6.3	11.3	7.3	61.3	− 25.6	19.7	12.0
log y, PR, RU	11.2	5.8	6.4	5.0	4.7	0.7	70.6	− 16.3	18.1	10.4
1939										
log y	30.3	12.8	11.9	7.5	18.4	5.4	36.9	− 17.9	32.8	5.1
log y, PR	23.5	6.0	10.8	6.4	12.7	− 0.3	45.4	− 9.4	31.0	3.3
log y, RU	26.6	9.1	11.2	6.8	15.4	2.4	42.2	− 12.6	31.2	3.5
log y, PR, RU	22.0	4.5	10.5	6.1	11.5	− 1.5	47.7	− 7.1	30.3	2.6
1950										
log y	32.7	12.0	13.1	8.8	19.6	3.2	30.9	− 20.2	36.4	8.2
log y, PR	25.8	5.1	11.9	7.6	13.9	− 2.5	39.4	− 11.7	34.7	6.5
log y, RU	29.4	8.7	12.4	8.1	17.0	0.6	35.6	− 15.5	35.0	6.8
log y, PR, RU	24.6	3.9	11.6	7.3	13.0	− 3.4	41.3	− 9.8	34.1	5.9

1959

log y	36.0	14.9	14.6	9.6	21.4	5.3	22.6	– 22.2	41.4	7.3
log y, PR	29.6	8.5	13.5	8.5	16.1	0.0	30.5	– 14.3	39.8	5.7
log y, RU	33.1	12.0	14.0	9.0	19.1	3.0	26.7	– 18.1	40.2	6.1
log y, PR, RU	28.6	7.5	13.3	8.3	15.3	–0.8	32.0	– 12.8	39.3	5.2

1965

log y	38.1	13.3	15.6	9.8	22.5	3.5	17.2	– 18.6	44.7	5.3
log y, PR	32.2	7.4	14.6	8.8	17.7	– 1.3	24.5	– 11.3	43.2	3.8
log y, RU	35.6	10.8	15.1	9.3	20.5	1.5	20.8	– 15.0	43.6	4.2
log y, PR, RU	31.4	6.6	14.4	8.6	17.0	–2.0	25.7	– 10.1	42.8	3.4

Source: Estimated shares, see source to Table 2; value of independent variables, Table 35. Actual shares, Table 34.

Table 37. Changes in Actual and Estimated Shares, Various Equations,
Subperiods, 1926-1965 (Percentage Points)

	S	C	OS	A	M
1926-1965					
Actual	19.4	4.4	15.0	−50.6	31.7
Estimated	20.2	8.0	12.3	−44.9	24.7
of which "explained" by[a]					
log y	13.0	6.5	6.4	−34.8	22.0
log y, PR	14.7	6.8	7.8	−36.8	22.3
RU	5.7	1.1	4.7	− 8.5	2.9
1926-1959					
Actual	15.7	3.6	12.1	−41.6	26.4
Estimated	17.4	6.9	10.6	−38.6	21.2
of which "explained" by[a]					
log y	11.0	5.5	5.3	−29.3	18.5
log y, PR	12.7	5.8	6.7	−31.3	18.8
RU	4.7	0.9	3.9	− 7.1	2.4
1926-1939					
Actual	12.1	3.0	9.0	−31.6	20.0
Estimated	10.8	4.1	6.8	−22.9	12.2
of which "explained" by[a]					
log y	6.1	3.1	3.0	−16.5	10.4
log y, PR	8.2	3.5	4.8	−19.0	10.8
RU	2.4	0.5	2.0	− 3.6	1.2
1939-1959					
Actual	3.6	0.6	3.1	−10.0	6.4
Estimated	6.6	2.8	3.8	−15.7	9.0
of which "explained" by[a]					
log y	4.7	2.4	2.3	−12.8	8.1
log y, PR	4.3	2.3	2.0	−12.3	8.0
RU	2.3	0.4	1.9	− 3.5	1.2
1959-1965					
Actual	3.7	0.8	2.9	− 9.0	5.3
Estimated	2.8	1.1	1.7	− 6.3	3.5
of which "explained" by[a]					
log y	2.0	1.0	1.0	− 5.5	3.5
log y, PR	2.0	1.0	1.0	− 5.5	3.5
RU	1.0	0.2	1.0	− 1.4	0.5

[a]Computed from the equation with all variables, e.g., the contribution of log y is obtained by putting the actual log y into the equation and keeping the other two variables at the level of the initial year of the period or subperiod.

Source: Actual change, Table 34.
Estimated change, Table 36 (the equation with all variables); for the "explanation" of the change, see note a.

changes are attributed to the various development variables. Table 38 presents the absolute changes in the gaps themselves. Finally, actual and estimated shares are compared and gaps are calculated for the whole group of countries (including socialist), with and without the *Sc* variable (Table 39).

Basic gaps are found in the S, C, and OS sectors in all the years investigated— 1926, 1939, 1950, and 1965; the 1959 findings are thus generalized for the Soviet period, at least since 1926. Also in accordance with the 1959 findings, the service gaps become smaller as *RU* and *PR* are added to log *y*. In this case the S, C, and OS gaps are cut by from one-half to two-thirds, in general by more than in 1959; when all the development variables are applied, the OS gap is completely closed and in some years reversed into a small surplus. In all the years the A shares are above the norm and the M gaps diminish by various degrees when all LED variables are taken into account; this also accords with the 1959 findings.

Turning to Table 39, there is again broad agreement with the 1959 findings that adding the *Sc* variable and the socialist countries to the regression does away with the gaps for the whole S sector; the C gaps become very small, and the negligible or zero OS gap turns into an excess. Adding *Sc* to the regression equations reduces the A sector surplus considerably, but except in 1939 the A share is still somewhat above normal even by socialist standards. This, if true, must be a result of local Russian conditions. *Sc* has a very small and nonsignificant effect on the M gap, an observation that is in line with the expected contradictory factors. As in 1959, *RU* and *PR* are in most cases partial substitutes for *Sc*.

Without entering more deeply into the details we can conclude that we have here a stationary industrial labor-force structure that is quite different from the normal. As in 1959, it can be explained by a different development structure,

Table 38. Changes in Deviations,[a] Subperiods, 1926-1965 (Percentage Points)

Period	S	C	OS	A	M
1926-1965	**0.8**	**3.6**	**−2.7**	**6.2**	**−7.0**
1926-1959	1.7	3.3	−1.5	3.5	−5.2
1926-1939	−1.3	1.1	−2.2	9.2	−7.8
1939-1959	3.0	2.2	0.7	−5.7	2.6
1939-1950	−0.6	1.2	−1.9	−2.7	3.3
1950-1959	3.6	1.0	2.6	−3.0	−0.7
1959-1965	−0.9	0.3	−1.2	2.7	−1.8

[a]Positive change is increase in gap (or decline in surplus); negative change is decline in gap (or increase in surplus).
Source: Table 36.

Table 39. *The Soviet Deviation from the Estimated Share (Including Socialist Countries), Selected Years, 1926-1965 (Percent)*

Independent variable	S		C		OS		A		M	
	Estimated share	Deviation: estimated minus actual share	Estimated share	Deviation: estimated minus actual share	Estimated share	Deviation: estimated minus actual share	Estimated share	Deviation: estimated minus actual share	Estimated share	Deviation: estimated minus actual share
1926										
log y	21.6	16.2	7.9	6.5	13.7	9.7	57.5	−29.4	21.0	13.3
log y, Sc	7.8	2.4	1.4	0.0	6.3	2.3	72.6	−14.3	19.7	12.0
log y, PR, RU	6.1	0.7	3.0	1.6	3.2	−0.8	77.0	− 9.9	16.5	8.8
log y, PR, RU, Sc	3.2	−2.2	0.6	−0.8	2.6	−1.4	79.2	− 7.7	17.6	9.9
1939										
log y	28.0	10.5	10.8	6.4	17.2	4.2	39.6	−15.2	32.4	4.7
log y, Sc	15.4	−2.1	5.0	0.6	10.4	−2.6	53.2	− 1.6	31.4	3.7
log y, PR, RU	17.8	0.3	7.7	3.3	10.2	−2.8	52.6	− 2.2	29.3	1.6
log y, PR, RU, Sc	13.9	−3.6	4.7	0.3	9.2	−3.8	55.3	0.5	30.8	3.1
1950										
log y	30.2	9.5	11.8	7.5	18.3	1.9	33.6	−17.5	36.3	8.1
log y, Sc	17.8	−2.9	6.1	1.8	11.7	−4.7	47.0	− 4.1	35.2	7.0
log y, PR, RU	20.4	−0.3	8.8	4.5	11.7	−4.7	45.9	− 5.2	33.3	5.1
log y, PR, RU, Sc	16.6	−4.1	5.9	1.6	10.7	−5.7	48.7	− 2.4	34.7	6.5

1959

log *y*	33.1	12.0	13.2	8.2	19.9	3.8	25.5	−19.3	41.5	7.4
log *y*, *Sc*	21.1	0.0	7.6	2.6	13.5	−2.6	38.5	−6.3	40.4	6.3
log *y*, *PR*, *RU*	24.6	3.5	10.4	5.4	14.2	−1.9	36.1	−8.7	39.2	5.1
log *y*, *PR*, *RU*, *Sc*	20.6	−0.5	7.5	2.5	13.1	−3.0	39.2	−5.6	40.1	6.0

1965

log *y*	35.2	10.4	14.2	8.4	21.0	2.0	19.6	−16.2	45.2	5.8
log *y*, *Sc*	23.3	−1.5	8.6	2.8	14.7	−4.3	32.9	−2.9	43.8	4.4
log *y*, *PR*, *RU*	27.7	2.9	11.8	6.0	16.0	−3.0	29.0	−6.8	43.0	3.6
log *y*, *PR*, *RU*, *Sc*	23.5	−1.3	8.7	2.9	14.8	−4.2	32.7	−3.1	43.8	4.4

Source: Estimated shares, see source to Table 32; actual share, Table 34.

that is, relatively low urbanization and high participation rates for given levels of per capita income, and by the effects of socialist growth strategy and structure. I shall not go here into some of the other factors such as labor force quality which may also contribute to the explanation.

Only one disturbing factor appears in this simplistic conclusion: the observation for 1926, which is more extreme than those of the later years, cannot be justified in terms of either socialist growth strategy or the structure and operation of a socialist system, neither of them fully present at that early date during the NEP period.

It seems to me, though, that a combination of some more ideological-doctrinal socialist factors, temporary effects of the turmoil of past years, and remnants of historical factors (together with some statistical biases in the wrong direction) creates the same picture for 1926 as that for later years. Although in 1926 the system was one of mixed economy, by that year a major part of the trade (external and internal) and money sectors had been nationalized along with large-scale industry, transport, and so on. There was some planning and a few centralized supply systems were in operation. Labor force participation of women was urged on ideological and practical grounds, and by 1926 they already made up 30 percent of the nonagricultural labor force. The ideological overtones against nonproductive work were strong and 1926 was too early for any serious work to be accomplished in the way of increasing health and educational services.

In addition it seems that the turmoil of past years did the most damage to the urban population and the service sector. By 1920 or 1921 between one-third and one-half of the previously urban population had left the cities and retired to the countryside. Not all of them had come back by 1926 and many small handicraft and trade businesses were never revived.

One could make a crude evaluation of the probable effect of these factors on the size of the S sector by comparing the industrial structure of 1926 with that of 1897 or, taking into account the discussion in Appendix E, 1913. Normally one would expect to find a considerable increase in the S share over 1897-1926, when output probably more than doubled. That no such increase occurred can be attributed to the above factors.

Two statistical factors may exaggerate the basic S gaps in 1926. One is the extremely inclusive practice in counting participants in the agricultural sector of the labor force. This, compared with later but not earlier years, tends to overstate the A share and to understate the S (and M) shares. Further, since this statistical inconsistency also exaggerates *PR,* we get more explanation for the (exaggerated) gaps. The second statistical bias may be that the normal S share—and hence the 1926 S gap—is, for reasons discussed earlier, overestimated; that is, the normal shares in the 1920s should be lower than those derived from cross-section analysis of the 1960s.

In addition, the remnants of some pre-Soviet factors may still have been at work in 1926 to reduce the size of the S sector and the proportion of urban population to below normal levels. Russia was late in developing a sizable third estate and a genuinely urban population; many of its cities remained administrative centers and winter residences for the nobility. Clearly the social changes of the late nineteenth century and of 1917 should have eliminated the causes of such a situation, but some of the effects may have continued up to 1926. However, there is no question that the events of the early 1930s did away with most of such lagging effects.

With these qualifications about using the 1926 observations as a starting point, we can now analyze how the S shares and the gaps changed over the period under discussion. Over 1926-1965 the estimated S share (estimated on the basis of all the development variables) changed almost as much as the actual share. For 1926-1959 the estimated share is only slightly smaller than the corresponding actual one. The overall dynamic picture is thus of a more or less stationary state with a relatively constant S gap. Bearing in mind the discussion on 1926, we can derive support from this finding for the general hypothesis that statically a socialist country has a peculiar industrial structure, but that dynamically changes occur according to more general development and growth factors.

This impression of a dichotomy between the "static" effect of the socialist system and the prevailing "dynamic" effect of the general development pattern is weakened when changes in the shares of subsectors of S and other sectors of the economy are observed or when changes over subperiods are examined. In most of these cases both sets of factors act together to present a mixed picture.

Over the whole period, the estimated C share rises faster and the estimated OS share more slowly than do the respective actual shares. This seems to be a manifestation of the characteristics of the socialist system discussed later: the tendency to replace commercial services by planning and administration and the exceptional emphasis on health and educational services.

In general, the actual changes in the S, C, and OS shares overtook the estimated changes in 1926-1939, fell behind in 1939-1959, and caught up again in the last subperiod, 1959-1965. The three subperiods correspond to a big leap forward, a period of sustained growth (after war and reconstruction), and a "modern" period which may be described as years of search for new ways. The excessive changes in the first period are explained by the need to make a major change in the structure of the economy and to overcome old obstacles to industrialization and urbanization and the establishment of the new socialist order. Part of the 1926 S gaps thus had to be closed, the part that originated in temporary and historical factors not connected with the socialist system. Had the socialist system not been established the gap-closing effects of the leap forward would probably have been larger. It should also be noted that of the total actual increase in the S and OS shares over 1926-1939, 3 percentage points reflect the increase in the share of the armed forces. Had the armed forces change been normal, the actual changes in both S and OS would have been very close to the estimated changes.

In the second period and especially during 1950-1959 the socialist strategy and system prevailed undisturbed, and the Soviet S shares lag behind the estimates based on normal patterns. In the late 1950s, problems arose, as higher income, national and personal, demanded a much higher level of the deficient services—mainly trade, planning of supply, and personal services. There was much talk and some steps were taken to alleviate the pressure, and the 1959-1965 findings show some effects of this. It may well be that the industrial structure of a socialist economy is much closer to the normal pattern once it has become affluent than in its periods of austerity.

Income per capita or per employee is the major factor raising the service shares over the whole period and its subperiods. This can be seen in the "explanation" lines of Table 37. Responsibility for the change in the shares is allocated on the basis of the regression coefficients in the equation that includes all the LED variables and thus carries the degree of significance that these coefficients do (see Table 2 above). The increase in the urbanization level over the period is responsible for up to a quarter of the total change in shares, and rather more in OS. *RU* is somewhat less important in 1926-1939 than in subsequent periods.

The changes in the A and M shares are generally similar to the changes in the S shares. Similar relationships held between the corresponding actual and estimated shares in the three subperiods: actual changes in A and M shares are larger than estimated for 1926-1939 and after 1959 but fall short of the estimated changes for 1939-1959. The only important difference in the behavior of the A and M shares is that over the whole period the tendency is for actual to be larger than estimated changes. For A, the difference is relatively small, with an actual decline of 50 percentage points compared with an estimated decline of 45 percentage points; for M the difference is greater—an actual rise of 32 percentage points compared with an estimated rise of 25 points. For 1926-1959 the differences between actual and estimated changes are even smaller. Taking into account what was said about 1926, such a small reduction in the gap does not appear to be inconsistent with our hypothesis which implies that the A share in socialist countries is higher than normal. Moreover, the *relative* A surplus is much higher in 1959 (or 1965) than in 1926.

This short investigation of changes in the Soviet industrial structure since 1926 in the main supports the hypothesis of this chapter that the socialist system is responsible for a persistent gap in the service industries accompanied by a surplus in A. Dynamically, we find that the effects of the socialist system mingle with the major development patterns that are common to most countries experiencing economic growth, socialist and nonsocialist.

9. The Socialist Economic System and the Level of Development: Conclusions and Prospects

The study concludes with a confrontation of the findings of the preceding chapter with the list of explanations offered for the service gaps throughout the book and adds some substantive explanations not so far mentioned and a short note summarizing the findings about the gap in public administration. My conclusion is that the existence of "socialist economic system" explains much, if not all, of the service gaps, not only empirically but also analytically.

Two further questions emerge from this conclusion. One is whether the connection between socialist economic system and service deficiencies is indispensable and systematic or whether it is merely a historical accident. Second, what is the connection between the effects of the socialist system and the effects of the growth forces of the economy. To answer this question we must decide whether the growth strategy discussed earlier is the only conceivable socialist strategy and, more important, whether one should expect a different gap structure at different stages of development. Finally, the conclusions of this chapter will help to evaluate the prospects of change in the industrial structure of the Soviet Union and the other socialist countries.

The Effect of the Economic System—A Survey

The discussion falls under three headings: growth strategy, the organization and operation of the system, and ideological forces.

The strategy of economic growth: The two main elements that, to my mind, define the socialist model of economic growth are first, the achievement of a high rate of economic growth, regardless of the current welfare of the population "as far as seems expedient," as it was put by A. Bergson in a slightly different context.[1] This is done by diverting economic resources as

1. A. Bergson, *The Economics of Soviet Planning* (New Haven, 1964), p. 7.

148

much as possible from present to future use. Though the definition of expediency may have widened somewhat in the late 1950s to include more than absolutely necessary concessions to current consumption, by the end of that decade the proportion of resources diverted to investment and to nonprivate uses was still higher than in most other countries.[2]

Second, this high rate of growth can be achieved by diverting a very large proportion of growth resources to heavy manufacturing industry, letting the other sectors, especially agriculture, lag behind so long as the growth process is not interrupted. To some extent this second strategy is consistent with the first goal, since manufacturing is the major producer of investment goods. It also results from a desire to achieve military power and to ensure that the regime controls the main economic resources of the country.

This growth strategy manifests itself in three main directions, in themselves partly related to and resulting from the strategy: the low level of urbanization, the high labor force participation rates, and the small share of GNP allocated to private consumption.

As stated in the last chapter, the low level of urbanization is achieved by keeping production techniques highly labor intensive in agriculture and capital intensive in manufacturing and by demanding maximum labor force participation, particularly of women, from those who move into the cities. A related factor tending to the same result is that under the Soviet system it is impossible for those who migrate to the cities to do so as independent petty retailers or craftsmen or suppliers of needed (or unneeded) personal services. This movement, which occurs in many developing countries (and which I have called "bulging" when it applies to services) is avoided in the Soviet Union and other socialist countries by the legal prohibition of private enterprise, by keeping agriculture permanently short of labor, and, if necessary, by explicit restriction on migration to the cities, especially the large ones. Thus, by avoiding bulging, keeping labor "reserves" on the farm, and reducing urbanization to a minimum in other ways as well, the socialist system can economize on services connected with an urban way of life—municipal, administrative, domestic, and other private services (all in OS), as well as the traditional sites of bulging, petty trade, and personal services.

The high labor participation rate, apart from keeping the level of urbanization lower than it would otherwise be, need not reduce the demand for services in any real sense; it only demonstrates that the normal service share for the Soviet Union estimated on the basis of income per capita alone is misleading since the product per worker in the Soviet Union is lower than income per capita indicates.

2. See above, note 22 in Chap. 6 and the adjacent text.

The large-scale employment of women,[3] however, is likely to increase in the real sense the demand for market services such as child care, laundries, restaurants, and shopping services, all services that take over some household tasks. The growth strategy argument in this respect joins forces with an important ideological principle of socialist doctrine. The transformation of the woman from a private person burdened with household chores into a social person involved equally with the man in the building of the socialist society—and at the same time the transformation of the family, a unit traditionally bound by the economic dependence of women, into a social union of equal partners—was and is one of the cornerstones of socialist thought.[4]

With this argument for employing women it is clear that as many household tasks as possible should be supplied by the market, so that women can be as free as men to work and participate in public and social life without worrying about household work. In principle and in the long run the contribution of women to socialist production and the change in their status and in their household burdens do not conflict but rather complement each other. The reason for this, the Soviet argument goes, is that the market production of household services is many times more efficient than their household production. Thus only a small fraction of the women going out to work will be needed to supply the equivalent amount of services to households, the rest being a surplus diverted to the productive sector.[5]

This theory, would, if translated into practice, obviously tend to increase the share of services in the Soviet economy. It is clear from the discussion of Chapter 7 that such a plan exists at present mainly on paper. Moreover, in addition to her regular work the Soviet woman on balance provides for herself and her household more services, and is able to buy or get less, than her counterpart in countries at a similar level of development. Only in the areas of child care, and to a smaller degree in catering, do more services seem to be available to her outside the household. With respect to all other services—trade, domestic and personal services, and household equipment—starting from the apartment itself, kitchen, laundry, cleaning appliances, cars and transport—the Soviet woman is much worse off.[6] The main and often the only incentive for women to go to work is the need for money, and they do go to work—in spite of the lack of adequate household services on the market and not in response

3. The Soviet participation rate for women is 41.5 percent LF(b) (39.4 percent for the urban population) or 49.3 percent for LF(a) (41.2 percent for urban population). This is one of the highest rates in the world (see *Census 1959,* p. 96, Table 30, and UN, *Demographic Yearbook 1963,* Table 18.) A detailed discussion of women's participation rates is to be found in Dodge, esp. chap. 3, and in *Indicators,* chap. VII, p. 92.

4. Dodge, chap. 4; Sonin 1965, chap. V.

5. See, e.g., Shishkina, pp. 145-146, and Sonin 1965, pp. 179-180.

6. Dodge, chap. 5. The gaps found in the labor shares of most of these services clearly demonstrate this situation.

to the incentive created by the few that are available. The need for additional labor and not the liberation of women is still the overriding force in the drive to get women to work. It also means that with the exception of some educational and catering services, we should not expect to find larger service shares as a result of substitution of marketing for household-supplied services. Rather, the opposite holds: in many areas (and also on balance in the service sector as a whole), there seems to be substitution of household-supplied services for market services not available in amounts comparable to those in other countries.

The main implication of the drive towards a high rate of growth is the high proportion of current production diverted to investment. When one adds to this the large expenditure on defense and public services, mainly education and health (the bulk of whose costs are covered directly from the budget), one is left with a relatively low proportion of current production going to private consumption. The effects of this allocation policy are considerable pressure on the population to work (the income effect) and a lower demand for services not supplied by the government, since disposable income per capita is low and services are assumed to have positive income elasticities. This policy also reduces the proportion of GNP consisting of goods sold to households, thus reducing the need for commercial services at both the wholesale and retail levels. The last aspect was discussed in detail in Chapter 6.

On the other hand, it appears that the supply of educational and health services, particularly the former, is above what the population would wish to *buy* at the Soviet level of income. The labor share of both these services was on the high side (see Table 10). The Soviet government has throughout clearly recognized the economic importance of investment in human capital. As a socialist central government it has been in a position to evaluate better and earlier than other governments the considerable external effects—external to individual users—or "public good" elements of education and health services and the potential contribution of investment in them towards the main goal— the drive for faster economic growth. The relatively heavy concentration of Soviet students in science and other practical subjects may serve as an indication that education is looked upon primarily as an investment.[7]

The organization and operation of the socialist economic system:[8] Of chief interest here are the costs in terms of labor inputs of linking together and

7. Dewitt, p. 509; *Dimensions,* p. 259, Table 8, and p. 261, Table 9. These services are considered less "nonproductive" since they directly affect efficiency of production. See, e.g., Shishkina, pp. 41-42, and I. I. Stoliarov, "Laws of the Development of the Non-productive Sphere During the Transition to Communism," *Problems of Economics,* 7.10:14-20 (February 1966).

8. The discussion here has benefited from H. S. Levine, "The Centralized Planning of Supply in Soviet Industry," *Comparisons,* part I, pp. 151-176, and from B. Ward, *The Socialist Economy.*

coordinating the production activities of different enterprises into one consistent system. More specifically, we are interested in estimating the differences in these inputs between a market and a socialist economy and thus to find out to what extent we can explain the Soviet gaps in public administration and in the "material technical supply" part of trade. The latter is the segment of wholesale trade that provides the links among production enterprises and the one excluded from the discussion of Chapters 6 and 7.

In a pure[9] centrally planned system many decisions made within the productive unit in a market system are made by higher agencies, which also control the operations of the productive units. As a result many more such links, to be called vertical, exist in a socialist than in a market economy. In principle some of these vertical links are substitutes for decision-making and control units that operate within the production enterprise in a market economy; this may explain the smaller proportion of white-collar personnel in enterprises in the Soviet Union when compared with market economies.[10] On the other hand, the enterprise in a centrally planned system needs extra personnel to receive commands from and furnish information to the superior agencies as well as to bargain with them, over and above the personnel needed for similar activities in enterprises in market systems. This difference thus results in more people in the public administration sector of a centrally planned system who deal with the operation of individual enterprises.

In a pure planning system, that is, one operating on the basis of central physical planning, the higher administrative agencies design for the enterprises not only their production plans but also their supply and sales plans. In a theoretical pure system every material to be supplied and every product to be sold is preplanned as to quantity, price, the supply enterprise and the receiving enterprise, and the time of supply and sales. The supply agencies need only execute a preplanned distribution program, and the sales and supply departments in enterprises turn into receiving and shipping clerks.

In the market economy, most of the functions of material supply and sales to firms and for firms are performed by trade enterprises as well as special departments within the enterprise. They have to find sources of supply at the lowest price, bargain on prices, find buyers for the products of the enterprise, and then, of course, execute the deals contracted. In the provision of these hori-

9. By a "pure" centrally planned system is meant a totally physically planned one (i.e., physical as distinct from monetary planning). By a "pure" market economy is meant one without government planning or intervention. It is of course still assumed that information has its costs and that the economy is of a monopolistic-competition oligopoly type rather than a perfect-competition system. Actual differences between the Soviet Union and other countries are usually less extreme.

10. See Table 11.

zontal links a market economy clearly puts more labor input into the trade industry while the centrally planned system will replace a considerable portion of trade workers by the staff of the central and local planning organs. In a centrally planned economy, we should thus expect to find, all other factors being equal, a smaller proportion of the labor force in trade and a higher proportion in public administration.

Under which system is the provision of horizontal links less expensive in terms of labor? It seems that the total amount of information needed for the efficient supply of all the horizontal links is smaller in the centrally planned economy, simply because the aggregate targets are given in the plan and do not have to be estimated from market behavior. Also, a large body of information on the probable behavior of competitors and suppliers is not needed here, since everybody simply executes the orders of the center. In addition, in a centrally planned economy each piece of information is collected and processed only once and is then presumably available to all who need it. In a market economy, however, the *same* market studies, cost analysis studies, sales estimations, and so on are made by different enterprises at the same time and such information is not shared.

On the other hand, the transfer of information is much more costly in a centrally planned system, since all the information has to arrive at one or relatively few centers, usually through successive agencies, while in a market economy most of the information needed for making the decisions on the execution of a linking operation is local and at hand.[11] It is difficult to evaluate the trade-offs between these two cost elements. My argument is, however, that the transmission of information and decisions in both directions (from the enterprise to the central agency and back) becomes more and more expensive per unit of value of transaction as the streams of information serve smaller and smaller transaction volumes. Although a general annual plan may be cheaper in a centrally planned economy, every small correction and adjustment in the supply plan is very costly since the information involved and the decision made must go through all the stages that the yearly plan goes through: from the enterprise up the ladder of authority and back down to the enterprise.

This rigidity of the centrally planned system is avoided in the market economy by applying different methods of marketing and supply to different sizes of transactions, thus reducing the fixed cost elements. Though in principle all the supplies for a given enterprise in a planned system, no matter how small, have to go through the same channels, supply departments of market economy enterprises vary their source of supply according to size of transaction, ur-

11. Ward (pp. 70-72) has a discussion along the same lines.

gency, and so on, and this allows them to save on the links. The absence of middlemen to provide for local shortage and price rigidity seem to be the most important sources of rigidity in a centrally planned system. Since the original plan is never fulfilled in all its details, the number of changes and adjustments that must be made over the plan period is large (it is augmented by the chain effects of the complete dependence of each transaction on many others); the cost of the horizontal links, per unit of supplied material, becomes exorbitant and many transactions simply fail to take place at all. The reaction of managers to this situation is to make their enterprise as self-sufficient as possible, and it pays them to produce many auxiliary materials at much higher cost than the established prices because they have to add to these established prices the costs, real and alternative, of getting the supply in—at all and on time. This may be one explanation of the fact that Soviet enterprises are larger on the average than enterprises in other countries and that the level of specialization is apparently lower. A larger enterprise seems to be also in the interest of the planning authorities, because the amount of planning, direction, control, supply plans, and so forth, per enterprise is fairly rigid regardless of its size. In this connection, one might mention the frequent discussion about forming—as distinct from actually forming—associations of firms; this can be understood in the light of the above planning problems. This also contributes to the impression that much of the increasing returns to scale said to exist in Soviet enterprises are concentrated at the firm level rather than at the plant and production-process levels.[12]

The high price of the outside link is only in part the result of the real distribution costs through the existing supply system, costs that reflect labor and other inputs. As I see it, the lack of apparatus assigned to execute many

12. The points made in the preceding passages rely mostly on the following sources: L. Smolinski, "The Soviet Economy in Search of a Pattern," *Survey,* no. 59 (April 1966), pp. 88-101, esp. pp. 89 and 97; Ya. Kvasha, "Kontsentratsia Proizvodstva i Malkaia Promyshelnost," *Voprosi Ekonomiki,* no. 5 (May 1967), pp. 26-31; T. Khachaturev and D. L. Lvov, "Ekonomicheskaia Effektivnost i Kachestvo," *Ekonomicheskaia Gazeta* (June 1967), p. 28. Despite the large size of enterprises average *run* sizes are small. Elsewhere Smolinski [L. Smolinski, Soviet Industrial Establishments: Scale and Performance (forthcoming)] shows that at least part of the increasing returns to scale of Soviet manufacturing industry is due to the supply advantages of large enterprise. I have also relied on Levine and on D. Granick, *Soviet Metal Fabrication and Economic Development* (Madison, Wis., 1967), chap. 7.

Some idea of the excessive price per link can also be obtained from JPRS-*Labor,* no. 155 (January 4, 1967), p. 16 (one example given is of screws produced by a nonspecialized enterprise at 14 times the cost of producing them in a specialized enterprise). See also *CDSP,* 10.49:11 (January 7, 1959), which mentions examples of restaurants being encouraged to grow their own food to reduce prices, and *CDSP,* 18.38:20-23 (October 12, 1966), where one writer describes the situation as moving backwards to the "times of independent principalities, to a closed barter economy."

needed connections ánd the high level of uncertainty about the execution of planned transactions are important elements of the high price; the alternative cost element, how much it will cost to get a given supply on time, according to the right specifications, and so forth, is a more important part of this price than the real costs of trying to execute the transaction. Thus, as the actual number of links is very small and the amount of inputs expended per link is not much above normal, the entire Soviet supply system should be smaller than normal.

The outcome of all these arguments is that the sector dealing with wholesale supply should be smaller than in market economies. This is both because the public administration sector takes over many of the functions of the supply agencies and because there seems to be a smaller number of links to connect, since the Soviet production enterprises are on the average larger and more self-sufficient than those in other countries. The public administration sector, which deals with economic planning and control, should be larger than in other countries, because it performs functions that other sectors perform in market economies.

Under a centrally planned system the collection and direction of resources allocated to investment are also handled mainly by the public agencies, with the help of a very small banking system. The handling and direction of investment funds are much simpler here than in a market economy where a great many transactions are needed first of all to solicit funds from the public, either in the form of savings or direct investment in the stock market, and where a similar number of transactions and deliberations is then required for the distribution of the funds among investors, plus a third large number of transactions for the distribution of the investment proceeds back to individuals. At least the first and third of these stages are almost entirely avoided in the Soviet Union because investment funds never reach individuals and thus do not have to be solicited back. The actual allocation of investment funds is also less expensive in a centralized system because all the targets and information are gathered in one place and there is no duplication of investment studies by different investment institutions. This explains the very low level of activity in the Soviet banking and money sectors; the rest of the explanation lies in ideological principles.

The ideological effects: It is difficult to estimate the importance of ideological-doctrinal considerations for the structure and development of the Soviet economy and society. Their somewhat secondary role can be deduced from the fact that growth strategy and economic system factors have turned out to be so important. Without entering upon a general debate on this point, let me point out here the probable ideological effects on the industrial structure of the Soviet labor force and on the service shares in particular.

The most important ideological conviction in this connection is the low social value attributed to "nonproductive" economic activities, which include all the services. This attitude, which can be traced back to Marx, has been somewhat modified as regards educational and health services, as it was recognized that they had a large element of investment in human capital. But the attitude towards public administrators and other clerical staff and trade and private service workers has remained unfavorable throughout.[13]

It seems to me that this Marxian concept of nonproductive work has blinded many prominent people in the Soviet Union to an understanding of the fundamental concept of the economic efficiency of labor, and especially the productivity involved in providing a good system of links among economic units. The bureaucratic tradition of Russia and the resentment against the "speculation" of which trade workers are constantly suspected may have added to this attitude.[14] The constant compaign to keep the administrative apparatuses in enterprises and government small is motivated by this doctrine. The constant harassment of trade workers as "speculators," which is apparently combined with low wages, makes it difficult for the industry to secure the required number of workers[15] and, what may be more important, workers of the right quality. There is presumably a connection between the relatively low quality of trade workers found in Chapter 5 (relative to the urban population and even to industrial workers) and the attitude towards their contribution to the economy.[16] In the early 1960s only the first voices heralding a change in this attitude were to be heard.[17]

The drive to enlist volunteers to perform administrative and economic services can be related to the conviction that public administration is a nonproductive service where paid staff should be cut to a minimum. Enlisting volun-

13. A fairly recent presentation of these doctrinal stands can be found in Stoliarov, pp. 14ff. Trade and public administration are ranked bottom among the nonproductive industries by society.

14. See Goldman 1963, chap. 8. A good example of the deep resentment towards traders is found in a collection of short articles on the role of the collective-farm market in *CDSP,* 18.7:21-24 (March 16, 1966).

15. On the connection of the attitude of society to the manpower shortage in trade see M. Sonin and P. Savranskaia, "Chelovek i Rabota," *Literaturnaia Gazeta,* no. 112 (September 22, 1966), pp. 1-2. See also *CDSP,* 17.15 (May 12, 1965).

16. More specific information for as late as 1966 on the quality of trade workers in the Soviet Union can be found in *CDSP,* 14.12:35 (April 19, 1967).

17. See Goldman 1963, chap. 8; Dikhtiar, pp. 45-52, asserts that, as trade and marketing will be necessary for a long time to come, even under communism, it is better to build a large and efficient trade industry. See also Sonin and Savranskaia, pp. 1-2.

teers for social activity is also valued for its educational merits and may also be looked upon as one of the "first steps" in the liquidation of the government that is another of the utopian dreams of the socialist ideology.

The ideological principles are also instrumental, as we have seen, in the high participation rate of women in the labor force. They have an important influence on the small amount of domestic services, and on the other hand may have some positive effect on the size of the educational services.

A Note on the Gap in Public Administration

The surprising gap in public administration cannot be investigated thoroughly here. Its importance and complexity alike warrant a special study. Nevertheless, some comments are in order. It has been argued that one would expect the sector to be relatively larger in the Soviet Union than in market economies because it should perform many functions elsewhere performed by other industries. This would make the gap to be explained even larger than that estimated in Chapter 3 (Table 8). It was no less surprising to find that "material production" branches, where we looked for concealed administrative employees, also suffered from administrative and clerical understaffing. This finding also increases the gap to be explained, in a more general sense.

Some of the gap in public administration was explained in previous chapters by (a) the existence of public administration workers in agriculture; (b) by unlisted volunteers (both in Chapter 4); and (c) by the probably higher quality of the public administration labor force. Though we do not have good estimates of either the size of the gap or of the elements of the explanation, the general orders of magnitude seem to indicate that after taking all these factors into account there is still a gap to be explained. Also to be explained is the apparent contradiction between the impression created by the Soviet literature of huge bureaucratic apparatuses and paper work and the finding that there is a gap. The following additional points may be made.

The administrative gap cannot be explained by superior techniques and equipment that increase labor productivity. Communication systems, which are a key factor in administrative efficiency, are at a low level, as are other aspects of office equipment, reproducing and calculating equipment and the like. The explanation must thus be found in the real quantity of services supplied.

It is probable that regular administrative services to the population are supplied at a low level, as is true for most of the other services to the population. Thus, there is a "reserve" of workers to deal with the economic planning and control.

The deep conviction of the Soviet authorities about the nonproductiveness of public administration[18] may have pushed them to too low a level of employment compared with their needs. The small number of clerical workers that they employ is noticeable, thus imposing many clerical jobs upon the executives and technical staff.

The same conviction may help also to explain the discrepancy between the impression one gets of the size of the administrative apparatus and its real size. Although the apparatus is not large, there is always the belief that it is and there is a continuous campaign to cut it. The Soviet press is persistently flooded by a stream of articles blaming inefficiencies in enterprises on the fact that there are too many administrative workers, charges that are difficult to prove. This is not to say that the existing administrative apparatus does not engage in superfluous and completely unnecessary paper work. I claim only that on the average it might not be as large as it sounds, and no larger than international standards indicate.

Confirmation of the last two points comes from, first, several articles, still in the minority, which point to *shortage* rather than surplus of administrative and clerical staff in various enterprises, though not in public administration agencies[19] and, second, from examination of some of the examples cited in the campaigns to cut down on paper work and administrative cadres. Several of them are worth mentioning:

Paper shuffling is one of the pernicious vestiges of the past. A piece of paper at times becomes an impenetrable and unsurmountable barrier between the manager and the actual business at hand. The volume of the so-called official correspondence is at times simply astounding. In the course of the past year the Khazakh Republic Council of Ministers received 42,000 documents (135 papers a day! [*sic*]) and sent out 57,000 documents to various agencies. The personnel of the Council of Ministers apparatus were writing 185 instructions a day![20]

And this is the government of a republic of more than ten million people. The correspondence of the economic council in the same republic was even smaller. And there are other examples of the same kind.[21] These are surprisingly small

18. See, e.g., V. Kostakov and P. Litviakov, "Utilization of Labor Resources in the Future," *Problems of Economics,* 5:30 (November 1962), and the references cited in notes 19 and 20 in this chapter.

19. See Chap. 4, note 5, and the discussion in the text there. See also *CDSP,* 15.19:21 (June 5, 1963).

20. *CDSP,* 16.5:25 (February 26, 1964).

21. See for example, *CDSP,* 12.4:26-27 (February 24, 1960), which describes a case very similar in its statistics to the one cited in the text; Khrushchev himself was the first to raise the matter, which was under investigation for a long time. See also *CDSP,* 16.31:11 (August 26, 1964); *CDSP,* 13.47:39-40 (December 20, 1961) and Kostakov and Litviakov, pp. 30ff.

volumes of correspondence, and one can legitimately raise the question of what these institutions are really doing. The one thing that they are not doing is precisely what they are so strongly charged with doing. As pointed out in Chapter 4 the same impression of huge administrative apparatuses is also created by the frequently cited figures for volunteers who serve in general only a small proportion of a full-time load. If public administration organs are not doing their job properly—and they are not—it is at least partly because they are understaffed rather than overstaffed.

Conclusions and Prospects

Has it been established that there is a general and necessary pattern of industrial structure in socialist countries; and that in general socialist systems need to have lower S shares and higher A shares? If such a pattern exists, what is the connection between it and level of development? Finally, how do we expect the industrial structure of the Soviet Union and other socialist countries to evolve?

The answer to the first question is to my mind partly in the affirmative. The most important reservation is the possibility that at a higher level of development the pattern might change. I myself think that it is likely that the socialist industrial structure will in the future tend towards the normal pattern.

To a large extent, moreover, the answer depends on how strictly one defines socialism as an economic system. If we define it simply as the system now prevailing in the Soviet Union, the affirmative answer is a tautology. If, at the other extreme, we accept a definition that contains only public ownership of the means of production, we should not expect the socialist industrial structure to depart very far from the norm. The question thus reduces itself to deciding what elements of the socialist system must be considered essential to the system in the real world of the present and what their impact is on the service shares. The discussion is confined to the stages of development in the socialist countries covered by the historical record.

In terms of what has here been defined as the socialist growth strategy it can be claimed that had the system been able to operate with less pressure on its resources, the high growth-rate target might have been achieved with a greater allocation for disposable income, tradable goods, leisure, and possibly a better balance between the growth of heavy industry and the growth of other sectors, notably agriculture. In this case, much of the service gap would be eliminated.

Judging from the historical record of the Soviet Union there are four ways in which the pressure of resources could be relaxed: reducing defense expenditures; increasing the general level of economic efficiency—at present considered by many students to be rather low; secular economic growth; and finally, making do with rather lower growth rates. High defense spending and low economic efficiency have up to now accompanied all leading socialist regimes: military strength has been partly an explicit target and partly a historical necessity; and one is still waiting for a really efficient socialist economy. Nevertheless, military spending and low efficiency cannot be considered as part of the definition of socialist system.

But, even granted a more efficient system with a smaller defense budget, I do not think that much would be changed; that is, the authorities would tend to devote the resources released to increasing the growth rate and they would keep the allocation between investment and consumption virtually unchanged. A high rate of economic growth has in modern times become a recognized target of many economies; what is specific to the socialist countries is that they, more than any other countries, are willing and able to achieve growth for growth's sake—to tolerate a longer waiting period between investment and the consumption of its fruits, to invest in producers goods designed to produce more producers goods. Under such conditions consumption will of course grow, but it will remain a lower proportion of GNP than normal. As regards secular growth, it is clear that additional resources created in this way have up to now always been devoted to further increasing growth by the socialist economies. Finally, it is clear that a merely "satisfactory" growth rate can be ruled out; within reasonable limits, it is the maximum that is aimed at.

A socialist economic system (especially one with a smaller defense budget) could divert more of its investment to agriculture and thus reduce the asymmetry between the rural and urban sectors. At least in early stages, this will always be done less than in market economies: socialist governments, unlike those in market economies, take into account the social costs of urbanization and the additional consumption entailed—both of which they try to minimize. In some cases political considerations of weakening the farmer class may also play a role. Because private enterprise is prohibited, no serious bulging is to be expected in the cities.

One can envisage at least two ways consonant with the structure and operation of a socialist system in which more workers can be employed in services, in particular such business services as planning, administration, and supply. One is to enlarge the planning, administrative, and supply agencies in order to enable them to perform their functions in a centrally planned system more efficiently than they do at present. Properly planned, such an expansion can undoubtedly produce very high rates of return, particularly in the supply agencies. Alternatively, a socialist system can operate in a less centralized fashion;

any decentralization would entail an increase in services employment above the requirements of the present relatively small central planning and supply systems (see below). This alternative implies a rather radical change in the system and may take place in the future. As regards the first alternative, one can adduce historical reasons why a better centralized system could not be implemented. The most important is the lack of experience in running such a system and the many occasions when enlarging the apparatus has only increased the confusion. Now that a considerable amount of the required experience is available there is no reason why it cannot be drawn on by a socialist regime. However, I believe that the ideological bias against so-called nonproductive activities—which stands in complete contradiction to the idea of central planning—has played an important part in preventing an increase in public administration employment.

Is this ideological bias against trade and administrative services really indispensable? No economist can justify such a bias, and there is no question that the economic system called socialist can both survive and remain socialist without it. From the economic viewpoint this bias is a historical accident, but it is also a reality of the present.

To summarize: If a socialist system is satisfied with something less than maximum growth, if it reduces the stress on heavy industry, increases the efficiency of its planning and supply mechanisms, and eliminates the ideological bias against services, then the S, and particularly the C, shares can move closer to the norm. I do not think it likely that such changes will occur at early stages of development, but they may occur once a certain level has been reached, for reasons to be discussed below.

Some remarks on the connection between factors originating in "socialist system" and those originating in "level of development" are in order here. At the end of Chapter 3 we concluded that the Soviet industrial structure tends to have a non-normal development structure, that is, that the relations between the values of the LED variables differ from the norm; after all LED variables were added there were still deficiencies in S and M and a surplus in A, and these remaining gaps suggest a lower level of development than was measured by the regression. Lastly, we saw that some of the gaps, particularly that in the C sector, do not respond to the LED variables.

The discussion of the socialist growth strategy clearly explains why the development structure is different, and how important the RU and PR variables are in this structure. Some of the explanations in terms of socialist system can be restated in terms of LED. First, private time spent by consumers directly explains a considerable part of the deficiency in retail services (Chapter 7). When translated into labor, this time input would have increased the value of PR and thus reduced the gaps even further. In the C sector itself, the private time input plays the same role as *PR* for the whole economy in demonstrating that the industry (economy) is less efficient than indicated by the output (income) alone. The volunteers, discussed in Chapter 4, have the same effect of raising the value of *PR.*

Second, the Soviet Union could be defined as "less developed" on account of the low proportion of disposable income and tradable goods in its GNP (Chapter 6). This cannot be done on the ground that these proportions increase with LED, because, as we have seen, they in fact tend to decline. It can be done in terms of growth strategy or the low level of efficiency of the Soviet system, part of which does not show up in the relation between income per capita and the labor force participation rate. If a country invests a higher than normal share of its GNP over an extended period, then, for a given level of per capita income (or better per worker income), one of two things (or a combination of both) must have occurred: either a considerable unused growth potential must have accumulated (in the form of capital stock), or the high investment rate is needed to produce a smaller than normal consumption share. The second possibility is a clear indication of inefficiency, and a country in which it occurs should be classified as less developed than indicated by all LED variables. If, on the other hand, a large growth potential is embodied in capital stock, the country may appear to be less developed than it actually is. I do not want to go into the question which of the two possibilities applies to the Soviet Union; I believe that both are present to some degree. (In this connection high defense outlay must be classed under the first head.) In either case, the consumption structure at least will resemble that found at a lower level of development, as so far defined. This amounts to taking per capita consumption as an additional LED variable. Presumably, it is this inclusive notion of development level that is commonly applied to the Soviet Union—hence the typical reaction of surprise to the information that the per capita income of the Soviet Union is (or was in 1959) around $1000.

Although we have thus somewhat extended the common ground between the development and socialist system factors, the whole of the gap can still not be explained by LED alone. Are there any dynamic relations between the socialist economic system and the level of development? It is to this question that we now turn in the ensuing discussion of future prospects.

During the period of the socialist regime the gaps, especially that in the C sector, did not close to any significant extent. Furthermore, there were similar gaps in other East European socialist countries, countries that differ in their level of economic development. Finally, even up to 1965 there are no clear signs that service gaps are closing in the Soviet Union despite a lot of talk on various economic reforms that should be oriented in such a direction. Adding all this together and assuming, as I do, that the socialist system will prevail— one must come to the conclusion that it is not likely that the service gaps will diminish much in the foreseeable future. It is only if one envisages radical changes in the characteristics of the socialist system that one can predict any narrowing of the S gaps. I believe that such important changes are in the making in the Soviet Union, that the socialist system is evolving, and that the main reason for this evolution is a combination of a qualitative change in the Soviet development process and, even more important, a belated recognition by the authorities of important quantitative as well as qualitative changes in the level of development. Much has been written on the possible connections between various aspects of the socialist system and the level of economic development, and I shall come back to this point briefly. Let me here say only that this connection, at least for leading socialist countries, is likely to be discontinuous in nature, that it takes a transformation from "developing" to "developed" and a recognition that the transformation has happened to move the authorities to reconsider such aspects of the system as have very heavy doctrinaire and traditional weights. To this rigidity of response one should add also the limitation of free discussion. Thus it can happen that response by way of economic reforms comes only when change is urgent and long overdue.

The late 1950s and early 1960s seem to be a period in which both necessary conditions are met; the Soviet Union could for the first time be considered a developed country in the late 1950s. At the same time, the change of rulers gave the opportunity for the regime to take stock of its achievements, position, and needed reforms. This could lead to a number of changes in the system which may affect the service gaps.

Of the three aspects of the socialist system—growth strategy, organization and planning techniques, and ideology—the first is mostly connected with the recognition that a socialist country has passed the stage of initial growth and reached the developed stage. At some point at this stage one would expect the socialist system to reduce the high pressures on the quantitative components of growth (mainly capital and labor) and to try to depend more on growth of efficiency and technological development. If this happens there is a chance for the share of private consumption and the proportion of tradable goods and private services to grow and with them to increase the need for and availability of commercial services. The pressures on the time resources of the population will also slacken, allowing them to buy more services on the market; working women, the proportion of whom we believe will stay relatively high for ideo- logical reasons, will eventually find more market substitutes for household services. This tendency is reinforced by the relative saturation in educational and health services which will make their rate of growth lower than it has been. The most important obstacle to this tendency is defense spending, an unpredictable element, but one that is getting a new push in recent years. The strategy of growth of developed socialist countries may change in another direction too—eventually emphasis is going to shift to developing agriculture (and light industry). The exploitation of hitherto neglected growth potentials in agriculture can become a major source of growth for a developed economy that has reached very high capital-output ratios in the heavy industries. But this exploitation must mean substitution of capital for labor and a drastic reduction in the A labor share and in the proportion of rural population. The result is to push the urbanization process and as a by-product increase the demand for services, as shown by our regression results. Similar growth potentials are available, in my view, also in the light industries—which when developed will increase the tradable goods proportion and the demand for commercial services.

At the present time it seems clear to most observers—inside as well as outside the Soviet Union—that with increasing complexity the now developed Soviet economy has long ago outgrown the traditional planning and supply systems. This is true of those who believe that the deficiency can be taken care of by broadening the central planning apparatus as well as of those who advocate new methods. The large backlog combined with a high rate of increase in the complexity of the Soviet economy as it moves towards light industry, agriculture, and the consumer is putting before the Soviet planner a hard choice between preserving a minimum level of efficiency or increasing the volume of activity of commercial or coordinating intermediaries.

The various reforms that are being implemented in the Soviet Union in the organization and working of the system seem to be slowly evolving in a direction that will call for more commercial services, more white-collar workers in production enterprises, and no decline in the administrative apparatus of central planning and control. Every measure of decentralization and increased autonomy and responsibility at the firm level is bound to call for more commercial intermediaries among firms and between production firms and retail outlets. This will occur when sales replace production as a major criterion of success for managers and when the number of centrally planned items is reduced; even the direct contacts between production and retail outlets are bound to increase and not reduce the number of trade workers—in the sales departments of enterprises and the buying departments of retail stores. The central planning and supply agencies are in my opinion barely large enough to deal effectively with the job of drawing up a general, overall, less detailed plan for the economy and to execute it. The additional intermediaries will help to provide the system with more of the hitherto largely lacking but essential flexibility.

On the ideological side, several developments seem to be taking place. First the ideological bias against commercial activity and to some extent also the bias against administrative activity seems to be diminishing. Secondly, it seems that the emphasis on women's labor force participation will prevail, but that the increase in the standard of living will make it necessary to offer more and better household-type services on the market (including domestic) to compensate for the declining inducement of the need for income to send women to work. Finally, saving and investment decisions will continue to be mostly centralized and ownership of productive capital will continue to be restricted to the government, the effect of both being that the banking sector will remain below normal. But even in this area, the partial decentralization of investment and the increasing importance of private saving may narrow the magnitude of the gap.

This discussion indicates some of the possible developments from the crossroads at which the Soviet economy stands at present. Despite the contradictory historical evidence, I would not be surprised if by the 1980s the industrial structure of the Soviet economy, in general and as regards the service sector, has gone a good part of the way towards the normal pattern.

Appendixes
Bibliography
Index

Appendix A.
The Regressions

Table A-1. Countries Included in the Regressions Ranked by Per
Capita Income, circa 1960 (1960 US dollars)

A. Sixty-two nonsocialist countries[a]

Group I

United States	2500	Jamaica	400
West Germany*	1879	Spain	400
Canada	1860	Panama	375
New Zealand	1850	Greece	360
Switzerland	1680	Mexico	340
Sweden	1660	Portugal	305
Australia	1550	Cuba*	289
Norway	1440	Turkey	265
France	1414	Costa Rica	260
United Kingdom*	1400	Colombia*	250
Belgium*	1260	*Group IV*	
Denmark	1260	Nicaragua	206
Netherlands	1140	Gabon*	203
Group II		Peru	200
Austria	860	Jordan	200
Italy	850	Ghana	195
Israel	757	Malaya*	193
Venezuela*	701	Honduras	185
Puerto Rico	680	Ecuador	185
Ireland	680	Iran	166
Finland	670	Ceylon	166
Uruguay	596	Algeria*	156
Trinidad*	580	Egypt	152
Argentina*	560	Morocco	145
Group III		Iraq §	141
Japan	430	El Salvador	135
Chile	410	Liberia*	127

169

Brazil*	125	B. Socialist Countries	
Ivory Coast*	118		
Philippines	118	Czechoslovakia	1300
Syria	118	East Germany	1130
South Korea	110	Soviet Russia	1000
Thailand	97	Hungary	750
Haiti*	95	Poland	640
Taiwan*	92	Bulgaria	520
Bolivia	85	Romania	500
Pakistan	74		
Sudan*	72	Yugoslavia	420

[a]Countries marked with an asterisk are not included in the regressions containing RU. Iraq (§) is not included in the LF(b) regressions.

Source: See source of Table 2 (nonsocialist countries) and Table 32 (socialist countries).

Appendix B.
The Adjusted Soviet Figures
(Derivation of Table 5 Data)

Table B-1. Civilian Labor Force, by Industry, 1959ᵃ (Thousands)

Industry	Census table 33 (1)	Census table 44 (2)	Census table 33 with table 44 breakdown (3)	Interitem shifts (table 5 columns)ᵇ Column (3)ᵈ (4)	Interitem shifts Columns (3) and (4) (5)ᵉ	Interitem shifts Column (4) (6)ᵉ	Adjusted figuresᶜ Column (3) (3)+(4)+(5) (7)	Adjusted figuresᶜ Column (4) (3)+(5)+(6) (8)
Material production	80,863							
3. Agriculture	38,426	38,716	38,426	+547	+548	-68	39,521	38,906
Subtotal (line 4 through line 7)	36,575	36,483	36,575					
4. Manufacturing		23,908	24,000ᶠ	-160	-8	-644	23,832	23,348
5. Construction		6,837	6,837	-279		+69	6,558	6,906
6. Transport		5,030	5,030			-91	5,030	4,939
7. Communications		708	708			+110	708	818
8. Electric power						+1,091	..	1,091
9. Other material production	691		691		-540	-151	151	..
10. Trade	5,171	4,884	5,171	-11		+21	5,160	5,192
Nonmaterial production	14,453							
Subtotal (13 plus 14)	9,793	9,339	9,793ᵍ					
13. Education, science, and art		6,163	6,463	-60		-596	6,403	5,867
14. Health and welfare		3,176	3,330	-25		-28	3,305	3,302
Other nonmaterial production (15 + 16 + 11 + 12)	4,660	3,978	4,660					

Line	(1)	(2)	(3)	(4)	(5)	(6)
15. Housing, personal, and domestic services	1,649	1,649	1,637	-12	+817	2,466
16. Unallocable services		682[h]	682		-682	–
Subtotal (11 plus 12)	2,329	2,329	2,329		+152	3,021[i]
11. Finance, credit, and insurance						260[j]
12. Government and local administration, social institutions, and social security						2,761
17. Not known	191	191	191			191
Total LF(b)	95,507	93,400	95,507	–		96,047

[a] Line numbers follow those of Table 5.

[b] Columns (4) and (5) show the adjustments made in order to arrive at the "Census 1959" figures shown in the third column of Table 5, for purposes of comparison with the annual-averages data. Columns (5) and (6) show the adjustments made in order to arrive at the "adjusted estimate" shown in the fourth column of Table 5, which serves as the basis for this discussion.

[c] As in Table 5, columns (3) and (4).

[d] Kolkhozniks classified under various occupations by the Census but all included in agriculture by the annual-averages data.

[e] See Table B-2.

[f] The difference of 92 in the subtotals (for lines 4 through 7) between columns (1) and (2) was arbitrarily allocated to manufacturing (line 4).

[g] The column (1) subtotal (lines 13 plus 14) was broken down in proportion to the detail shown in column (2).

[h] This is the difference between the columns (1) and (2) "other nonmaterial production" subtotal. See also note d to Table 7.

[i] In addition to the adjustment shown in column (6), there is an estimate of 540,000 for militarized police [the estimate is for 1955, see M. Borenstein et al., Soviet National Accounts for 1955 (Ann Arbor, 1961; mimeograph), p. 52]. The information in Census Tables 44 and 47 suggests that these people are not included in the civilian figures. It may, however, be assumed that they are included in the army figure of 3,623,000 shown in Census Table 33.

[j] The figure for finance, credit, and insurance (line 11) is from annual-averages data in Indicators, p. 72, Table VI-4. The figure in line 12 is the residual.

Source: Census 1959 (Moscow, 1962), pp. 104-109, Table 33; pp. 46-58, Table 44; pp. 161-166, Table 47. The figure for workers in private subsidiary lots (line 2 of Table 5, not shown here) is from p. 96, Table 30.

Table B-2. Details of Interitem Shifts in Table B-1[a]

Line from	to	Number employed (thousands)	Description
9	3	411*	Forestry
	3	25*	Hunting (according to Census Table 47)
	3	93	Collection of berries and nuts (this is the residual of line 9)
	4	104*	Literature and publishing
	10	58	Secondary and scrap materials[b] (estimate, see Weitzman and Elias).
		691	Total line 9, other material production
3	8	51	
4		644	
5		73	
6		91	Workers in various industries whose occupation is given
10		37	as power plant worker
13		66	
14		28	
15		83	
11+12		18	
		1091	Total line 8, electric power
3	7	110	Rural mail carriers
4	3	112*	Fishing industry
13	15	530	Culture and entertainment
15	5	142	Construction workers
15	11+12	170	Municipal-type workers
16	15	682	Unallocable services (see note d to Table 7).

[a]These are the shifts shown in columns (5) and (6) of Table B-1. The column (5) adjustments are marked with an asterisk. Unless otherwise stated, the adjustments were made according to Census Table 44.
[b]Estimate, see M. S. Weitzman and A. Elias, *The Magnitude and Distribution of Civilian Employment in the U.S.S.R: 1939-1959*, U.S. Department of Commerce, Bureau of the Census. Foreign Demographic Analysis Division Publication Series P-95, no. 58 (Washington, D.C., 1961), memeograph.

Appendix C. Formal Presentation of the Quality Adjustments

I. The symbols

X_{kij} level of quality k in industry i and country (group) j

X_{kj} all-industry average level of k in country (group) j

    (i) age and sex

       X_{aij} proportion of labor force ij prime ages

       X_{sij} proportion of males in labor force ij

    (ii) education

       X_{eij} average years of schooling of labor force ij

x_{kij} Absolute difference in level of quality k between industry i and the average for the total labor force[1]

$$x_{kij} = X_{kij} - X_{kj}$$

P_{kj} "productivity weight" (shown in part II of this Appendix).

    (i) age and sex

       $1 - P_{kj}$ is index of productivity of persons outside the favorable category, with productivity of favorable category = 1

    (ii) education

       P_{ej} = percentage added to output by additional year's schooling

Q_{kj} Standard output for labor force of average quality k

$$Q_{kj} = (X_{kj}) (P_{kj}) + (1 - P_{kj})$$

x_{kij}^{*} relative quality difference between industry and average[2]

$$x_{kij}^{*} = x_{kij} / Q_{kj}$$

q_{kij} weighted quality advantage

    $q_{kij} = (x_{kij}^{*}) (P_{kj})$ percent added to output by quality advantage

q_{ki} relative quality advantage

$$q_{ki}^{*} = q_{kij_{\circ}} - q_{kij}$$

R_{ij} adjustment coefficient for industry i, country (group) j, all qualities combined

$$R_{ij} = \prod_k (q_{kij} + 1) - 1$$

r_i coefficient for adjusting the change in share of industry i, going from j to j_0

$$r_i = \prod_k (q^*_{ki} + 1) - 1$$

W_{ij} labor share of industry i, country (group) j
W^*_{ij} adjusted labor share[3]

$$W^*_{ij} = (R_{ij} + 1)(W_{ij})$$

II. Productivity weights

$1 - P_a$ (age)[4]
    Country groups I through IV   0.7
    Soviet Union   1.0
$1 - P_s$ (sex)[4]
    Country groups I through IV   0.6
    Soviet Union   0.2
P_e (education)[5]
    Country groups I   5.0
                II-III   8.3
                IV   ..
    Soviet Union   13.8

1. Age and sex in percentage points; education in years.
2. For education, $x^*_{eij} = x_{eij}$ (since there is no "unfavored" category $Q_{ej} = 1$).
3. E.g., if industry i has a share of 25 percent of labor force and an adjustment coefficient of 1.05 (i.e., its combined quality advantages add 5 percent to output) then without the advantage it would require $25 \times 1.05 = 26.25$ percent of labor force to achieve the same output.
4. Index of productivity of persons outside favorable category, with favorable category = 1.
5. Percent added to output by additional year's schooling.

III. Tables

Table C-1. Relative Quality Differences, by Country Groups[a]

	A	M+S	M	S	C	OS
A. Sectors compared with total labor force						
Group I						
Age (8)	0.0	0.0	3.2	−4.0	−5.6	−3.2
Sex (11)	12.6	−2.4	12.6	−22.2	−13.4	−27.8
Education (4)	−0.8	0.1	−0.4	0.4	0.1	0.7
Group II						
Age (4)	−0.8	0.0	0.8	−2.3	−3.9	0.0
Sex (11)	10.0	−4.1	10.9	−17.4	−0.8	−28.3
Group III						
Age (6)	−1.5	2.3	2.3	3.1	5.4	2.3
Sex (9)	6.5	0.8	13.0	−13.0	3.3	−21.1
Group II-III[b]						
Education (2)	−1.4	0.5	0.1	1.0	0.3	1.5
Group IV						
Age (10)	−0.8	0.8	1.6	0.8	6.8	−2.2
Sex (19)	2.6	−4.3	4.3	−11.4	−6.1	−11.4
B. Sectors compared with M+S labor force						
Group I						
Age (8)			3.2	−4.0	−5.6	−3.2
Sex (11)			15.2	−20.0	−11.1	−25.6
Education (4)			−0.5	0.3	0.0	0.6
Group II						
Age (4)			0.8	−2.3	−3.9	0.0
Sex (11)			15.2	−13.6	3.4	−24.6
Group III						
Age (6)			0.0	0.8	3.1	0.0
Sex (9)			12.2	−13.8	2.5	−21.8
Group II-III[b]						
Education (2)			−0.4	0.5	−0.2	1.0
Group IV						
Age (10)			0.8	0.0	6.0	−3.0
Sex (19)			8.8	−7.2	−1.8	−7.2

[a]The figures are x_{kij}^*'s (see above, part I of this Appendix). Figures in parentheses give the number of countries. For complete list of countries in each group see Appendix Table A-1.

[b]Average of Argentina (group II) and Japan (group III).

Source: Age and sex, Table 15; education, unpubl. data of M. Zymelman.

Table C-2. Relative and Interindustry Quality Differences[a]
in the Soviet Union

	A	M+S	M	S	C	OS
1. General weights						
LF(a)						
Percent aged 25-64[b]	−0.9	0.3	−3.2	7.6	6.7	8.0
Percent males[c]	−10.7	8.5	19.1	−12.0	−9.9	−12.5
Education						
(years of schooling)[d]	−1.3	1.2	0.6	2.2	1.0	2.7
LF(b)						
Percent aged 25-64[b]	−0.8	0.1	−3.4	7.4	6.4	7.7
Percent males[c]	−5.2	3.5	13.9	−16.6	−14.6	−17.1
Education						
(years of schooling)[d]	−1.1	1.0	0.4	2.0	0.8	2.5
M+S						
Percent aged 25-64[b]			−3.5	7.3	6.3	7.6
Percent males[c]			10.2	−19.8	−17.9	−20.3
Education						
(years of schooling)[d]			−0.6	1.0	−0.2	1.5
2. Soviet weights						
LF(a)						
Percent aged 25-64[b]	−0.8	0.3	−2.9	7.0	6.1	7.3
Percent males[c]	−14.7	11.7	26.3	−16.5	−13.7	−17.2
Education						
(years of schooling)[d]	−1.3	1.2	0.6	2.2	1.0	2.7
LF(b)						
Percent aged 25-64[b]	−0.7	0.1	−3.1	6.8	5.9	7.1
Percent males[c]	−7.0	4.7	18.5	−22.1	−19.4	−22.8
Education						
(years of schooling)[d]	−1.1	1.0	0.4	2.0	0.8	2.5
M+S						
Percent aged 25-64[b]			−3.2	6.7	5.8	7.0
Percent males[c]			13.3	−25.8	−23.2	−26.4
Education						
(years of schooling)[d]			−0.6	1.0	−0.2	1.5

[a] $x_{ki\ (su)}$

[b] The by-industry age distribution of the labor force excluding workers on private plots [Table 39 of source (1)] was aggregated to major sectors by using the industrial distribution of the labor force in Table 33 of source (1). The 25-29 age group was assumed to be half of the 20-29 group, and 60-64 was assumed to be two-thirds of 60+.

For workers on private plots, Table 32 of source (1) provides information on the number of women aged 15-54 and the number of men aged 16-59. We assume that one-third of women aged 55+ belong to 55-59; and that persons aged 16-24 account for 18 percent of the 16-69 group (this is the proportion in agriculture aged 16-19 and is half the proportion in agriculture aged 20-24). Finally, two-thirds of persons aged 60+ are assumed to belong to the 60-64 group, as with the rest of the labor force.

[c] Based on Table 33 of source (1) and source (4) for LF(a), and Table 30 of source (1) for LF(b).

[d] Data on educational level by type of school attended or completed [Table 40 of source (1)] were converted to years of schooling as follows:

Type of school	Years
1. University graduates	15
2. Did not complete university	13
3. Specialized secondary	10½
4. Categories 2 and 3 combined (weighted 20 and 80 percent, respectively)	11
5. Completed general secondary	10
6. Did not complete secondary	7-8
7. Categories 5 and 6 combined (weighted 20 and 80 percent respectively)	8
8. Did not complete 7-year school	44
9. Other, complete and incomplete 4-year school, no school	3

In determining the number of years for each type of school we relied on source (2); for the "did not complete" categories we relied on source (3). The main Census source (Table 40) gives lines 1, 4, 7, and 8 (Category 9 derived as a residual). For weighting the number of years attributed to lines 2, 3, 5, and 6, we used additional data from source (1), Table 36.

Source: (1) *Census 1959*, pp. 96-97, Table 30; pp. 98-101, Table 32; pp. 104-105, Table 33; p. 115, Table 36; pp. 117-118, Table 38; and pp. 123-124, Table 40.

(2) N. Dewitt, *Educational and Professional Employment in the USSR* (Washington, 1961), Chart 1, facing p. 22.

(3) *Dimensions*, p. 244, Table 4.

(4) *Indicators*, p. 103, Table VII-5.

Table C-3. Relative Labor Quality, by Industry
Soviet Union[a] and Group II

	A	M+S	M	S	C	OS
A. $x^*_{ki(su)} - x^*_{ki(II)}$						
1. Total labor force						
Age	-0.1	0.3	-4.0	9.9	10.6	8.0
Sex	-20.7	12.6	8.2	5.4	-9.1	15.8
Education	0.1	0.7	0.5	1.2	0.7	1.2
2. M+S						
Age			-4.3	9.6	10.2	7.6
Sex			-5.0	-6.0	-21.3	4.3
Education			-0.2	0.5	0.0	0.5
B. q^*_{ki}						
1. Total labor force						
Age	-0.0	0.1	-1.2	3.0	3.2	2.4
Sex	-8.3	5.0	3.3	2.2	-3.6	6.3
Education	0.8	5.8	4.1	10.0	5.8	10.0
2. M+S						
Age			-1.3	2.9	3.1	2.3
Sex			-2.0	-2.5	-8.5	1.7
Education			-1.7	4.1	0.0	4.1
C. r_i						
1. Total labor force	-7.5	11.2	6.3	15.7	5.2	19.7
2. M+S			-4.9	4.5	-5.7	8.4

[a]LF(a), using general weights.

IV. Notes on the productivity weight estimates

1. Age criterion

The estimate is derived as follows: First, weights are computed for three age groups (14-19, 20-24, and 60+) compared with the 35-44 group. Each of the three ratios is a weighted average of the relative wages of workers differing in quality characteristics. The weights are estimated from data on labor force distribution by quality characteristics of countries participating in the analysis [UN, *Demographic Yearbook 1964* (New York, 1965), Table 9 (age and sex), and Denison 1967, p. 85, Table 8-3 (education)]. The three productivity weights are then combined in the proportions 45:45:10 for the 14-19, 20-24, and 60+ age groups, respectively (the proportions represent the average age structure of the countries in the analysis). Although Denison uses a different computation, his figure is quite close to ours.

Denison distinguishes only between ages 16-19 and the rest of the labor force. His productivity weight for males at this age (compared with males in the prime-age group) is one-third. Our comparable coefficient is one-half, but we corrected for differences in educational level, which Denison did not have to do according to his quality estimation method. As the educational level of workers at the ages of 16 to 19 years is lower than the average for the prime-age workers, this could explain all or part of the difference between one-third and one-half. Our final age weight is above half because we added two age groups with higher relative wages and because our weight includes females for whom wage differentials are usually lower. See Denison 1962, chap. 8, pp. 80-83, especially note 4; and Denison 1967, pp. 71-74.

2. Sex criterion

The estimate is arrived at in the same way as the age weight and it is also based on wage differentials in the United States in 1960. Denison uses almost the same figure for a slightly different comparison. When the differences are taken into account, his weight comes out somewhat lower than 0.6.

We compare all females to all males and thus include young age groups in which the female/male ratio in the labor force is higher than for adults. Denison compares only adults. Also, differences in educational level (in favor of women) are included in Denison's productivity weight. See Denison references in the preceding note.

3. Education criterion

Our figure is derived from US Census data. Denison found a somewhat higher differential for the United States in 1949, but his figure apparently includes some differences that do not belong to education (see Denison 1962, p. 72 and the discussion of this point in Schwartzman, chap. 4, p. 10, note 11).

There is much discussion in the literature about how much of the wage differential between different educational levels should be attributed to education and how much to natural ability (Denison 1962, pp. 73-74, and Denison 1967, pp. 83-85). This distinction does not interest us, as it is the combined effect of both factors that accounts for interindustry differences in labor quality. It should only be remembered that we are measuring more than the direct effects of education. Note also that the wage differentials associated with education are always measured within countries. We do not claim that international differences on educational level are associated with differences in "ability."

Appendix D. The Derivation of Tables 23 and 24

I. MTGS by country group (Table 23)

Computed as MTGS = Z − (FT + FIK), where Z is the percent of consumer commodities in GNP at current market prices, FT is the share in GNP of the value added of trade, and FIK is the share in GNP of farm income in kind (throughout, as in the text, we refer to GNP excluding final trade services). Some of the elements of the computation require explanation:

1. Z was computed as the product:
(percent commodities in private consumption) (percent private consumption in GNP).

The first element was computed from the "composition of private consumption" country tables in the UN source. Some of the items listed there (Nos. 6, 8, 9, 10, 11, 13-14) are mixed goods-services categories (e.g., transport, which includes public services as well as purchase of cars, etc.). We employ two assumptions about these mixed items [columns (1) and (2) in Table 23]: (i) that 40 percent of the commodities in these items are goods in all countries; and (ii) that in group I countries the goods percentage is 33 percent, and in the other countries 20 percent.

In making these assumptions we have relied on UN, *A System of National Accounts and Supporting Tables* (New York, 1964), where a more detailed classification key is presented which distinguishes between goods and services. In the UN tables the mixed items cover between 15 and 30 percent of private consumption, and the proportion is in general lower for the less developed countries; an error of 10 percent in the proportion of goods can hardly give rise to an error in MTGS of more than 2 percentage points.

2. The estimate of GNP share of FIK assumes arbitrary proportions of agricultural product in kind, the proportions ranging from 10 percent in developed countries to 25 percent for the least developed ones.

II. TGS, Soviet Union and other countries (Table 24)

1. Group II figures from Table 23 were converted into 1955 dollars over the implicit exchange rates based on the relative prices of Gilbert's "other OEEC countries" whose price structure we believe to be not much different from that of group II countries (see also note 11, in Chap. 6). The exchange rates are US $1.34/"European" $1 (for GNP) and US $1.10/"European" $1 (for consumption of goods).

2. United States figures at Soviet factor cost are computed in two stages.
   (a) US market price figures were computed from Bergson (see source).
   (b) The market price figures were converted to factor cost by applying the Soviet ratio of factor cost to market price figures.
The resulting exchange rates are 0.893 rubles/US $1 (for GNP) and 1.11 rubles/US $1 (for consumption of goods.)

3. The derivation of the Soviet figures is shown in Appendix Table D-1.

III. Source for data of Tables 23 and 24 and Appendix Table D-1.

The principal international source is UN, *Yearbook of National Accounts Statistics, 1964,* as follows:

Proportion of commodities in private consumption, country tables; private consumption as percent of GNP at market prices, pp. 358-370, International Table 3.

For some countries other sources are used:
United States, U.S., Department of Commerce, *Survey of Current Business,* 42.2:11 (February 1962).
Switzerland, Chile, Morocco, Iraq, and the Philippines, ILO, *Yearbook of Labour Statistics, 1965* (Geneva, 1965), Table 28.
Argentina, UN, *Statistical Bulletin for Latin America* (New York, 1964), vol. 2, pp. 180-181, Table 72.
Soviet Union, 1955—Bergson 1969, except for value added in trade, from M. Borenstein et al., pp. 78, 84. 1959—A. S. Becker, *Soviet National Income and Product 1958-1962 Part Two. N.I. at Factor Costs and Constant Prices* (Santa Monica, 1966), p. 33, Table 2; except for value added in trade from S. H. Cohn, *Derivation of 1959 Value-Added Weights for Originating Sectors of Soviet GNP* (McLean, Virginia, 1966), p. 21; and except for exchange rates which are from Bergson 1969.

Table D-1. Derivation of Soviet Figures Used in Table 24

	1955			1959		
	Market prices[a]	Factor prices		Market prices[a]	Factor prices	
		Domestic[a]	1955 $[b]		Domestic[a]	1955 $[b]
1. GNP	114.3	93.48	180	167.77	140.57	268
2. Retail sales to households	52.8	32.44	38.5	73.82	49.76	58.4
3. Retail sale as per cent GNP	46.2	35.7	21.4	44.0	35.4	21.8
4. Trade value added as per cent of GNP	..	5.0	5.0	..	5.3	5.3
5. TGS[c]	..	31.3	17.3	..	31.8	16.6
Exchange rates (rubles per $)[d]						
GNP	0.635	0.519	..	..	..	
Retail sales	1.370	0.840	..	..	..	

[a]Lines 1 and 2 in billions of new rubles.
[b]Line 1 and 2 in billion of 1955 dollars.
[c]Computed as lines [(3)−(4)]/[100−(4)].
[d]For 1959 the figures in lines 1 and 2 are independent estimates; the exchange rates derivable from them are almost the same as the 1955 rates.
Source: See part III of this appendix.

Appendix E. Historical Changes
in the Industrial Structure
of Russia
and the Soviet Union

A Note on the 1913 Industrial
Distribution in Russia

The changes that occurred in Russia over the period are broadly similar to trends in other countries that have experienced economic growth and development during the last century or two. The proportion of labor engaged in agriculture declined over the period to half or less of its 1897 share; the labor force share of the M sector increased by 20-30 percentage points and by the end of the period was two to three times the initial level; the rise in the share of manufacturing was even more dramatic. The labor share of the S sector also increased sharply and probably more than doubled. The changes within the S sector demonstrate more specific aspects of the country and period than the changes in the major sectors. Still, at least in their direction of change, they conform to the historical experience of other countries. It is clear that the dominant explanatory factor for the structural changes is the economic development of Russia and the Soviet Union. A few comments are warranted about the 1913 data, which make a break in the trend.

According to Table E-1, only one of the changes really started before 1913, which means in effect, before the revolution. From 1897 to 1913 there was no decline in the A share (possibly there was even an increase), the M share declined, and only the S share may have increased somewhat, mainly as a result of a jump in the share of trade. If we accept these observations at face value and go one step further and associate them with economic growth in the prerevolutionary period, we have to conclude that no economic growth occurred in Russia during this period. The large increase in the proportion of labor engaged in trade would then have to be explained by other factors and may signify a weakening of economic strength rather than an improvement in the economy. It may indicate, especially at early stages of development, a superfluous mushrooming of commercial activities without any real increase in production.[1]

The labor distributions in 1913 and 1926 show that very important changes

1. Ofer, pp. 130-137 (on bulging in services).

had taken place even at this early stage of the revolution. The A share shows its first decline, and the M share rose by more than 50 percent. On the other hand, the rising service share trend is reversed, owing mainly to the steep fall in the share of trade to below the 1897 level. In addition, the rapid increase in the share of public services (line 7) was already under way in this period.

Some of the conclusions based on these observations contradict what is considered common knowledge about the economic growth of Russia and the Soviet Union during these two periods. It is generally accepted that real industrial production more than doubled between 1897 and 1913 and barely reached the 1913 level by 1926.[2] According to fragmentary labor force statistics from other sources, the number of workers and employees in manufacturing and mining rose by 33 percent during 1897-1913, while the population increased by only 23 percent; in 1913-1926 there was no change in the number of employees in this industry. The number of employees in trade went up by about 22 percent in 1897-1913 or not more than the population increase and less than the increase in manufacturing and mining.[3] In 1924 more than 50 percent of all trade sales was in private hands (and only 24 percent in 1928),[4] so that nationalization cannot yet have had its full effect.

Combining these pieces of evidence and re-examining the structural changes during the two periods, one comes to the conclusion that some of the changes attributed by Table E-1 to 1913-1926 really belong to the earlier period. All the extreme changes in the share of trade indicated in both periods seem economically implausible, though it is understandable that the nationalization of most trade enterprises along with the decline in international trade and the general disruptions of the economy could have reduced the proportion of trade workers in the labor force.

Since the 1897 and 1926 data are derived from fully documented population censuses and since I was not able to go back to the source from which the Soviet Statistical Yearbook derived its 1913 data (presented in exactly the same form as in Table E-1), it must be concluded that the 1913 figures are too low for at least the M sector and too high for at least the trade sector. The true figures should show that the M share rose more in the first period than in the second and that the trade share rose less than the table shows in the first period, and declined less in the second.

2. Alexander Gerschenkron, "The Rate of Industrial Growth in Russia Since 1885," *Journal of Economic History,* 7:146, 161 (supplement, 1947).

3. Frank Lorimer, *The Population of the Soviet Union* (Geneva, 1946), Tables 4 and 7, and the notes on pp. 20, 22; A. G. Rashin, *Formirovnie Rabochego Klassa Rossie Istorii Ekonomicheskie Ocherki* (Moscow, 1958), pp. 62, 153.

4. R. Nazarov, "Stanovleni i Rasvitie Kolkhoznoi Torgovli," *Sovetskaia Torgovlia,* no. 2 (February 1967), p. 20.

Table E-1. Industrial Distribution of the Labor Force,ᵃ Russia and Soviet Union, Selected Years, 1897-1964 (Percent)

Industry	1897 (i)	1897 (ii)	1913	1926	1937	1940	1950	1958	1959	1960	1964
1. Agriculture	64	77	75	71	56	54	48	42	41	39	33
2. Manufacturing and construction	18	10	9	14	24	23	27	31	32	32	35
3. Transport and communications	2	2	2	4	5	5	5	7	6	7	8
4. Trade	5+	4	9	3	4	5	5	5	5	6	6
5. Public administration	1+	1	..ᵇ	2	3	3	3	2	3	2	2
6. Education and health	1+	1	1	4	5	6	8	10	10	11	13
7. Other services	7	5	4	2	3	4	4	3	3	3	3
8. A (line 1)	64	77	75	71	56	54	48	42	41	39	33
9. M (lines 2 plus 3)	20	12	11	18	29	28	32	38	38	39	43
10. S (lines 4 through 7)	16	11	14	11	15	18	20	20	21	22	24
11. Total civilian labor force (lines 8 through 10)	100	100	100	100	100	100	100	100	100	100	100
12. M/S ratio	1.2	1.1	0.8	1.6	1.9	1.6	1.6	1.9	1.8	1.8	1.8

ᵃThe definitions and coverage of the data for the various years are not entirely consistent. Figures for 1897 (col. i), 1926, and 1959 are, broadly speaking for the LF(b) definition: 1897 (i) includes one worker per family business; 1926 excludes all family workers and 1959 excludes workers on private plots, but both count all persons reported as workers in the censuses. At least for the later years, there seems to be little difference between "family workers" and "workers on private plots" (cf. 1958, 1959 and 1960).

The remaining figures fall somewhere between our LF(a) and LF(b) concepts. 1897 (col. ii) is based on the distribution of the total population and thus "favors" agriculture to the extent that rural families are larger than urban. It appears to conform with the definitions of later years better than 1897 (i). The figures for 1913, 1937-1958, 1959, 1960 are based on annual full-time equivalents and include family workers also as full-time equivalents.

ᵇIncluded in other services.

Source: 1897–Census 1897, vol. II, Tables 20 and 21 [variant (i)], and Census 1897, II, 4, Table 1.
1913, 1937–Narkhoz 1959, p. 583.
1940, 1950, 1960, 1964–Narkhoz 1964, p. 543.
1926, 1959– see source to Table E-2.

Table E-2. *Industrial Distribution of the Soviet Labor Force*[a]*, 1926 and 1959 Censuses*

Industry	Thousands		Percent of total				Percent of M+S		Percent of S	
			Lf(a)		Using Nimitz A data[b]					
	1926	1959	*1926*	*1959*	1926	1959	1926	1959	*1926*	*1959*
1. Agriculture (a)	71,735	48,822	*87.6*	*46.2*	77.5[c]	38.6[c]				
2. Manufacturing	4,593	23,992	*5.6*	*22.7*	10.2	25.9	45.2	42.2		
3. Construction	390	6,979	*0.5*	*6.6*	0.8	7.5	3.8	12.3		
4. Transport	1,249	5,030	*1.5*	*4.7*	2.8	5.4	12.3	8.8		
5. Communications	95	818	*0.1*	*0.8*	0.2	0.9	0.9	1.4		
6. Trade and credit	1,157	5,489	*1.4*	*5.2*	2.5	5.9	11.4	9.6	*30.1*	*27.3*
7. Public administration	662	2,779	*0.8*	*2.6*	1.5	3.0	6.5	4.9	*17.2*	*13.8*
Of which: Internal security	*95*	*839*	*0.1*	*0.8*	0.2	0.9	*0.9*	*1.5*	*2.5*	*4.2*
8. Education	865	6,463	*1.1*	*6.1*	1.9	7.0	8.5	11.4	*22.5*	*32.2*
9. Health	363	3,330	*0.4*	*3.2*	0.8	3.6	3.6	5.9	*9.4*	*16.6*
10. Housing, personal, and domestic services	717	2,019	*0.9*	*1.9*	1.6	2.2	7.0	3.5	*18.7*	*10.1*
Housing and hotels	*158*	*1,044*	*0.3*	*1.0*	0.4	1.1	*1.5*	*1.8*	*4.1*	*5.2*
Personal services	*106*	*293*	*0.1*	*0.3*	0.2	0.3	*1.0*	*0.5*	*2.8*	*1.5*
Domestic services	*453*	*682*	*0.5*	*0.6*	1.0	0.8	*4.5*	*1.2*	*11.8*	*3.4*
11. Religious institutions[d]	79	..	*0.1*	..	0.2	..	0.8	..	*2.1*	*..*
12. Not known	807[e]	191	—	—	—	—	—	—	—	—

	1926	1959						
13. A (line 1)	71,735	48,822	87.6	46.2	—	—		
14. A (Nimitz's figures)f	35,000	35,800	—	—	77.5	38.6		
15. M (lines 2 through 5)	6,327	36,819	7.7	34.8	14.0	39.7	62.2	64.7
16. S (lines 6 through 11)	3,843	20,080	4.7	19.0	8.5	21.7	37.8	35.3
17. M+S (lines 15 plus 16)g	10,170	56,899	12.4	53.8	22.5	61.4	**100.0**	**100.0**
18. Total LF(a)h (lines 13 plus 17)	81,905	105,721	**100.0**	**100.0**				
19. Total with Nimitz A data (lines 14 plus 17)	45,170	92,699			**100.0**	**100.0**		

aThe figures are based on concept LF(a), i.e., they include all family workers (in and out of agriculture). The source figures for both years have been adjusted in order to make them comparable as far as possible. In Table E-1 (the time series) some of these adjustments have been omitted because they could not be carried through for all years. It should also be noted that the 1959 figures of Table 5 include additional adjustments which could not be made for 1926.

bSee note f.

cThe absolute figures underlying these percentages are those in line 14.

dReligious services are not included in the labor force in 1959 (see note d to Table 7).

eThese are day laborers who may be employed in any industry.

fThese are Nimitz's figures for full-time equivalent. We believe that these figures provide a better comparison between 1926 and 1959. In addition, they come closer to the LF(b) concept.

gThe M/S ratios are 1.6 in 1926 and 1.8 in 1959.

hExcluding line 12 (not known).

Source: 1926—*Census 1926*, vol. 34 Tables II, IV, V, and VI.
1959—see source to Table 5.
N. Nimitz, *Farm Employment in the Soviet Union, 1928-1963* (Santa Monica, 1965), p. 7, Table 1.

Table E-3. *Industrial Distribution of Nonagricultural Employees,* [a] *Selected Years, 1928-1964 (Percent)*

Industry	1928	1932	1937	1940	1950	1959	1964
1. Manufacturing	41.7	40.8	42.4	38.6	40.4	40.2	40.3
2. Construction	8.0	11.7	6.6	5.5	7.3	9.5	8.4
3. Transport	14.0	10.3	11.1	12.0	11.7	11.9	11.0
4. Communications	1.0	1.2	1.6	1.6	1.5	1.3	1.4
5. Trade	6.4	11.2	10.5	11.6	8.6	8.8	8.9
Catering	*0.6*	*3.2*	*2.0*	*2.7*	*1.9*	*2.0*	*2.2*
Retail	*..* [b]	*4.4*	*5.2*	*4.8*	*3.8*	*4.1*	*4.4*
Wholesale	*5.8*	*3.6*	*3.3*	*4.1*	*2.9*	*2.7*	*2.3*
6. Credit and insurance	1.0	0.7	0.8	0.9	0.8	0.6	0.5
7. Public administration	11.2	8.4	6.2	6.4	5.2	2.6	2.1
8. Education, culture, and science	8.9	7.4	10.0	10.6	11.6	12.0	13.6
Education and culture	*7.9*	*6.5*	*8.8*	*9.3*	*9.5*	*9.1*	*9.7*
Scientific institutions	*0.8*	*0.7*	*1.0*	*1.0*	*1.3*	*2.9*	*3.9*
Scientific services	*0.2*	*0.2*	*0.2*	*0.3*	*0.8*	*..* [c]	*..* [c]
9. Health	4.5	3.4	4.6	6.1	6.7	6.3	6.4
10. Housing and personal services	1.6	3.4	4.3	4.3	3.4	3.4	3.5
11. Other [d]	1.7	1.5	1.9	2.4	2.8	3.4	3.9
12. M sector (lines 1 through 4) [e]	65.8	65.0	63.0	59.3	62.8	65.2	63.7
13. S sector (lines 5 through 10) [e]	34.2	35.0	37.0	40.7	37.2	34.8	36.3
14. Total M+S	**100.0**	**100.0**	**100.0**	**100.0**	**100.0**	**100.0**	**100.0**
15. M/S ratio	1.9	1.9	1.7	1.5	1.7	1.9	1.8

[a]See note 1, Chap. 3.
[b]Included in line 5c.
[c]Included in line 8b.
[d]Includes: capital repair, drilling, project survey organizations, literature and publishing, art, etc. See also note e.
[e]Total M and S include, respectively, 2/3 and 1/3 of line 11, "other."
Source: New Directions, pp. 770-772, Table A-1.

Bibliography

Adelman, I. and Taft-Morris, C. "A Factor Analysis of the Interrelationship Between Social and Political Variables and Per Capita Gross National Product," *Quarterly Journal of Economics,* 79:555-578 (November 1965).

Austria. Oesterreichisches Statistisches Zentralamt. *Volkzählungs Ergebnisse 1961: Heft 15 Die Berufstätigen nach Ihrer Wirtschaftlichen Zugehörigkeit* (Census of population, 1961). Vienna: 1964.

Baum, Samuel, and Jerry W. Combs, Jr. *The Labor Force of the Soviet Zone of Germany and the Soviet Sector of Berlin.* U.S., Department of Commerce, Bureau of the Census. Foreign Demographic Analysis Division Publication Series P-90, no. 11. Washington: 1959.

Becker, A. S. *Soviet National Income and Product 1958-1962 Part Two. N.I. at Factor Costs and Constant Prices.* (Memorandum RM-4881-PR.) Santa Monica, RAND Corporation, 1966.

Becker, Gary S. "A Theory of the Allocation of Time," *Economic Journal,* 75:493-517 (September 1965).

Beckerman, W., and R. Bacon. "International Comparisons of Income Levels: A Suggested New Measure," *Economic Journal,* 76:519-536 (September 1966).

Bergson, Abram. *The Real National Income of Soviet Russia since 1928.* Cambridge, Mass.: Harvard University Press, 1961.

_____ *The Economics of Soviet Planning.* New Haven: Yale University Press, 1964.

_____ "The Comparative National Income of the USSR and USA: Appendixes and Abbreviations." Unpublished data prepared for the 1970 Conference on Research in Income and Wealth, at Toronto. October 1969 (mimeograph).

Berliner, J. S. *Factory and Manager in the USSR.* Cambridge, Mass.: Harvard University Press, 1957.

Biuleten Ispolnitelnogo Komiteta Moskovskogo Gododskogo Soveta Depitagov Trudiashchikhia, no. 5 (March 1962), p. 5.

Borenstein, M., P. E. Anderson, B. N. Merguerian, and C. B. Krueger, *Soviet National Accounts for 1955.* (Center for Russian Studies.) Ann Arbor: University of Michigan, 1961 (mimeograph).

CDSP. See Joint Committee on Slavic Studies.

Census 1897. See Russia.

Census 1926. See Soviet Union. TsSU.

Census 1959. See Soviet Union. TsSU.

Chenery, Hollis B. "Patterns of Industrial Growth," *American Economic Review,* 50:624-654 (September 1960).

_____ and Lance Taylor. "Development Patterns: Among Countries and Over Time," *Review of Economics and Statistics,* 50.4:391-416 (November 1968).

Clark, Colin. *The Conditions of Economic Progress.* 3rd ed. London: Macmillan, 1957.

Cohn, S. H. *Derivation of 1959 Value-Added Weights for Originating Sectors of Soviet GNP.* McLean, Virginia: Research Analysis Corporation, 1966.

Comparisons. See U.S., Congress.

Denison, E. F. *The Sources of Economic Growth in the United States.* (Supplementary Paper 13.) New York: Committee for Economic Development, 1962.

_____ *Why Growth Rates Differ: Postwar Experience in Nine Western Countries.* Washington: The Brookings Institution, 1967.

Dewitt, N. *Educational and Professional Employment in the USSR.* Washington: National Science Foundation, 1961.

Dikhtiar, G. "Soviet Trade in the Period of the Full-Scale Building of Communism," *Problems of Economics,* 5. 4:45-52 (August 1962).

Dimensions. See U.S., Congress.

Dodge, N. T. *Women in the Soviet Union.* Baltimore: The Johns Hopkins Press, 1966.

Ekonomicheskaia Gazeta (Economic Gazette).

France. Institut National de la Statistique et des Etudes Economiques, *Recensement Général de la Population de 1961. Résultats du Sondage au 1/20 pour la France Entière: Population Active* (Census of population, 1961). Paris: 1964.

Fuchs, Victor R. *Productivity Trends in the Goods and Service Sectors, 1929-61: A Preliminary Survey.* (National Bureau of Economic Research: Occasional Paper 89.) New York and London: Columbia University Press, 1964.

_____ *The Growing Importance of the Service Industries.* (National Bureau of Economic Research: Occasional Paper 96.) New York and London: Columbia University Press, 1965.

_____ "A Statistical Analysis of Productivity in Selected Service Industries in the United States, 1939-63," in Victor R. Fuchs and Jean Alexander Wilburn, *Productivity Differences within the Service Sector.* (National Bureau of Economic Research: Occasional Paper 102.) New York and London: Columbia University Press, 1967.

_____ *The Service Economy.* (National Bureau of Economic Research: General Series No. 87.) New York and London: Columbia University Press, 1968.

_____ ed. *Production and Productivity in the Service Industries.* (National Bureau of Economic Research: Studies in Income and Wealth Vol. 34.) New York and London: Columbia University Press, 1969.

George, K. D. *Productivity in Distribution.* (Department of Applied Economics Occasional Paper 8.) Cambridge: Cambridge University Press, 1966.

Gerschenkron, Alexander. "The Rate of Industrial Growth in Russia Since 1885," *Journal of Economic History,* 7:144-174 (Supplement, 1947).

Gilbert, Milton, and Associates. *Comparative National Products and Price Levels.* Paris: OEEC, 1958.

Ginor, Fanny. "The Impact of Capital Imports on the Structure of Developing Countries," *Kyklos,* 22:104-123 (Fasc. 1, 1969).

Goldman, M. I. "Product Differentiation and Advertising: Some Lessons from Soviet Experience," *Journal of Political Economy,* 68:346-357 (August 1960).

_____ *Soviet Marketing.* Glencoe, Ill.: The Free Press, 1963.

_____ "The Reluctant Consumer and Economic Fluctuations in the Soviet Union," *Journal of Political Economy,* 73:366-380 (August 1965).

_____ *The Soviet Economy: Myth and Reality.* Englewood Cliffs, New Jersey: Prentice-Hall, 1968.

Granick, David. *The Red Executive.* Garden City, N.Y.: Doubleday, 1961.

_____ *Soviet Metal Fabrication and Economic Development.* Madison: University of Wisconsin Press, 1967.

Hall, M., J. Knapp, and C. H. Winsten. *Distribution in Great Britain and North America.* Oxford: Oxford University Press, 1961.

Horovitz, M. H., M. Zymelman, and I. L. Herrnstadt. *Manpower Requirements for Planning: An International Comparison Approach.* Vol. II: *Statistical Tables.* (Department of Economics.) Boston: Northeastern University, 1966.

Indicators. See U.S., Congress.

International Labour Organization (ILO). *Year Book of Labour Statistics 1964* and *1965.* Geneva: 1964 and 1965.

Japan. Bureau of Statistics, Office of the Prime Minister. *1960 Population Census of Japan; Part 3: Labor Force Status, Industry, Employment Status, Hours Worked and Unemployment.* Tokyo: 1963.

Jefferys, J. B., and D. Knee. *Retailing in Europe.* London: Macmillan, 1962.

Joint Committee on Slavic Studies, *Current Digest of the Soviet Press.* Weekly. (Referred to as *CDSP.*)

JPRS. See U.S., Department of Commerce.

Khachaturev, T., and D. L. Lvov. "Ekonomicheskaia Effektivnost i Kachestvo" (Economic efficiency and quality), *Ekonomicheskaia Gazeta.* June 1967, pp. 28-29.

Komarov, V. "O Ratsionalnom Ispolzovani Kadrov Spetsialistov" (On the rational utilization of specialist cadres), *Voprosi Ekonomiki.* September 1966, pp. 15-25.

Konnik, I. "Plan i Rynok v Sotsialisticheskom Khoziaistve" (Plan and market in a socialist economy), *Voprosi Ekonomiki.* May 1966, pp. 18-30.

Kostakov, V., and P. Litviakov. "Utilization of Labor Resources in the Future," *Problems of Economics,* 5. 7:30-36 (November 1962).

Kunin, S. "Shire Privlekat Obshchesvenost k Uluchsheniu Ucheta i Otchetnosti" (To draw public attention to improving accounting), *Vestnik Statistiki,* February 1962, pp. 16-22.

Kuznets, Simon. "Quantitative Aspects of the Economic Growth of Nations II. Industrial Distribution of National Product and Labor Force," *Economic Development and Cultural Change,* vol. 5 (supplement to no. 4, July 1957).

_____ "Quantitative Aspects of the Economic Growth of Nations III. Industrial Distribution of Income and Labor Force by States, United States, 1919-1921 to 1955," *Economic Development and Cultural Change,* vol. 6 (no. 4, part II, July 1958).

_____ "Quantitative Aspects of the Economic Growth of Nations VII. The Share and Structure of Consumption," *Economic Development and Cultural Change,* vol. 10 (no. 2, part II, January 1962).

_____ "A Comparative Appraisal," in Abram Bergson and Simon Kuznets, eds., *Economic Trends in the Soviet Union.* Cambridge, Mass.: Harvard University Press, 1963.

_____ *Modern Economic Growth Rate Structure and Spread.* New Haven: Yale University Press, 1966.

_____ *Economic Growth of Nations: Total Output and Production Structure.* Cambridge, Mass.: The Belknap Press of Harvard University Press, 1971.

Kvasha, Ya. "Kontsentratsia Proizvodstva i Malkaia Promyshelnost" (Concentration of production and small-scale production), *Voprosi Ekonomiki,* May 1967, pp. 26-31.

Lengellé, M. *The Growing Importance of the Service Sector in Member Countries: Changes in Employment Structure.* Paris: OECD, 1966.

Levine, H. S. "The Centralized Planning of Supply in Soviet Industry," *Comparisons of the United States and Soviet Economies.* U.S., Congress (86th, 1st Sess.), Joint Economic Committee. Washington: 1959.

Liniichuk, Ia. "Some Problems of Internal Rural Trade Turnover," *Problems of Economics,* 8. 7:45-52 (November 1965).

Lorimer, Frank. *The Population of the Soviet Union.* Geneva: League of Nations, 1946.

Lukianov. A. I., and B. M. Lazarev. *Sovetskoe Gosudarstvo i Obshchestvennie Organizatsi* (The Soviet state and social organization). Moscow: 1960.

Morozov, V. "Development of Commodity-Money Relations in the Countryside," *Problems of Economics,* 8. 7:32-44 (November 1965).

Narkhoz. See Soviet Union. TsSU.

Nazarov, R. "Stanovlenie i Rasvitie Kolkhoznoi Torgovli" (The formation and growth of kolkhoz trade), *Sovetskaia Torgovlia,* February 1967.

Nemchenko, V. "Certain Problems in the Rational Utilization of Soviet Labor Resources," *Translations on USSR Labor.* U.S., Department of Commerce. Joint Publications Research Service (JPRS). no. 95 (December 7, 1965).

New Directions. See U.S., Congress.

Nimitz, N. *Farm Employment in the Soviet Union, 1928-1963.* (Memorandum RM-4623-PR.) Santa Monica: RAND Corporation, 1965.

Ofer, Gur. *The Service Industries in a Developing Economy: Israel as a Case Study.* (Praeger Special Studies in International Economics and Development.) Jerusalem and New York: Frederick A. Praeger in cooperation with the Bank of Israel, 1967.

OECD. *Supplement to Manpower Problems in the Service Sector.* Paris: 1966.
_____ *Manpower Problems in the Service Sector.* (International Seminars 1966-2.) Paris: 1967.
Patrushev, V. D. *Intensivnost Truda Pri Sotsializme* (Intensity of work under socialism). Moscow: Izdatelstvo Ekonomicheskoi Literaturi, 1963.
_____ *Vremia Kak Ekonomicheskaia Kategoria* (Time as an economic factor). Moscow: Misl, 1966.
Petrosian, G. S. *Vnerabochee Vremia Trudiashchikhsia v SSSR* (Nonworking time of working people in the USSR). Moscow: Ekonomika, 1965.
Pigalev, P. "Obshchestvennie Nachala v Rabote Partiinykh Organov" (Social basis of the work of the party organs), *Kommunist,* no. 7, May 1962, pp. 60-69.
Plotnikov, K. "Certain Problems of the Development of Finance and Credit in the Process of Building Communism," *Problems of Economics,* 7. 10:31-40 (February 1965).
Prochazka, Zora. *The Labor Force of Bulgaria.* U.S., Department of Commerce, Bureau of the Census. Foreign Demographic Analysis Division Publication Series P-90, no. 16. Washington: 1962.
Prudenski, G. A. *Vremia i Truda* (Time and work). Moscow: Misl, 1964.
_____ "Opit Ekonomiko-Sotsiologicheskikh Issledovani" (Experiment in socio-economic research), *Ekonomicheskaia Gazeta,* no. 2, 1966, pp. 10-12.
_____ "Biudzhet Vnerabochego Vremeni" (Budget of nonworking time), *Ekonomicheskaia Gazeta,* no. 17, April 1967, pp. 6-7.
Pryor, F. L., and G. J. Staller. "The Dollar Values of the Gross National Products in Eastern Europe 1955," *Economics of Planning,* 6. 1:1-26 (1966).
Rashin, A. G. *Formirovnie Rabochego Klassa Rossie: Istorii Ekonomicheskie Ocherki* (The formation of the working class in Russia: Studies in economic history). Moscow: Akademia Nauk SSSR Institut Istorii, 1958.
Russia. Tsentralni Statisticheski Komitet. *Paspredelenie Naselenia po Vidam Glavnikh Zaniatii i Vozrasnim Gruppam po Otdelnim Territorialnim Raionam.* St. Petersburg: 1905. *(Census 1897 I.)*
_____ *Pervia Vseobshchaia Perepis Naselenia Rossiiskoi Imperii 1897 g.* Vol. 8. St. Petersburg: 1905. (Referred to as *Census 1897 II.*)
Sanborn, Henry. "Pay Differences Between Men and Women," *Industrial and Labor Relations Review,* 17:534-550 (July 1964).
Schwartzman, David. *The Decline of Service in Retail Trade: An Analysis of the Growth of Sales Per Manhour, 1929-1963.* (Bureau of Economic and Business Research, Study no. 48.) Pullman, Wash.: Washington State University, 1971.
Shishkina, H. N. *Trudovie Resursi SSSR* (Labor resources in the USSR). Moscow: Isdatelstvo Ekonomicheskoi Literaturi, 1961.
Smolinski, L. "The Soviet Economy in Search of a Pattern," *Survey,* no. 59 (April 1966), pp. 88-101.
_____ Soviet Industrial Establishments: Scale and Performance (forthcoming).
Sonin, M. *Aktualnie Problemi Ispolzovania Rabochei Sili v SSSR* (Current problems of labor force utilization in the USSR). Moscow: Misl, 1965.

_____ "Some Problems in Increasing the Efficiency of Utilization of Labor Resources," *Problems of Economics*, 9:3-14 (No. 8, December 1966).

_____ and P. Savranskaia. "Chelovek I Rabota" (Man and work), *Literaturnaia Gazeta*, September 22, 1966, pp. 1-2.

Sotsialisticheski Trud (Socialist labor).

Sovetskaia Torgovlia (Soviet trade).

Soviet Union. Tsentralnoe Statisticheskoe Upravlenia (TsSU). *Itogi Vsesoiuznoi Perepisi Naselenia 1959 g. SSSR.* (Census of Population 1959.) Moscow: Gosstatizdat, 1962. (Referred to as *Census 1959.*)

_____ *Narodnoe Khoziaistvo SSSR* (The national economy of the USSR). 1959, 1960 and 1964 issues. Moscow: 1960, 1961, and 1965. (Referred to as *Narkhoz.*)

_____ *Selskoe Khoziaistvo SSSR* (The agricultural economy of the USSR). Moscow: 1960.

_____ *Sistematicheski Slovar Zaniatii* (Occupational classification). Moscow: 1959.

_____ *Slovar po Otrasliam* (Industrial classification). Moscow: 1959.

_____ *Sovetskaia Torgovlia: Statisticheski Svornik* (Soviet trade: Statistical handbook). Moscow: 1964. (Referred to as *Sovtorg 1964.*)

_____ *Vsesoiuznaia Perepis Naselenia 1926 g.* Vol. 34. Moscow: 1932. (Referred to as *Census 1926.*)

_____ *Vsesoiuznaia Perepis Naselenia 1959 g.* (Census instructions.) Moscow: 1958.

_____ RSFSR. *Sovetskaia Torgovlia v RSFSR* (Soviet trade in the RSFSR). Moscow: 1958.

Sovtorg. See Soviet Union. TsSU.

Stigler, G. J. *Trends in Employment in the Service Industries.* (National Bureau of Economic Research: General Series No. 59.) Princeton: Princeton University Press, 1956.

Stoliarov, I. I. "Laws of Development of the Nonproductive Sphere During the Transition to Communism," *Problems of Economics*, 7. 10:14-20 (February 1965).

Struev, A. "The Trade Branch," *Problems of Economics*, 8. 11:17-20 (March 1966).

_____ "Kazhdi Den-Chastitsa Iubileinogo Goda" (Every day is part of jubilee year), *Sovetskaia Torgovlia*, no. 2, 1967, pp. 2-7.

Sukharevski, B. "Development of the Sphere of Services and the Building of Communism," *Problems of Economics*, 7. 10:21-30 (February 1965).

Szalai, A. et al. "Multinational Comparative Social Research," *American Behavioral Scientist*, 10. 4:1-31 (December 1966). Appendix to this article in separate supplement to this issue.

Temin, P. "A Time-Series Test of Patterns of Industrial Growth," *Economic Development and Cultural Change*, 15. 2:174-182 (part 1, January 1967).

Tiukov, V. "Soviet Trade in the Period of Full-Scale Building of Communism," *Problems of Economics*, 5. 6:3-10 (October 1962).

UN, *Demographic Yearbook.* New York: various issues.

_____ *Statistical Bulletin for Latin America.* Vol. 2, No. 1.

_____ *A System of National Accounts.* (Studies in Methods, Series F No. 2 Rev. 2.) New York: 1964.

_____ *Yearbook of National Accounts Statistics 1964.* New York: 1965.

U.S., Congress. Joint Economic Committee, *Comparisons of the United States and Soviet Economies.* 86th Cong., 1st Sess., 1959. (Referred to as *Comparisons.*)

_____ *Dimensions of Soviet Economic Power.* 87th Cong., 2nd Sess., 1962. (Referred to as *Dimensions.*)

_____ *Current Economic Indicators for the U.S.S.R.* 89th Cong., 1st Sess., 1965. (Referred to as *Indicators.*)

_____ *New Directions in the Soviet Economy.* 89th Cong., 2nd Sess., 1966. (Referred to as *New Directions.*)

_____ *Economic Developments in Countries of Eastern Europe.* 91st Cong., 2nd Sess., 1970.

U.S., Department of Commerce. *Translations on Consumer Goods and Domestic Trade.* Joint Publications Research Service. (Referred to as JPRS-*Consumer Goods.*) Various issues.

_____ *Translations on USSR Labor.* Joint Publications Research Service. (Mimeograph.) (Referred to as JPRS-*Labor.*) Various issues.

_____ *Survey of Current Business.*

_____ *The National Income and Product Accounts of the United States: 1929-1965. Statistical Tables.* (Supplement to *Survey of Current Business.*) Washington: 1966.

_____ Bureau of the Census. *Statistical Abstract of the United States 1962* and *1965.* Washington: 1962 and 1965.

_____ *United States Census of Population 1960; United States Summary, Detailed Characteristics.* Washington: 1963.

_____ *United States Census of Population 1960; Occupational Characteristics.* Washington: 1963.

Vakulov, A. "Za Pliushevim Kanatom" (Behind the counter), *Ekonomicheskaia Gazeta,* no. 38, September 1966.

Vasileev, A. A. *Kolkhoznaia Torgovlia i Zagotovki* (Trade and procurement in kolkhozes). Moscow: Gosstatizdat, 1960.

Ward, B. N. *The Socialist Economy: A Study of Organizational Alternatives.* Berkeley, Calif.: University of California and Random House, 1967.

Weitzman, M. S. *Comparison of U.S. and U.S.S.R. Employment in Industry, 1939-1958.* U.S., Department of Commerce, Bureau of the Census. Foreign Demographic Analysis Division Publication Series P-95, no. 60. Washington: 1963.

_____ and A. Elias. *The Magnitude and Distribution of Civilian Employment in the U.S.S.R: 1939-1959.* U.S., Department of Commerce, Bureau of the Census. Foreign Demographic Analysis Division Publication Series P-95, no. 58. Washington: 1961 (mimeograph).

Yanowitch, Murray. "Soviet Patterns of Time Use and Concepts of Leisure," *Soviet Studies,* 15:17-37 (July 1963).

Ypsilantis, James N. *The Labor Force of Czechoslovakia.* U.S., Department of Commerce, Bureau of the Census. Foreign Demographic Analysis Division Publication Series P-90, no. 13. Washington: 1960.

Index